M000206485

To

....

From

....

Date

....

365 Devotions on the
POWER OF
PRAYER
for Men

Daily Inspiration from Classic Prayers

BARBOUR
PUBLISHING

Published by Barbour Publishing, Inc., 1810 Barbour Drive, Uhrichsville, Ohio 44683, www.barbourbooks.com

Our mission is to inspire the world with the life-changing message of the Bible.

Member of the
Evangelical Christian
Publishers Association

Printed in China.

INTRODUCTION

For thousands of years, people of faith have penned powerful prayers, for themselves and the masses. Now, 365 of these classic prayers are available under one cover for men who want to tap into the power of the ages. Each daily reading begins with a short devotional and a supporting Bible verse, followed by a classic prayer that can reach across the oceans of time to touch the heart, lift the spirit, embolden the soul, brighten the mind, and strengthen the faith. And each day's entry concludes with a prayer starter to initiate your own time of communion with God.

Included in the back of this book are brief biographies of the authors of the classic prayers. There you will also find an index of topics—such as adversity, aging, blessings, contentment, discouragement, faith, fear, guidance, hope, joy, plans, purpose, relationships, thoughts, truth, and more—so you can access specific help any day of the year!

May this book be a blessing in your life, energizing your own prayers, fueled by the belief that:

> *All things, whatsoever ye shall ask in*
> *prayer, believing, ye shall receive.*
> MATTHEW 21:22

Each morning we choose which path we are going to follow: our own or God's. If we choose our own, we may find ourselves drifting off course in turbulent waters. But if we align our will with God's at the outset and listen for His voice throughout the day, we know we'll be cruising in the right direction, with God at the helm. Which course will you choose as you launch yourself into this day?

> *And therefore will the LORD wait, that he may be gracious unto*
> *you, and therefore will he be exalted, that he may have mercy*
> *upon you. . .blessed are all they that wait for him. . . . Thine ears*
> *shall hear a word behind thee, saying, This is the way, walk ye*
> *in it, when ye turn to the right hand, and when ye turn to the*
> *left. . . . And the LORD shall cause his glorious voice to be heard.*
>
> ISAIAH 30:18, 21, 30

Afresh I seek thee. Lead me—once more I pray—
Even should it be against my will, thy way.
Let me not feel thee foreign any hour,
Or shrink from thee as an estranged power.
Through doubt, through faith, through bliss, through stark dismay,
Through sunshine, wind, or snow, or fog, or shower,
Draw me to thee who art my only day.
GEORGE MACDONALD

MY PRAYER STARTER: Father in heaven, may I choose Your way today and every day. Please guide me in Your best path.

Each day we take pains to make sure we look good on the outside. But we all know beauty (or perhaps we should say "handsome") is only skin deep. What lies in our heart is the true teller of who we are. Spend some moments today on your heart health by seeking to follow Jesus' example. It will change your life.

Keep thy heart with all diligence; for out of it are the issues of life.
PROVERBS 4:23

Dear Lord,
May I be no man's enemy, and may I be the friend
of that which is eternal and abides.
May I never quarrel with those nearest me; and
if I do, may I be reconciled quickly.
May I never devise evil against any person. If any devise evil against
me, may I escape uninjured and without the need of hurting them.
May I love, seek and attain only that which is good.
May I wish for all humanity's happiness and envy none.
May I, to the extent of my power, give all needful help to my friends
and to all who are in want.
May I respect myself.
May I always keep tame that which rages in me.
May I accustom myself to be gentle, and never be angry with people
because of circumstances.
May I never discuss who is wicked and what wicked things he
has done, but know good people and follow in their footsteps.
EUSEBIUS OF CAESAREA

MY PRAYER STARTER: Creator God, please cleanse and purify the heart You've given me. Make me more like Jesus today.

God requires our obedience. Not because He wants to make life difficult, but because He alone knows what's good for us. When we are walking in His will and way, we're able to avoid the pitfalls and predicaments that distract and discourage. In fact, when we live in obedience, we find ourselves enjoying all God has planned for us. Whether or not we think, from our limited knowledge, what He's saying makes sense, and whether or not we understand, with our limited perspective, where He's leading, we can trust that the Father sees all and truly does know best.

> *By faith Abraham, when he was called to go out into a place*
> *which he should after receive for an inheritance, obeyed; and he*
> *went out, not knowing whither he went. By faith he sojourned in*
> *the land of promise, as in a strange country. . . : for he looked for a*
> *city which hath foundations, whose builder and maker is God.*
>
> HEBREWS 11:8–10

Almighty and everlasting God, only speak to us that we may hear thee. Then speak to us again and yet again so that when in our hearts we answer thee by saying No, we may at least know well to whom we say it, and what it costs us to say it, and what it costs our brothers, and what it costs thee.

FREDERICK BUECHNER

MY PRAYER STARTER: Lord God, faith demands that I obey You in every particular. Please increase my faith, and my pleasure in obedience.

God wants our hearts totally devoted to Him. Yet sometimes His gifts get in the way. When we're healthy, full, and successful in our work and relationships, we may begin making God a secondary priority. But when those gifts are removed, when we're facing illness, hunger, or failure, we may find ourselves suddenly on our knees, crying out to God, making Him our *first* priority. Remember that all you have—health, food, success, and more—is not yours but God's. And none of those gifts should stand between you and Him. God is giving you all of Himself. And that's what He wants back—all of you. For then His strength becomes fully active.

> *For the eyes of the LORD run to and fro throughout*
> *the whole earth, to shew himself strong in the behalf*
> *of them whose heart is perfect toward him.*
>
> 2 CHRONICLES 16:9

Lord, you gave me health and I forgot you. You take it away and I come back to you. What infinite compassion that God, in order to give himself to me, takes away his gifts which I allowed to come between me and him. All is yours. You are the Lord. Dispose everything, comforts, success, health. Take all the things that possess me instead of you that I may be wholly yours.
FRANÇOIS FÉNELON

MY PRAYER STARTER: Loving Father, thank You for Your gifts that I have undeservedly received. Fill me with the burning desire to offer my entire existence in return.

Nothing will happen today that God hasn't already seen coming. So rest assured that God's got you. That His constant thoughts toward you are filled with peace as He works out His plans for your life. Secure in that knowledge, you can have patience and peace, no matter what the day brings. You and your life are in God's hands.

For I know the thoughts that I think toward you, saith the Lord, *thoughts of peace, and not of evil, to give you an expected end. Then shall ye call upon me, and ye shall go and pray unto me, and I will hearken unto you. And ye shall seek me, and find me, when ye shall search for me with all your heart.*

JEREMIAH 29:11–13

I do not know, O God, what will happen to me today, I only know that nothing will happen to me but what has been foreseen by you from all eternity, and that is sufficient, O my God, to keep me in peace. I adore your eternal designs. I submit to them with all my heart. I desire them all and accept them all. I make a sacrifice of everything. I unite this sacrifice to that of your dear Son, my Saviour, begging you by His infinite merits, for the patience in troubles, and the perfect submission which is due to you in all that you will and design for me.

ÉLISABETH OF FRANCE

MY PRAYER STARTER: All-knowing God, even though Your plan is mysterious to me, I know it is perfect and full of peace. Grant me the faith and courage to follow.

Why not make your whole being—mind, body, soul, and spirit—a united expression of gratitude to God! Give Him a standing ovation for all the blessings He's showered upon you—within and without, seen and unseen. Thank Him for every tangible and intangible blessing you've received. Thank Him for all the blessings in His storehouse, waiting to pour down upon you. You'll be blessed when you do. For praising God gladdens not only you but Him as well!

> *Come before his presence with singing. Know ye that the*
> *LORD he is God: it is he that hath made us, and not we*
> *ourselves; we are his people, and the sheep of his pasture.*
> *Enter into his gates with thanksgiving, and into his courts*
> *with praise: be thankful unto him, and bless his name.*
>
> PSALM 100:2–4

May my whole being, O God, be one thanksgiving unto Thee;
may all within me praise Thee and love Thee; for all which Thou
hast forgiven, and for all which Thou hast given; for Thine unknown
hidden blessings, and for those which, in my negligence or thought-
lessness, I passed over; for any and every gift of nature or of grace;
for my power of loving; for all blessings within and without;
and for all which Thou hast yet in store for me; for everything
whereby Thou hast drawn me to Thyself, whether joy or sorrow;
for all whereby Thou willest to make Thine own forever. Amen.
EDWARD B. PUSEY

MY PRAYER STARTER: God, I am a finite man, but You deserve an infinite degree of gratitude. So fill every fiber of my mind and body with over-flowing thankfulness directed toward You and You alone.

Silence. It can be hard to come by these days. But within this calmness you can find your way to God's presence, to a place where you can hear His still, small voice and feel His touch. Jeanne Guyon, the French mystic and author of *Experiencing the Depths of Jesus Christ*, advised people to "practice silent prayer for a long, uninterrupted period of time." For someone new to this idea, she suggested combining "spoken prayer with silent prayer." Below today's Bible verse are three different expressions Guyon said you can offer to the Lord—but they must spring from the heart. See if one speaks to your inner spirit. Then take it with you as you enter the silence of heaven and come before your loving Lord.

And when he had opened the seventh seal, there was silence in heaven about the space of half an hour. . . . And another angel came and stood at the altar, having a golden censer; and there was given unto him much incense, that he should offer it with the prayers of all saints.

REVELATION 8:1, 3

- "Oh my God, let me be wholly Yours."
- "Let me love You purely for Yourself, for You are infinitely lovely."
- "Oh my God, be my all! Let everything else be as nothing to me."

JEANNE GUYON

MY PRAYER STARTER: Lord, Sustainer of peace, be my anchor as I walk upon this troubled earth. Amid the noise, lead me to Your blessed silence and fill me with Your calm.

Where do you go when trouble knocks at your door? To whom or what do you turn for courage to face calamity? In the prayer below, Oswald Chambers reminds you to run to God. To look to Him for all the help you need. To draw strength from God's promise that He is your helper. He will never leave nor forsake you. God says so. So you know it's the truth. You know it's a solid promise. Because God will never leave you, you can boldly declare, "I will not fear." Proclaim it this second, this moment, this day, this life! When you do, God will not fail you. His help is not on its way—it's within you now!

He hath said, I will never leave thee, nor forsake thee.
So that we may boldly say, The Lord is my helper,
and I will not fear what man shall do unto me.

HEBREWS 13:5–6

The Lord is my helper, I will not fear—I will not be haunted by apprehension. . . . I will remember God's say-so. I will be full of courage. . . . "The Lord is my Helper, this second, in my present outlook. . . . I will not fear." It does not matter what evil or wrong may be in the way, He has said—"I will never leave thee. . . . I will in no wise fail you." The Lord is my helper.

OSWALD CHAMBERS

MY PRAYER STARTER: All-powerful Father, thank You for Your never-ending faithfulness. Even during my darkest moment, grant me the strength to be faithful to You as well.

Troubles, abounding for believers and nonbelievers alike, can be downright depressing, making us feel like we're in the belly of Jonah's whale. Deep waters engulf us. Seaweed wraps around our heads. But just before we sink, we remember God—His love for us and ours for Him. And we pray. We become quiet, awaiting God's deliverance and knowing it will come. Then, once we're spit out on the shores, we find our footing on the Rock of our faith.

> *The waters compassed me about, even to the soul: the depth*
> *closed me round about, the weeds were wrapped about my*
> *head. . . . When my soul fainted within me I remembered*
> *the LORD: and my prayer came in unto thee.*
> JONAH 2:5, 7

O Lord, my God! The amazing horrors of darkness were gathered about me, and covered me all over, and I saw no way to go forth; I felt the depth and extent of the misery of my fellow-creatures separate from the Divine harmony, and it was heavier than I could bear, and I was crushed down under it; I lifted up my hand, I stretched out my arm but there was none to help me; I looked round about, and was amazed. In the depths of misery, O Lord, I remembered that Thou art omnipotent; that I had called Thee Father; and I felt that I loved Thee, and I was made quiet in my will, and I waited for deliverance from Thee.
JOHN WOOLMAN

MY PRAYER STARTER: Faithful Lord, You've saved me from sin and punishment, so I know You can handle whatever life throws at me. Let me never doubt Your ability to rescue.

God instructs you to "work with your own hands" so that you'll "have lack of nothing" (1 Thessalonians 4:11–12). Sounds like a good plan, for you know that if you do your work for God's pleasure, He will say to you, "Well done, good and faithful servant" (Matthew 25:23). Yet problems may arise when you focus on the results of your work instead of the work itself. God wants you neither distracted by what prospers you nor worried about the outcome of your efforts. He also doesn't want you to compare your own work to others'. Instead, endeavor to leave all the results of your work in God's hands, to keep your attention on Him alone, and to improve upon the talents He's given you.

> *In the morning sow thy seed, and in the evening withhold*
> *not thine hand: for thou knowest not whether shall prosper,*
> *either this or that, or whether they both shall be alike good.*
> ECCLESIASTES 11:6

O God, who has commanded that no man should be idle, but that we should all work with our hands the thing that is good; grant that I may diligently do my duty in that station of life to which thou hast been pleased to call me. Give me grace, that I may honestly improve the talents thou hast committed to my trust, and that no worldly pleasures may ever divert me from the thoughts of the life to come, through Jesus Christ our Lord.
SABINE BARING-GOULD

MY PRAYER STARTER: Father, I know that You have given me a set of skills and the responsibility to use them. Guide my actions, helping me use these talents for Your glory.

God is exactly what you need when and where you need it. He's the pillar of fire going before you, leading you through the dark wilderness path. He's the star above you, the bright light guiding you to the infant King. He's the smooth path below you, steadying your feet. He's the good and gentle shepherd behind you, steering you to still waters, where He can restore your soul. God is all these things before, above, below, and behind you at every moment. He will never take away His guidance, provision, or promises, nor will He remove Himself from you. Allow this all-encompassing God to meet your needs right now, to be what and where you need Him to be today, tonight, and forever.

And the Lord went before them by day in a pillar of a cloud, to lead them the way; and by night in a pillar of fire, to give them light; to go by day and night: he took not away the pillar of the cloud by day, nor the pillar of fire by night, from before the people.

EXODUS 13:21–22

Be thou a bright flame before me,
Be thou a guiding star above me,
Be thou a smooth path below me,
Be thou a kindly shepherd behind me,
Today—tonight—and forever.

SAINT COLUMBA OF IONA

MY PRAYER STARTER: Ever-present God, I constantly need Your guidance to stay on Your holy path. Fill me with comfort, wisdom, and endurance as You lead me closer home.

A society begins to fracture when children no longer respect or obey their fathers. That's why God made it one of the ten commandments—and the only one with a promise! When kids respect their elders, life goes a lot more smoothly—for you, them, and society. At the same time, fathers are not to provoke or aggravate their kids.

If you have an argument with your own parents or children, be humble enough to consider that you might be wrong. Consider apologizing, if needed. And forgive them, just as God forgives you. Respect is a two-way street. Bless your children and parents. Love them. Pray for them. When you do, harmony will exist between you, them, and God.

Children, obey your parents in the Lord: for this is right. Honour thy father and mother; which is the first commandment with promise; that it may be well with thee, and thou mayest live long on the earth. And, ye fathers, provoke not your children to wrath: but bring them up in the nurture and admonition of the Lord.

EPHESIANS 6:1–4

Give, I pray Thee, to all children grace reverently to love their parents, and lovingly to obey them. Teach us all that filial duty never ends or lessens; and bless all parents in their children, and all children in their parents.
CHRISTINA ROSSETTI

MY PRAYER STARTER: God, help me be a loving father to my children, just as You are to me. Help me also to set an example for them by loving and respecting my own parents.

Discouragement can bring you down, so low that you feel as if God's too far to reach. But it's not He who's moved; it's you. Remember, God is constantly pouring out His love upon you, yearning for you to raise your eyes toward Him. When you do, you'll find that He's there, ready to satiate your hunger and quench your thirst for Him. Look up.

As the hart panteth after the water brooks, so panteth my soul after thee, O God. My soul thirsteth for God, for the living God: when shall I come and appear before God? My tears have been my meat day and night, while they continually say unto me, Where is thy God?

PSALM 42:1–3

O Lord, our God, we desire to feel Thee near us in spirit and in body at this time. We know that in Thee we live and move and have our being, but we are cast down and easily disquieted, and we wander in many a sad wilderness where we lose the conscious experience of Thy presence. Yet the deepest yearning of our hearts is unto Thee. As the hart panteth after the waterbrooks, so pant our souls after Thee, O God. Nothing less than Thyself can still the hunger or quench the thirst with which Thou hast inspired us. Power of our souls! enter Thou into them and fit them for Thyself, making them pure with Christ's purity, loving and lovable with His love.
SAMUEL MCCOMB

MY PRAYER STARTER: Lord, when my soul loses its spark of hope, You are the only One who can kindle it anew. Take my eyes off my fleeting problems and fix them on Your unchanging goodness.

How awesome that nothing can overcome the light of Jesus (John 1:5) and that He has charged you to spread His light among others (Matthew 5:16). Even more amazing—because you're a believer who's given himself up for Jesus Christ, you, like Him, are a sweet, fragrant sacrifice to God. Today, pray for Jesus to totally possess you so that you become more like Him, more of a shining and fragrant conduit of His light and aroma. Once you do, others will look at you but see and smell only Jesus.

Now thanks be unto God, which always causeth us to triumph in Christ, and maketh manifest the savour of his knowledge by us in every place. For we are unto God a sweet savour of Christ, in them that are saved.

2 CORINTHIANS 2:14–15

Dear Jesus, help me to spread Thy fragrance everywhere I go. Flood my soul with Thy spirit and love. Penetrate and possess my whole being so utterly that all my life may only be a radiance of Thine. Shine through me and be so in me that every soul I come in contact with may feel Thy presence in my soul. Let them look up and see no longer me but only Jesus. Stay with me and then I shall begin to shine as you shine, so to shine as to be a light to others.
MOTHER TERESA

MY PRAYER STARTER: Radiant Father, let Your light of love and righteousness infiltrate my soul. Transform me into a mirror that reflects Your attributes for everyone to see.

Do you pray with a sense of expectancy? Do you believe that God has heard your prayers and that He will, if your desire is in line with His, answer them with a resounding yes? Know this: God *requires* you to live in a state of expectancy. For Jesus Christ has promised, "If we ask any thing according to his will, he heareth us: and if we know that he hear us, whatsoever we ask, we know that we have the petitions that we desired of him" (1 John 5:14–15). That means God *will* answer you. And you'll put more power behind your prayers once you expect God to reply. . .and go beyond what you've imagined. Andrew Murray writes, "Beware in your prayers, above everything else, of limiting God, not only by unbelief, but by fancying that you know what He can do." That's powerful stuff.

So don't delay. Pray. Expect. And believe God will do more than you could ever ask.

> *I will look unto the LORD; I will wait for the*
> *God of my salvation: my God will hear me.*
> MICAH 7:7

Teach us, O gracious Lord, to begin our daily tasks with
fear, to go on with obedience, and to finish them in love,
and then to wait patiently in hope, and with cheerful
confidence to look up to thee, whose promises are faithful
and rewards infinite; through Jesus Christ our Lord.
GEORGE HICKES

MY PRAYER STARTER: Gracious Lord, may my prayers always spring from a deep trust in Your promises. May I eagerly anticipate Your response, even when I don't know what it will be.

God knows exactly what you need before you even ask Him. It's true! Jesus says so (Matthew 6:8)! Yet He still wants you to come to Him, to put your desire into words so that your petition is clear. And God Himself will separate the good desires from the bad, making sure you get all the best. What God *doesn't* want you to do is worry about when, what, where, or how He's going to provide for you. Be content to leave all those details to Him. Just keep seeking, praising, and worshipping your Provider. Trust Him for all. He's got you covered!

O taste and see that the LORD is good: blessed is the man that trusteth in him. O fear the LORD, ye his saints: for there is no want to them that fear him. The young lions do lack, and suffer hunger: but they that seek the LORD shall not want any good thing.

PSALM 34:8–10

Almighty God, who knowest our necessities before we ask, and our ignorance in asking: Set free thy servants from all anxious thoughts for the morrow; give us contentment with thy good gifts; and confirm our faith that according as we seek thy kingdom, thou wilt not suffer us to lack any good thing; through Jesus Christ our Lord.
SAINT AUGUSTINE

MY PRAYER STARTER: Father, You already know what I will need tomorrow, yet You still want me to ask. Thank You for such an opportunity to communicate with You.

God has been with you since the day He created you in your mother's womb. He's still with you today, even as you read these words. He'll be with you tomorrow and the next day, until you are old and gray—and then He'll be with you in the heavenly beyond. So keep on trusting God, no matter what the days bring.

O Lord God: thou art my trust from my youth. . . . Cast me not off in the time of old age; forsake me not when my strength faileth. . . . Now also when I am old and greyheaded, O God, forsake me not; until I have shewed thy strength unto this generation, and thy power to every one that is to come.
PSALM 71:5, 9, 18

Almighty God, by whose mercy my life has continued for another year, I pray that, as my years increase, my sins may not increase. As age advances, let me become more open, more faithful and more trusting in you. Let me not be distracted by lesser things from what is truly important. And if I become infirm as I grow old, may I not be overwhelmed by self-pity or bitterness. Continue and increase your loving kindness towards me so that, when you finally call me to yourself, I may enter into eternal happiness with you, through Christ my Lord. Amen.
SAMUEL JOHNSON

MY PRAYER STARTER: Eternal God, You've always been with me, even when I've tried to push You away. Help me stay by Your side, leaning on You for my every need.

What do you do when faced with the seemingly unconquerable? Pray, right? That's what King Jehoshaphat did when armies threatened to invade his kingdom. On his knees, he sought God's face and prayed for deliverance. He proclaimed his own helplessness and his faith in God, saying, "We have no might against this great company that cometh against us; neither know we what to do: but our eyes are upon thee" (2 Chronicles 20:12). God responded, "No problem. I've got this." The next day, the king told his people to believe. Then he ordered his singers (praise) to travel ahead of his army (strength), and "when they began to sing and to praise" (2 Chronicles 20:22), God began to work, defeating the enemy and leaving the spoils for Jehoshaphat's people.

The point? It's great to pray, but always end your prayer in praise. God will bring the victory!

Believe in the LORD your God, so shall ye be established; believe his prophets, so shall ye prosper. . . . He appointed singers unto the LORD, and that should praise the beauty of holiness, as they went out before the army, and to say, Praise the LORD; for his mercy endureth for ever.

2 CHRONICLES 20:20–21

Open wide the window of our spirits and fill us full of light;
open wide the door of our hearts, that we receive and
entertain Thee with all our powers of adoration and love.
CHRISTINA ROSSETTI

MY PRAYER STARTER: Almighty Deliverer, may I always entrust my problems to You. And even before the answer comes, may I learn to thank You in advance.

Waiting *continually* on God (Hosea 12:6) with calm endurance seems almost impossible. And it is—without His help. But with God, all is possible. Psalm 37 gives some tips on how to get there: Trust in God and do good where you are. Feed on your faith while you're waiting. Rest in God without worry, knowing He's working things out according to His plan and has everything under control. Just keep calmly walking on the path He's laid out for you. Before long, your worry will vanish, replaced by God's peace.

> *Trust in the LORD, and do good; so shalt thou dwell in the land,*
> *and verily thou shalt be fed. . . . Rest in the LORD, and wait*
> *patiently for him: fret not thyself. . . . Wait on the LORD,*
> *and keep his way, and he shall exalt thee to inherit the land.*
>
> PSALM 37:3, 7, 34

God, teach me to be patient, teach me to go slow,
Teach me how to wait on You when my way I do not know.
Teach me sweet forbearance when things do not go right
So I remain unruffled when others grow uptight.
Teach me how to quiet my racing, rising heart
So I might hear the answer You are trying to impart.
Teach me to let go, dear God, and pray undisturbed until
My heart is filled with inner peace and I learn to know Your will.
HELEN STEINER RICE

MY PRAYER STARTER: Father, I know that impatience is often a sign of doubt. Strengthen my faith as I pray, enabling me to patiently endure my trials in anticipation of Your glorious reply.

It's great to read the Bible, memorize verses, study passages, and hear sermons. But if you don't put the message of God's Word to work, both you and the world will suffer. So don't just love the Word—live it. Be God's hands and feet. Put His plans, will, and ideas above your own. Let His light shine through you and onto the people around you. Follow as Jesus follows. Speak as He speaks. Love as He loves. Shine as He shines. Glow as He glows. When you put the Word into action, everyone prospers.

> *But be ye doers of the word, and not hearers only, deceiving*
> *your own selves. For if any be a hearer of the word, and*
> *not a doer, he is like unto a man beholding his natural face*
> *in a glass: for he beholdeth himself, and goeth his way, and*
> *straightway forgetteth what manner of man he was.*

JAMES 1:22–24

We most humbly beg you to give us grace not only to be hearers of the Word, but doers also of the same; not only to love, but also to live your gospel; not only to favor, but also to follow your godly doctrine; not only to profess, but also to practice your blessed commandments, to the honor of your Holy Name, and the health of our souls.
THOMAS BECON

MY PRAYER STARTER: Lord, our perfect Guide, let me never see Your instructions as trivial advice. Continuously remind me of their importance and enable me to follow them.

Thank God for the Spirit who leads you into truth, interpreting your groans and relaying your true needs to the Lord of all. Pray today's classic prayer with all your heart.

We know not what we should pray for as we ought: but the Spirit itself maketh intercession for us with groanings which cannot be uttered.

ROMANS 8:26

O God, forgive the poverty, the pettiness, Lord, the childish folly of our prayers. Listen not to our words, but to the groanings that cannot be uttered. . . . So often we pray for that which is already ours. . . ; so often for that which never can be ours; so often for that which we must win ourselves; and then labour endlessly for that which can only come to us in prayer. How often we have prayed for the coming of Thy kingdom, yet when it has sought to come through us we have sometimes barred the way; we have wanted it without in others, but not in our own hearts. We feel it is we who stand between man's need and Thee; between ourselves and what we might be; and we have no trust in our own strength, or loyalty, or courage. O give us to love Thy will, and seek Thy kingdom first of all.
WILLIAM EDWIN ORCHARD

MY PRAYER STARTER: Compassionate Father, thank You for understanding not just my words but the heart from which they spring. May I always entrust You with the deepest parts of my soul.

Often preoccupied with our own little fiefdoms, we forget we're to be working as servants in *God's* kingdom—not lording over ours! Instead of making things go our way, we're to ensure they go *God's* way. When Jesus taught us how to pray, He began by having us acknowledge who God is. And the next sentence is about God's kingdom coming, His will being done on earth, just as in heaven. Letting God have full reign is His primary purpose for us. Make it your purpose today—and every day—till His kingdom comes.

Pray ye: Our Father which art in heaven, Hallowed be thy name.
Thy kingdom come, Thy will be done in earth, as it is in heaven.
MATTHEW 6:9–10

O God, our leader and our Master and our Friend, forgive our
imperfections and our little motives, take us and make us one
with Thy great purpose, use us and do not reject us, make us
all servants of Thy kingdom, weave our lives into Thy struggle
to conquer and to bring peace and union to the world.
We are small and feeble creatures, we are feeble in speech,
feebler still in action, nevertheless let but Thy light shine upon us,
and there is not one of us who cannot be lit by Thy fire and who
cannot lose himself in Thy salvation. Take us into Thy purposes,
O God. Let Thy kingdom come into our hearts and into this world.
H. G. WELLS

MY PRAYER STARTER: Righteous King, Your wisdom and power are infinitely greater than mine. Let my life be a vessel, built for the sole purpose of spreading Your kingdom on earth.

When the storms of life rise up, hunker down into your refuge, the rock of God. Cry out, and He'll protect you. Even better, He'll still the waves and calm the wind. Jesus did it for His disciples when their boat was rocked. He'll do it for you too. So flee to the One who has power over all creation. Let Him calm you. When you do, you'll reach that haven you've been striving for—peace in God within, no matter what befalls you without.

> *Then they cry unto the LORD in their trouble, and he bringeth them out of their distresses. He maketh the storm a calm, so that the waves thereof are still. Then are they glad because they be quiet; so he bringeth them unto their desired haven.*
>
> PSALM 107:28–30

Almighty God, the Refuge of all that are distressed, grant unto us that, in all trouble of this our mortal life, we may flee to the knowledge of Thy lovingkindness and tender mercy; that so, sheltering ourselves therein, the storms of life may pass over us, and not shake the peace of God that is within us. Whatsoever this life may bring us, grant that it may never take from us the full faith that Thou art our Father. Grant us Thy light, that we may have life, through Jesus Christ our Lord. Amen.
GEORGE DAWSON

MY PRAYER STARTER: Almighty Deliverer, I am sometimes rocked by life's tumultuous sea. May I always seek refuge by turning to You in prayer.

Lady Jane Grey wrote the prayer below while imprisoned in the Tower of London, shortly before her execution in 1554. What a testament of faith amid adversity! Although you may never have your head on a chopping block, troubles will come. But there's a way out: looking to God for the strength and peace to endure, come what may.

> *I will love thee, O LORD, my strength. The LORD is my rock, and my fortress, and my deliverer; my God, my strength, in whom I will trust; my buckler, and the horn of my salvation, and my high tower.*
>
> PSALM 18:1–2

O Merciful God, be Thou now unto me a strong tower of defence, I humbly entreat Thee. Give me grace to await Thy leisure, and patiently to bear what Thou doest unto me; nothing doubting or mistrusting Thy goodness towards me; for Thou knowest what is good for me better than I do. Therefore do with me in all things what Thou wilt; only arm me, I beseech Thee, with Thine armour, that I may stand fast; above all things, taking to me the shield of faith; praying always that I may refer myself wholly to Thy will, abiding Thy pleasure, and comforting myself in those troubles which it shall please Thee to send me, seeing such troubles as are profitable for me; and I am assuredly persuaded that all Thou doest cannot but be well; and unto Thee be all honour and glory. Amen.
LADY JANE GREY

MY PRAYER STARTER: Faithful God, You endured terrible suffering to make my salvation possible. May I follow in Your footsteps, bearing whatever pain is necessary to stay faithful to You.

Anxious thoughts can so easily lead a man astray, creating fear and turmoil within. The solution? Run to God, your defense and your rock of refuge—the one place you can go when your foot begins slipping, when you start losing your spiritual balance. As you flee to His side, the God of all creation will help you navigate your anxious thoughts. In His might He will break up the fears amassed around your soul. Wait upon the Lord, calling on Him from deep within your heart. He is not only your hope but your ultimate Comforter. He will give you the power to stay calm amid your days of trouble (Psalm 94:13).

When I said, My foot slippeth; thy mercy, O LORD, held me up. In the
multitude of my thoughts within me thy comforts delight my soul. . . .
The LORD is my defence; and my God is the rock of my refuge.

PSALM 94:18–19, 22

O Lord, my God, be not Thou far from me; my God, have regard to help me, for there have risen up against me sundry thoughts, and great fears, afflicting my soul. How shall I pass through unhurt? How shall I break them to pieces? This is my hope, my one only consolation, to flee unto Thee in every tribulation, to trust in Thee, to call upon Thee from my inmost heart, and to wait patiently for Thy consolation. Amen.

THOMAS À KEMPIS

MY PRAYER STARTER: Lord, Comforter of my soul, prevent me from slipping beneath the sea of anxiety and fear. Calm the storm and let Your promises keep me afloat.

How wonderful it is to live with a heart open to the Spirit—His moving, His breathing, His knocking. When you possess this open awareness and accept that whatever happens is for your good, you'll find joy. For then you're living for God, not for what He may provide. So open your heart's door, and welcome in His light and love!

> *I stand at the door, and knock: if any man hear my*
> *voice, and open the door, I will come in to him.*
> REVELATION 3:20

O Thou Divine Spirit that, in all events in life, art knocking at the door of my heart, help me to respond to Thee. I would not be driven blindly as the stars over their courses. I would not be made to work out Thy will unwillingly, to fulfil Thy law unintelligently, to obey Thy mandates unsympathetically. I would take the events of my life as good and perfect gifts from Thee; I would receive even the sorrows of life as disguised gifts from Thee. I would have my heart open at all times to receive Thee—at morning, noon and night; in spring, and summer, and winter. Whether Thou comest to me in sunshine or in rain, I would take Thee into my heart joyfully. Thou art Thyself more than the sunshine; Thou art Thyself compensation for the rain; it is Thee and not Thy gifts I crave; knock, and I shall open unto Thee.
GEORGE MATHESON

MY PRAYER STARTER: Generous Creator, You have blessed me with far more than I deserve. However, even if my material blessings are taken away, let me cling to You, the only One who can give meaning to my life.

God has a task for you, one He has uniquely qualified you to perform. It's one you have been created for. Are you in a position to hear God's message? Have you gone and lain down in your place? When you do—when you're silent and still before Him—the Lord will come and stand before you. He'll call out your name. Answer Him with the words "Speak, Lord, I'm listening," and God will then give you *His* words, telling you His plan and what He wants you to do. And as His servant, you'll perform whatever task He gives.

Try it today. Go to God. Sit down in your secret place. Lay yourself before Him. Once your heart, mind, soul, and spirit are in tune with God's—once you hear Him call your name—respond by saying, "Speak, Lord, I'm listening." Then willingly do as He instructs.

Samuel went and lay down in his place. And the LORD came,
and stood, and called as at other times, Samuel, Samuel.
Then Samuel answered, Speak; for thy servant heareth.

1 SAMUEL 3:9–10

Speak, gracious Lord, oh speak; thy servant hears;
For I'm thy servant and I'll still be so;
Speak words of comfort in my willing ears;
And since my tongue is in thy praises slow,
And since that thine all rhetoric exceeds;
Speak thou in words, but let me speak in deeds!
ALEXANDER POPE

MY PRAYER STARTER: God, You are not only my Savior but the Lord of my life, so the least I can do is obey Your every command. Reveal what You want me to do—I am listening.

There are days when you feel empty. When your faith feels weak at best. When your heart is cold toward others, perhaps even toward yourself and God. When your doubts seem stronger than your trust.

Amazingly enough, Martin Luther—the former priest, monk, and leader of the Protestant Reformation—felt all those things. So did the disciples. At times, Jesus referred to them as "ye of little faith" (Matthew 8:26). So if you find yourself feeling spiritually bereft, don't be ashamed. Instead, take all that you're experiencing to God. Be humble before Him. Tell Him where you're lacking and ask Him to fill the need. Jesus Christ will meet you where you are—and replenish you until your cup runneth over once again.

And he said unto me, My grace is sufficient for thee: for my strength is made perfect in weakness. Most gladly therefore will I rather glory in my infirmities, that the power of Christ may rest upon me.
2 CORINTHIANS 12:9

Behold, Lord, an empty vessel that needs to be filled. My Lord, fill it. I am weak in the faith; strengthen me. I am cold in love; warm me and make me fervent, that my love may go out to my neighbor. I do not have a strong and firm faith; at times I doubt and am unable to trust you altogether. O Lord, help me. Strengthen my faith and trust in you.
MARTIN LUTHER

MY PRAYER STARTER: God, Assurer of my salvation, my faith's fire grows dim at times. In these moments, kindle my belief again with Your breath, setting my soul ablaze with love for You.

Today's classic prayer is similar to Psalm 139:23–24—"Search me, O God, and know my heart: try me, and know my thoughts: and see if there be any wicked way in me, and lead me in the way everlasting"—but it has one big difference: the author is not just asking God to test him and know all his innermost thoughts, purposes, and ambitions; he's actually asking God to help *him* know and understand them. He's not just asking God to reveal a harmful path to him, but to lead him away from it and onto God's way. The speaker is begging God to search him well and then reveal himself to himself! Pray to know yourself today.

> *O Lord, thou hast searched me, and known me. Thou knowest*
> *my downsitting and mine uprising, thou understandest*
> *my thought afar off. Thou compassest my path and my*
> *lying down, and art acquainted with all my ways.*
>
> PSALM 139:1–3

Search me, oh God, and know my heart and help me know it; try me and know my innermost, undermost thoughts and purposes and ambitions, and help me know them; and see what way there be in me that is a grief to Thee; and then lead me. . .out of that way unto *Thy* way, *the* way everlasting. For Jesus' sake; aye for men's sake, too.
S. D. GORDON

MY PRAYER STARTER: All-knowing Father, as I peer through the mirror of Your Word, reveal to me who I truly am, erase my pride, and give me strength to change the imperfections I see.

Oh, to be free of temptation. To not be enticed to lie, to smoke that cigarette, or to watch that ungodly media. Temptation itself isn't evil, but giving in to it is. When temptation is satisfied, God is not. When a man is drawn away by temptation, the urge soon morphs into a habitual, besetting sin that begins to control his life. So ask God to cool your desire. Pray for Him to be with you in the storm of temptation. He'll lead you away!

And lead us not into temptation, but deliver us from evil: For thine is the kingdom, and the power, and the glory, for ever. Amen.
MATTHEW 6:13

Blessed are all Thy saints, O God and King, who have travelled over the tempestuous sea of this life and have made the harbour of peace and felicity. Watch over us who are still on our dangerous voyage; and remember such as lie exposed to the rough storms of trouble and temptations. Frail is our vessel, and the ocean is wide; but as in Thy mercy Thou hast set our course, so steer the vessel of our life towards the everlasting shore of peace, and bring us at length to the quiet haven of our heart's desire, where Thou, O God, art blessed and livest and reignest for ever. Amen.
SAINT AUGUSTINE

MY PRAYER STARTER: Father, I know that the lure of temptation can be more than I can bear. Fill me with Your power in these moments of weakness and save me from sin's destructive force.

British author Caryll Houselander wrote, "The one thing that [Mary] did and does is the one thing that we all have to do, namely, to bear Christ into the world." And her prayer below—equally applicable to men—is a perfect place to start. It's about presenting yourself to God so that you can become like Jesus and bear Him into your world. That means giving Him your body, eyes, mind, feet, hands, and heart in exchange for His humanity, vision, thoughts, path, prayer, and will to love. The more you give of yourself to enter Jesus' state, the more you will actually become like Him. He will increase and you will decrease. And although lessening yourself sounds scary, it's actually a miraculous paradox. For in that process, you will become *more* yourself, more the man you were created to be. Praise God!

I beseech you therefore, brethren, by the mercies of God, that
ye present your bodies a living sacrifice, holy, acceptable
unto God, which is your reasonable service.

ROMANS 12:1

Be born in us
Incarnate Love
take our flesh and blood and
give us Your humanity;
take our eyes and
give us Your vision;
take our minds and
give us Your pure thought;
CARYLL HOUSELANDER

take our feet and
set them in Your path;
take our hands and
fold them in Your prayer;
take our hearts and
give them Your will
to Love.

MY PRAYER STARTER: Almighty Creator, fill me with Yourself, displacing every ounce of my ego and replacing it with Your motives and Your love.

Today's prayer by Corrie ten Boom is simple. But to truly understand its power, one needs to examine its author. Corrie ten Boom lived with her sister Betsie and her watchmaker father, Casper, in the Netherlands. There, in their own home, they hid Jews in their closet, provided for them in a time of severe rationing, and helped them escape the Nazi Holocaust during World War II. The ten Booms' efforts to shield God's people from evil became known as the Dutch Resistance. When their subterfuge was discovered, the entire ten Boom family was arrested and sent to a German prison. Casper died ten days later. Corrie and Betsie landed in a German work camp where Betsie eventually died. Before leaving this world, she told her sister, "There is no pit so deep that He [God] is not deeper still." After her experiences, Corrie wrote the book *The Hiding Place.*

That's the history behind this powerful prayer. Now you can make it part of your own. Know that God is where you can hide from any evil that comes against you. Know that He is your ultimate protector. Hope in Him and His Word with the assurance that there's no pit so deep that God is not deeper still.

Thou art my hiding place and my shield: I hope in thy word.
PSALM 119:114

Thank you, Lord Jesus, that you will be our
hiding place, whatever happens.
CORRIE TEN BOOM

MY PRAYER STARTER: Lord, Refuge of our souls, this fallen world often resembles an inescapable ravine. Strengthen my footing, save me from the darkness, and hide me from the terrors within.

God is not just interested in *who* you are. He's also interested in *where* you are. And not just sometimes—but at *all times*. Yet it seems easy to get so caught up in your own plans for who and where you want to be in the world that you find yourself forgetting that God's plans should always override your own. So go to God in the morning. Seek out and hear His loving voice. Tell Him you trust Him to lead you down the right path. Then ask Him to reveal His desires to you, to tell you who and where He wants you to be—in both your inner and outer self. Lift yourself up to Him and He will tell you all you need to know.

> *Cause me to hear thy lovingkindness in the morning;*
> *for in thee do I trust: cause me to know the way wherein*
> *I should walk; for I lift up my soul unto thee.*
> PSALM 143:8

O God, grant that at all times you may find me as you desire me and where you would have me be, that you may lay hold on me fully, both by the Within and the Without of myself, grant that I may never break this double thread of my life.
TEILHARD DE CHARDIN

MY PRAYER STARTER: Lord God, align my plans with Yours. And if my plan runs contrary to Your will, reveal Your own plan to me and strengthen my resolve to follow it instead.

When you've made a misstep, you may find it difficult to ask God for His forgiveness. Yet that's exactly what you should do. For when you ask Him to forgive you, God blots out of His mind whatever you've done. He does this because He *wants* you to turn to Him—for all things amid all circumstances! So if you've intentionally or unintentionally stepped out of His way by turning to the dark instead of staying in His light—if you've left a brother or sister wounded, if you've preferred your plans over His, if in your impatience you've outrun Him, if you've broken a commandment, if you've injured those you love, or if you've muttered something against His will for your life—go to God. Ask Him to forgive you. Immediately, you'll be back in His good graces.

I have blotted out, as a thick cloud, thy transgressions, and,
as a cloud, thy sins: return unto me; for I have redeemed thee.

ISAIAH 44:22

If my soul has turned perversely to the dark;
If I have left some brother wounded by the way;
If I have preferred my aims to Thine;
If I have been impatient and would not wait;
If I have marred the pattern drawn out for my life;
If I have cost tears to those I loved;
If my heart has murmured against Thy will,
O Lord, forgive.

F. B. MEYER

MY PRAYER STARTER: Merciful Lord, thank You for pardoning my many mistakes. Let me never forget to ask for Your forgiveness whenever I slip.

Imagine living with the awareness that God's strength is continually flowing into you. That this holy strength, this power from your Creator and the Source of all things, is enough to meet your every need.

God gives—and is constantly exuding—all power. He's the source of all the strength you'll ever need to meet your challenges. *Your* job is to look for it, to hope for it, to expect it. That's what it means to wait upon God. And when you do, He'll power you up. He'll make you stronger than you ever thought possible. He'll raise you up like an eagle. You'll run and never tire. You'll walk where He has you go and not stumble into exhaustion. Make today's classic prayer your constant belief, your mantra, every moment of every day. And finalize it with an *amen*—a "so be it." And it will be!

> *He giveth power to the faint; and to them that have no might he increaseth strength. . . . They that wait upon the LORD shall renew their strength; they shall mount up with wings as eagles; they shall run, and not be weary; and they shall walk, and not faint.*
>
> ISAIAH 40:29, 31

God's strength flows into me continually, and is sufficient for my every need. . . . So be it; amen!
AGNES SANFORD

MY PRAYER STARTER: Mighty God, my own strength is not enough to fulfill the plans You have for me. Empower me, working through these limbs to display Your glory and love to others.

According to today's science, ending the day with a prayer of thanksgiving to God positively impacts you spiritually, emotionally, mentally, and physically. But the ancient writer of Psalm 4 knew this all along.

Don't stop at thanksgiving! Continue your prayer by asking God to bless those you love. Then put yourself in God's hands and lie down in peace, knowing He'll watch over you tonight and prepare you for a good day tomorrow.

> *Thou hast put gladness in my heart. . . . I will both lay me down in peace, and sleep: for thou, LORD, only makest me dwell in safety.*
> PSALM 4:7–8

We come before Thee, O Lord, in the end of thy day with thanksgiving. Our beloved in the far parts of the earth, those who are now beginning the labours of the day what time we end them, and those with whom the sun now stands at the point of noon, bless, help, console, and prosper them. Our guard is relieved, the service of the day is over, and the hour come to rest. We resign into thy hands our sleeping bodies, our cold hearths, and open doors. Give us to awake with smiles, give us to labour smiling. As the sun returns in the east, so let our patience be renewed with dawn; as the sun lightens the world, so let our loving-kindness make bright this house of our habitation.
ROBERT LOUIS STEVENSON

MY PRAYER STARTER: Father, thank You for Your protection, salvation, and peace. Direct my steps at day, keep me safe through the night, and remind me constantly of Your love.

C. S. Lewis, along with fellow Christians Charles Williams and Hugo Dyson, belonged to a literary group known as the Inklings. When Williams died, Lewis recorded Dyson as saying, "It is not blasphemous to believe that what was true of Our Lord is, in its less degree, true of all who are in Him. They go away in order to be with us in a new way, even closer than before."

Let today's classic prayer—and the idea that the one you've lost is still with you in some way—hearten you when you mourn the physical death of your loved one. Just as Jesus is still with you, so is the dear one who resides with Him now.

Lo, I am with you always, even unto the end of the world. Amen.
MATTHEW 28:20

Lord, my loved ones are near me.
I know that they live in the spirit.
My eyes can't see them because they have left their bodies for a moment, as one steps out of one's clothing. . . .
But in you, Lord, I hear them calling me. . . .
For they are now more vividly present.
Before, our bodies touched but not our souls.
Now I meet them when I meet you.
I receive them when I receive you.
I love them when I love you.
MICHEL QUOIST

MY PRAYER STARTER: Compassionate God, losing loved ones can be emotionally scarring. Help me believe that if they trusted You, they are now rejoicing in Your presence and waiting for me to join them.

This is a noisy world. It's easy to get caught up in the din of media and the voices and gossip of others. It's even hard to find a decent role model, whether on TV, in the movies, or in "real life." Fortunately, the apostle Paul gives some good advice in Colossians. He urges you to seek things above, not below. To set your heart, desires, and eyes on heavenly matters. To shut out all worldly distractions by thinking, talking, and focusing on the higher things. Because, after all, you've been called to a higher life in Jesus Christ. When you change your thoughts and mindset to Him, you lift the world.

If ye then be risen with Christ, seek those things which are above, where Christ sitteth on the right hand of God. Set your affection on things above, not on things on the earth. For ye are dead, and your life is hid with Christ in God.

COLOSSIANS 3:1–3

We pray shut us out from the world's clamour and the wagging tongues and the noisy booming voices, and the example that would lead us not toward Thee, but toward the world. Save us from it and shut us in with Thee, and may we think and talk and meditate on holy things today. This message now with Thy blessing may grace and mercy and peace be with us through Jesus Christ our Lord.

A. W. TOZER

MY PRAYER STARTER: Glorious Father, take my thoughts and motives away from the petty and temporal things of life. Fix them instead on Your glory and truth, which will last forever.

You have an idea in mind. And it seems like a good one. So you concoct a plan and the steps you would take to get there. But somehow, things aren't working out. Even plan B seems to miss the mark. You keep hitting a wall. You begin to wonder what's happening, what to do.

The same thing happened to Paul and Timothy. They thought they should go one way, but the Holy Spirit forbade them to do so. Then they determined to go another, but the Spirit prevented that step too. Finally, Paul had a vision, and they concluded that God was leading them in a different direction (see Acts 16:6–10).

If you find doors of opportunity being shut in your face, if you've come to a place where you don't know your next step, turn to God. He'll let you in on His plans. . .if not today, then tomorrow. Just when the timing is absolutely right in His eyes, He'll let you know what He's trying to teach you. He'll direct your steps down the right path.

A man's heart deviseth his way: but the LORD directeth his steps.
PROVERBS 16:9

Lord, we've tried everything we can think of. Every road has seemed a dead end. Doors have been so consistently shut in our faces that You must be trying to teach us something. Tell us what it is.
CATHERINE MARSHALL

MY PRAYER STARTER: All-knowing Lord, thwart my plans whenever they contradict Your will. My temporary discomfort will be forgotten when Your full, eternally significant plan is unveiled.

Worry can eat up your life. In fact, the word *fret*, a synonym for *worry*, comes from the Old English *fretan*, which means to "devour, feed upon, consume"!

The remedy for worry is to go to the God who resides within your heart. Spend time in His calming presence. Reawaken your awareness of how much bigger than your troubles He is. In Him you'll find all the hope and power you need to ward off worry—and more.

For God is not the author of confusion, but of peace.
1 CORINTHIANS 14:33

God of our secret life, weary of ourselves, we come to Your shelter. Our span of troubled days we bring within Your calm eternity. . . . In the strife of life and the sadness of mortality, we find a spirit of power and of hope in Your providence. Infinite Ruler of creation, whose spirit dwells in every world: we look not to the heavens for You, though You are there; we search not in the oceans for Your presence, though it murmurs with Your voice; we wait not for the wings of the wind to bring You near, though they are Your messengers; for You are in our hearts, O God. You make Your abode in the deep places of our thought and love. In each gentle affection, each contrite sorrow, each noble aspiration, we would worship You.
JAMES MARTINEAU

MY PRAYER STARTER: Lord, as long as You are by my side, worry has no place in my heart. Let Your peace replace my anxious thoughts, and remind me of Your power.

Jesus stopped at Martha's house. While "Martha was cumbered about much serving" (Luke 10:40), Mary "sat at Jesus' feet, and heard his word" (Luke 10:39). When Martha implored Jesus to tell Mary to help her, He replied, "Martha, Martha, thou art careful and troubled about many things: *but* one thing is needful: and Mary hath chosen that good part, which shall not be taken away from her" (Luke 10:41–42, emphasis added).

Whenever Jesus begins with a "but," He's calling your attention to something important. "*But* seek ye first the kingdom of God." That's the number-one priority God wants you to have. When you put sitting at His feet and listening above all things, everything else falls into place.

> But *seek ye first the kingdom of God, and his righteousness;*
> *and all these things shall be added unto you.*
> MATTHEW 6:33, EMPHASIS ADDED

O Father, calm the turbulence of our passions; quiet the throbbings of our hopes; repress the waywardness of our wills; direct the motions of our affections; and sanctify the varieties of our lot. Be Thou all in all to us; and may all things earthly, while we bend them to our growth in grace, dwell lightly in our hearts, so that we may readily, or even joyfully, give up whatever Thou dost ask for. May we seek first Thy kingdom and righteousness; resting assured that then all things needful shall be added unto us.
MARY CARPENTER

MY PRAYER STARTER: Heavenly Father, let me be a man of action when the time is right. But when You call me to sit at Your feet and listen, may I obey and surrender my urge to intervene.

God's Word is your doorway to knowledge. It's what gives you direction as it enfolds you, enlightening your spirit, informing your mind, stirring your heart, and guiding your soul. When you stay within the light of God's Word, it keeps you from going astray, from walking out of the path He's set before you—the one you alone were designed to walk.

When you bring God's Word before Him, He delights in your quest for knowledge, your thirst for hearing what He has to say. So seek God's wisdom and knowledge every day. Allow His Word to unfold before you. Ask Him to reveal the pattern you are to abide by. Meditate on His precepts, the ideas He is laying upon your heart. And then as you look up from the words He's written for you, follow that light, the one that leads you to life everlasting.

> *Thy word is a lamp unto my feet, and a light unto*
> *my path. . . . The entrance of thy words giveth light;*
> *it giveth understanding unto the simple.*
> PSALM 119:105, 130

Lord, thou hast given us thy Word for a light to shine upon our path; grant us so to meditate on that Word, and to follow its teaching, that we may find in it the light that shines more and more until the perfect day; through Jesus Christ our Lord.
SAINT JEROME

MY PRAYER STARTER: Lord, my eternal Guide, let Your Word be the light I need to traverse this dark world. Illuminate its pages, revealing to me the wisdom that lies within.

In Jeremiah 23:23–24, God says: "Am I a God at hand, saith the LORD, and not a God afar off? Can any hide himself in secret places that I shall not see him? saith the LORD. Do not I fill heaven and earth? saith the LORD." Three times the words "saith the LORD" appear. Sounds as if God is making a point.

There is nowhere you can go where God is not near. He's within you, around you, above you, and below you. He's at your right hand and your left. Beneath your feet and above. He's nearer than your own breath.

God is closer than you can imagine. For only in Him do you live and move and have your being (Acts 17:28). Live with that knowledge embedded deeply in your heart and mind.

Whither shall I go from thy spirit? or whither shall I flee from thy presence? If I ascend up into heaven, thou art there: if I make my bed in hell, behold, thou art there. If I take the wings of the morning, and dwell in the uttermost parts of the sea; even there shall thy hand lead me, and thy right hand shall hold me.

PSALM 139:7–10

Lord, you are closer to me
than my own breathing,
nearer than my hands and feet.
SAINT TERESA OF ÁVILA

MY PRAYER STARTER: God, I know You are always inseparably close. Whenever I feel alone, remind me of Your presence.

When you lose your God focus, you may become distracted and perhaps stumble. To regain your sight, ask God to show you the one thing *He* wants you to do.

After Saul was blinded on the road to Damascus, God said to the believer Ananias, "Arise, and go. . .and enquire" (Acts 9:11). Following God's specific directions, Ananias found Saul and laid his hands upon him—and the scales fell from Saul's eyes!

God wants you to follow Ananias's example. To open your eyes to the visions He imparts. To then eagerly and determinedly perform what He calls you to do. Who knows whose sight will be restored when you open your *own* eyes and obey?

> *To him said the Lord in a vision, Ananias. And he said, Behold, I am here, Lord. And the Lord said unto him, Arise, and go. . .and enquire. . .for one called Saul of Tarsus: for, behold, he prayeth, and hath seen in a vision a man named Ananias coming in, and putting his hand on him, that he might receive his sight.*
>
> ACTS 9:10–12

Grant me, O Lord, the single eye, that I may see the one thing needful, the thing that you want done. Don't let my vision be blurred by looking at too many things, or longing to please anyone but you. Give me simplicity of heart, quiet confidence in you, and eagerness to know and do your will.
GEORGE APPLETON

MY PRAYER STARTER: All-seeing God, sometimes my vision is blurred by the mundane. Clarify Your divine purpose for me, allowing me to spot opportunities to share Your light with others.

Author E. M. Bounds said, "Prayers are deathless. They outlive the lives of those who uttered them." It's true! Your prayers ascend to heaven, where angels hold golden bowls full of incense "which are the prayers of saints" (Revelation 5:8). The prayers are then hurled back to earth and sprayed among God's people (Revelation 8:3–5). All cries to God go *eternally* full circle!

Today's prayer of blessings for you, written by Saint Thérèse, is still alive! It exists for you to read and draw strength from, especially when you doubt where you are or where you're headed. Allow the saint's prayer to supply the peace you need. Trust that you're *exactly* where God wants you. Be encouraged to hope, use your talents, pass on God's love, and live in contentment. Then bring yourself and your own prayers before God, settling into the reality of His presence and the foreverness of prayer.

And the smoke of the incense, which came with the prayers of the saints, ascended up before God out of the angel's hand.

REVELATION 8:4

May today there be peace within.

May you trust God that you are exactly where you are meant to be.

May you not forget the infinite possibilities that are born of faith.

May you use those gifts that you have received,

and pass on the love that has been given to you.

May you be content knowing you are a child of God.

SAINT THÉRÈSE OF LISIEUX

MY PRAYER STARTER: Ever-listening Creator, may my prayers be like trees, rising to You and flowering with blessings that You pour down upon others.

Imagine being totally yielded up to God! To allow Him to use you as He would. To obey His every command. To leave all of your plans, ideas, and steps up to Him, knowing He's wiser than you. Have you utterly given yourself—your life and all that you are—up to God?

Pray for that today. God has chosen you for a specific purpose, one you alone can fulfill when you let Him work through you unobstructed. When you willingly give Him all of you—mind, spirit, body, soul, and heart—you'll be amazed at the freedom in which you'll abide, the answers to prayer you'll receive, and the blessings that will flow through you and into the world!

Ye have not chosen me, but I have chosen you, and ordained you, that ye should go and bring forth fruit, and that your fruit should remain: that whatsoever ye shall ask of the Father in my name, he may give it you.

JOHN 15:16

O Lord, I give myself to thee, I trust thee wholly. Thou art wiser than I, more loving to me than I myself. Deign to fulfil thy high purposes in me whatever they be; work in me and through me. I am born to serve thee, to be thine, to be thy instrument. Let me be thy blind instrument. I ask not to see, I ask not to know, I ask simply to be used. Amen.

JOHN HENRY NEWMAN

MY PRAYER STARTER: Father, let me be an obedient son to You. Direct my every thought, word, and action, and let nothing prevent me from following Your lead.

Few things are more precious than the friends God has put into your life. Think about them today. Thank God for connecting your paths. Then, in love, offer up your prayer for them to the greatest friend you'll ever have—Jesus.

This is my commandment, That ye love one another, as I have loved you.
JOHN 15:12

O blessed Lord and Saviour, who hast commanded us to love one another, grant us grace that, having received Thine undeserved bounty, we may love every man in Thee and for Thee. We implore Thy clemency for all; but especially for the friends whom Thy love has given to us. Love Thou them, O Thou fountain of love, and make them to love Thee with all their heart, with all their mind, and with all their soul, that those things only which are pleasing to Thee they may will, and speak, and do. . . . Measure not to them Thy goodness by the dulness of our devotion; but as Thy kindness surpasseth all human affection, so let Thy hearing transcend our prayer. Do Thou that they. . .may attain in the end to everlasting life.
SAINT ANSELM

MY PRAYER STARTER: Lord, thank You for giving me friends to accompany me in my journey home. Bless them with Your peace and give them the endurance to keep walking onward.

Some days, your mind may be too crowded with thoughts of what you should do. Unfortunately, such thoughts are often followed by worry over where you'll get the strength for your next task. Here's where God must enter the equation.

Open your mind to God's presence. Ask Him to shine His light on your thoughts. To flood your mind with the beams of His wisdom. To revise your plans for today so that they align with His goal for your life. Then know He'll give you the power to do what He's called you to do—for the glory of God, His Son, and His Spirit.

> *[I pray] that the God of our Lord Jesus Christ, the Father of glory, may give unto you the spirit of wisdom and revelation in the knowledge of him: the eyes of your understanding being enlightened; that ye may know what is the hope of his calling, and what the riches of the glory of his inheritance in the saints, and what is the exceeding greatness of his power to usward.*
> EPHESIANS 1:17–19

We beseech thee, O Lord, to enlighten our minds and to strengthen our wills, that we may know what we ought to do, and be enabled to do it, through the grace of thy most Holy Spirit, and for the merits of thy Son, Jesus Christ our Lord.
WILLIAM BRIGHT

MY PRAYER STARTER: Lord, God of all wisdom, penetrate the fog of confusion in my mind with Your clarity. Illuminate my path, one step at a time.

DAY 49

Not only does worry rob you of energy, it robs you of your life. It blinds you from seeing what the Son is doing, inwardly and outwardly. So turn your anxious thoughts into thanks of wonder! By doing so, you won't miss where the Light is leading you.

Therefore I say unto you, Take no thought for your life. . . .
Which of you by taking thought can add one cubit unto his stature?
MATTHEW 6:25, 27

O God, we thank Thee for this universe, our great home; for its vastness and its riches, and for the manifoldness of the life which teems upon it and of which we are a part. We praise Thee for the arching sky and the blessed winds, for the driving clouds and the constellations on high. We praise Thee for the salt sea and the running water, for the everlasting hills, for the trees, and for the grass under our feet. We thank Thee for our senses by which we can see the splendor of the morning, and hear the jubilant songs of love, and smell the breath of the springtime. Grant us, we pray Thee, a heart wide open to all this joy and beauty, and save our souls from being so steeped in care or so darkened by passion that we pass heedless and unseeing when even the thornbush by the wayside is aflame with the glory of God.
WALTER RAUSCHENBUSCH

MY PRAYER STARTER: Magnificent Creator, I am amazed by the intricate world You've made. In light of such splendor, let my thoughts rise above my worries and toward Your greatness.

When you feel weak—tired of your work, your pleasures, your postponed hopes, and your very own self—go to the One who sees you, knows you, and longs to bring you out of yourself and into Him. Go to Jesus. He'll be your hiding place, the One who shelters you from the wind and storms of life. Your Lord, your King, looks upon you with compassion and tenderness. He wants to be the Rock you look to, the One you stand on. The Rock that will provide you with shade when the sun is at its hottest. Allow Him to be all that—and more. He'll gently draw you to Himself, giving you the true rest you need in this wearying land.

> *Behold, a king shall reign in righteousness, and princes shall rule in judgment. And a man shall be as an hiding place from the wind, and a covert from the tempest; as rivers of water in a dry place, as the shadow of a great rock in a weary land.*
> ISAIAH 32:1–2

O Lord, who art the shadow of a great rock in a weary land, who beholdest thy weak creatures, weary of labour, weary of pleasures, weary of heart from hope deferred, and weary of self. In thine abundant compassion and unutterable tenderness bring us we pray thee, unto thy rest, through Jesus Christ, thy Son, our Saviour.
CHRISTINA ROSSETTI

MY PRAYER STARTER: Lord, my great Provider, when I grow too weary to stand, let me lean on You. Guide me into my home of ultimate rest.

Sometimes, you may find your eyes glazing over at the name *God*. Perhaps because you use it so often in your prayers, it's lost its power for you. If so, consider using a name the Hebrews used for Him, one that reflects His many aspects, one that sparks your heart and fits your current need.

As the shepherd David penned Psalm 23, he thought deeply about his own occupation and compared it to his relationship with God. Since David, like his sheep, trusted God for guidance and protection from his enemies, he referred to God as The Lord Our Shepherd.

You too can address God by His many aspects. Here are a few: The Lord Is There, The Lord Will Provide, Strong Tower, God Most High, The God who Watches Over Me, Refuge, Shield, Fortress, The Lord Is Peace, The Lord My Rock, and Dwelling Place. Call God by a name that will bring more power to your heart and prayer life!

We will walk in the name of the LORD our God for ever and ever.
MICAH 4:5

God, this word we call you by
is almost dead and meaningless,
transient and empty
like all the words men use.
We ask you
to renew its force and meaning,
to make it once again
a name that brings your
HUUB OOSTERHUIS

promise to us.
Make it a living word
which tells us
that you will be for us
as you have always been—
trustworthy and hidden
and very close to us,
Our God, now and for ever.

MY PRAYER STARTER: Lord, whose name rests above all names, may I always find new ways to praise You through the many titles that belong to You. May my prayers never grow stale.

Some days, you may find yourself so wrapped up in your daily business, so driven by the stress of your day, so involved in running to and from appointments or from deadline to deadline that you have drifted away from Jesus—not physically, but mentally, emotionally, and spiritually. That's when you need to pray for Jesus to draw you to Himself. For when your awareness of Him fills every thought and space of your spirit and heart, you will become more His—more open to His voice, direction, love, peace, and light.

When under stress, look up to the One who can take you out of yourself and into Him. Allow Jesus to enfold you in His arms, carry you close to His chest, and gently lead you into His peace of heart and mind (Isaiah 40:11).

> *No man can come to me, except the Father which hath sent me*
> *draw him: and I will raise him up at the last day. . . . And I,*
> *if I be lifted up from the earth, will draw all men unto me.*
>
> JOHN 6:44; 12:32

Yea, Lord Jesus Christ, whether we be far off or near, far away from Thee in the human swarm, in business, in earthly cares, in temporal joys, in merely human highness, or far from all this, forsaken, unappreciated, in lowliness, and with this the nearer to Thee, do Thou draw us, draw us entirely to Thyself.
SØREN KIERKEGAARD

MY PRAYER STARTER: Constant Father, anchor my soul with Your Word. May the petty details of life never nudge me away from Your presence.

In Matthew 25:31–40, Jesus told a parable about a King who, upon His return, will say to the ones right with God, "You are blessed because when I was hungry, you fed me; when I was thirsty, you gave me a drink. When I was a stranger to you, you welcomed me. When I was naked, you dressed me. When I was sick or in prison, you came to see me." And the people asked, "When did we see you hungry, thirsty, a stranger, naked, and sick or imprisoned, then feed, quench, welcome, clothe, and visit you?" And the King replied, "When you did those things for the lowest of the low, you did them for me."

In other words, Jesus says that whatever you do for someone else, you do for Him. So when you look at that person—friend or foe, stranger or relative—you're to see Jesus. You're to love all whom you encounter. To see them as God Himself. This is not only love personified—it is love perfected!

Ask God to give you the power to see His face in everyone else's.

No man hath seen God at any time. If we love one another,
God dwelleth in us, and his love is perfected in us.

1 JOHN 4:12

Grant me to recognize in other men, Lord
God, the radiance of your own face.
TEILHARD DE CHARDIN

MY PRAYER STARTER: God, Creator of humanity, You made us all in Your image. Help me to see this image when I look into the eyes of my neighbor, never failing to love them as You love me.

The Holy Three—God, Jesus, and the Spirit—are an unfathomable mystery, but They are there for you, deep within. Spend time exploring the truth of Their presence today.

> *And I will pray the Father, and he shall give you another Comforter,*
> *that he may abide with you for ever; even the Spirit of truth; whom*
> *the world cannot receive, because it seeth him not, neither knoweth*
> *him: but ye know him; for he dwelleth with you, and shall be in you.*
>
> JOHN 14:16–17

You, O eternal Trinity, are a deep sea, into which the more I enter the more I find, and the more I find the more I seek. . . . As the hart desires the springs of living water, so my soul desires to leave the prison of this dark body and see you in truth.

O abyss, O eternal Godhead, O sea profound, what more could you give me than yourself? You are the fire that ever burns without being consumed; you consumed in your heat all the soul's self-love; you are the fire which takes away cold; with your light you illuminate me so that I may know all your truth. Clothe me, clothe me with yourself, eternal truth, so that I may run this mortal life with true obedience, and with the light of your most holy faith.

CATHERINE OF SIENA

MY PRAYER STARTER: Mysterious Lord, help me to revel in Your mystery. Stay by my side, and never let me grow bored with Your awe-inspiring truth and presence.

You rise from prayer to begin your duties. You feel set to meet the challenges before you, with God at the forefront of your eyes, ears, and thoughts. But then you actually *begin* your work, get caught up in the busyness of your day, and your consciousness of God takes flight!

Today's classic prayer addresses that contingency. It admits to God that a busy day lies ahead. But it asks, before the worker enters it, for God to keep his duties in line with God's. To keep his spiritual life on God's course whether or not he is actively aware of God's presence. You may want to pray today's prayers *every* day to keep your duties on God's track!

> *Commit thy works unto the LORD,*
> *and thy thoughts shall be established.*
> PROVERBS 16:3

O Lord, I have a busy world around me; eye, ear, and thought will be needed for all my work to be done in that busy world. Now, before I enter upon it, I would commit eye, ear, and thought, to thee! Do thou bless them and keep their work thine, such as, through thy natural laws, my heart beats and my blood flows without any thought of mine for them, so may my spiritual life hold on its course at those times when my mind cannot consciously turn to thee to commit each particular thought to thy service. Hear my prayer for my dear Redeemer's sake. Amen.
THOMAS ARNOLD

MY PRAYER STARTER: Father, let Your Word be so ingrained into my mind that I instinctively follow its instructions, even when life is at its busiest. May I never run out of time to pray.

When your own power is gone and you feel hopeless, that's the time to go to the unchanging One. Seek God—without Him, you're powerless. Ask Him to remove all that's not of Him and to fill you with the fruits of His Spirit. Flee to the Refuge who holds all promise for your life, and trust He'll bring you through. As you wait on God, He'll renew you and power you up. He'll be your arm of strength—your defense every morning—and help you meet whatever your day brings.

O LORD, be gracious unto us; we have waited for thee: be thou their arm every morning, our salvation also in the time of trouble.

ISAIAH 33:2

O Lord, reassure me with Your quickening Spirit;
without You I can do nothing.
Mortify in me all ambition, vanity, vainglory,
worldliness, pride, selfishness, and resistance from God,
and fill me with love, peace, and all the fruits of the Spirit. . . .
I would surrender myself to You,
trusting Your precious promises
and against hope believing in hope.
You are the same yesterday, today, and forever;
and therefore, waiting on Thee, Lord,
I trust that I shall at length renew my strength.
WILLIAM WILBERFORCE

MY PRAYER STARTER: Dependable Lord, be with me as I start the day. Let Your Spirit guide my actions and empower me to face whatever happens.

God searches us. He sees beyond our disguises. His love bears all our missteps, overlooks all our mistakes, and helps us see ourselves as we truly are. Only then, when our vision is totally clear, can we see *others* as they truly are. For then, we're looking through the eyes of God.

Allow today's prayers to draw you near to God. Let Him search you from top to bottom. He'll show you the truth, give you the strength to bear it, and raise you fearless in Him.

> *But God hath revealed them unto us by his Spirit: for the*
> *Spirit searcheth all things, yea, the deep things of God.*
> 1 CORINTHIANS 2:10

O God, whose spirit searcheth all things, and whose love beareth all things, encourage us to draw near to Thee in sincerity and in truth. Save us from a worship of the lips while our hearts are far away. Save us from the useless labour of attempting to conceal ourselves from Thee who searchest the heart.

Enable us to lay aside all those cloaks and disguises which we wear in the light of day and here to bare ourselves, with all our weakness, disease and sin, naked to Thy sight.

Make us strong enough to bear the vision of the truth, and to have done with all falsehood, pretence, and hypocrisy, so that we may see things as they are, and fear no more.
WILLIAM EDWIN ORCHARD

MY PRAYER STARTER: All-seeing God, help me bare my emotions and deepest thoughts to You. Then implant Your love in my heart so that I can show it to others.

Your character is determined by what you allow to reign over you. Is Jesus Christ on the throne of your life, thoughts, and spirit, or has something else taken possession of you, leading you down the wrong path? Although you may have no power to resist the thoughts that war against the law of your mind, Jesus does. So call Him in! Invite the King of Peace to take over the throne of your mind once again. He *will* deliver you!

> *But I see another law in my members, warring against the law of my*
> *mind, and bringing me into captivity to the law of sin which is in*
> *my members. . . . Who shall deliver me from the body of this death?*
> *I thank God through Jesus Christ our Lord. So then with the mind*
> *I myself serve the law of God; but with the flesh the law of sin.*
>
> ROMANS 7:23–25

O Lord, come quickly and reign on Thy throne, for now oft-times something rises up within me, and tries to take possession of Thy throne: pride, covetousness, uncleanness, and sloth want to be my kings; and then evil-speaking, anger, hatred, and the whole train of vices join with me in warring against myself, and try to reign over me. I resist them, I cry out against them, and say, "I have no other king than Christ." O King of Peace, come and reign in me, for I will have no king but Thee! Amen.

SAINT BERNARD

MY PRAYER STARTER: Righteous King, rule over the kingdom of my heart. Conquer any sinful attitudes or habits that might have creeped in, and transform me into Your trusted servant.

When worry stirs up a hurricane of unease within, your sole recourse is to turn to God. He's the only One powerful enough to calm the troubled sea of your heart. And once His peace overrides your storm, you can focus your all on Him, your Refuge.

> *O Lord, thou art my God; I will exalt thee, I will praise thy name; for thou hast done wonderful things. . . . For thou hast been a strength to the poor, a strength to the needy in his distress, a refuge from the storm, a shadow from the heat.*
>
> ISAIAH 25:1, 4

Oh, Lord, unto whom all hearts are open, Thou canst govern the vessel of my soul far better than I can. Arise, O Lord, and command the stormy wind and the troubled sea of my heart to be still, and at peace in Thee, that I may look up to Thee undisturbed, and abide in union with Thee, my Lord. Let me not be carried hither and thither by wandering thoughts; but, forgetting all else, let me see and hear Thee. Renew my spirit; kindle me in Thy light, that it may shine within me, and my heart may burn in love and adoration towards Thee. Let Thy Holy Spirit dwell in me continually, and make me Thy temple and sanctuary, and fill me with divine love and light and life, with devout and heavenly thoughts, with comfort and strength, with joy and peace. Amen.
JOHANN ARNDT

MY PRAYER STARTER: Father, when the winds of fear and anxiety start blowing in my mind, send Your Spirit to calm the storm. Keep my eyes locked on You, lest I slip beneath the waves.

Oh, how often our thoughts go wild, leading us astray from God's reality. Based on the sight before us, we consider an idea—usually a mistaken one that feeds our fears. Then we are driven to add on to that mistaken premise with even more wild imaginings that we choose to treat as facts! Before we know it, our false notions have constructed an entirely false scenario, a dark, fabricated castle of resentment, despair, and doubt.

To keep yourself thinking correctly, pray for God to help you live in *His* reality—not yours! Ask Him for more faith, for Him to exchange your thoughts for His. Know that only His reality and His words can lead you to the truth, restoring your faith in Him.

I have spread out my hands all the day unto a rebellious people,
which walketh in a way that was not good, after their own thoughts.
ISAIAH 65:2

Oh, let me live in thy realities,
Nor substitute my notions for thy facts,
Notion with notion making leagues and pacts;
They are to truth but as dream-deeds to acts,
And questioned, make me doubt of everything.
"O Lord, my God," my heart gets up and cries,
"Come thy own self, and with thee my faith bring."
GEORGE MACDONALD, *Diary of an Old Soul*

MY PRAYER STARTER: God of all truth, I know that my mind can play tricks on me. Let me never trust my own flawed reasoning skills over Your perfect wisdom.

Your heart is an important part of you. It's your very center. Out of it flow your feelings, thoughts, and will. As such, you're to guard it above all other things (Proverbs 4:23).

And when it comes to seeking God, to making Him an indispensable part of your life, you're to use your *entire* heart.

Because your heart is so important, pray that God would give you one that's true to Him alone. Ask Him to give you a heart that cannot be conquered by trouble or waylaid by something unworthy of His plan for your life.

With such a pure heart that beats for and seeks only God, you'll find a faithfulness that envelops God with an unimaginable degree of love and passion.

> *But if from thence thou shalt seek the LORD thy God, thou shalt find him, if thou seek him with all thy heart and with all thy soul.*
> DEUTERONOMY 4:29

Give me, O Lord, a steadfast heart, which no unworthy affection may drag downwards; give me an unconquered heart, which no tribulation can wear out; give me an upright heart, which no unworthy purpose may tempt aside.

Bestow upon me also, O Lord my God, understanding to know Thee, diligence to seek Thee, wisdom to find Thee, and a faithfulness that may finally embrace Thee. Amen.
SAINT THOMAS AQUINAS

MY PRAYER STARTER: Lord, let my heart be a compass that always points toward You. Let me be faithful to You, for You've been perfectly faithful to me.

Even when you're not sure where you're going or where God's leading you, trust Him. After God called Abraham to go to a place he'd never seen before, Abraham obeyed because he had complete trust in God. He believed in God's promises. He walked, keeping his eyes on his Source. And God credited it to him as righteousness (Genesis 15:6)! Determine in your heart and soul to do the same.

> *By faith Abraham, when he was called to go out into a place which*
> *he should after receive for an inheritance, obeyed; and he went*
> *out, not knowing whither he went. By faith he sojourned in the*
> *land of promise, as in a strange country. . . : for he looked for a*
> *city which hath foundations, whose builder and maker is God.*
> HEBREWS 11:8–10

O Thou Eternal, in Whose appointment our life standeth! Thou hast committed our work to us, and we could commit our cares to Thee. May we feel that we are not our own, and that Thou wilt heed our wants, while we are intent upon Thy will. May we never dwell carelessly or say in our hearts, "I am here, and there is none over me"; nor anxiously, as though our path were hid; but with a mind simply fixed upon our trust, and choosing nothing but the dispositions of Thy Providence.
JAMES MARTINEAU

MY PRAYER STARTER: Faithful God, let me trust You enough to keep walking forward, even when I can't see the ground. Give me the faith to follow You impulsively, never questioning Your motives.

How wonderful that you have Someone who not only loves you throughout your life but will continue to love you when the storms of life have passed! His name is God. And because of His Son, Jesus, there's a place waiting for you in heaven.

Even now, you've already entered into this heavenly existence because of Jesus. In Him, nothing can touch your spirit. So sprint into the arms of the Shepherd. He's waiting to guide, protect, and carry you. He'll still the seas, calm the waves of worry. He'll hide you when you need a refuge, and then He'll renew and strengthen you as you wait out the storm. And at the end, He will bring you to your haven, where there'll be no more pain or sorrow—only light and love.

> *Blessed be the God and Father of our Lord Jesus Christ,*
> *which according to his abundant mercy hath begotten us*
> *again unto a lively hope by the resurrection of Jesus Christ*
> *from the dead, to an inheritance incorruptible, and undefiled,*
> *and that fadeth not away, reserved in heaven for you.*

1 PETER 1:3–4

Jesus, Lover of my soul,
Let me to Thy bosom fly,
While the nearer waters roll,
While the tempest still is high:
Hide me, O my Saviour, hide,
Till the storm of life is past;
Safe into the haven guide,
O receive my soul at last.
CHARLES WESLEY

MY PRAYER STARTER: God, bring down Your kingdom of peace into my heart. Let me endure whatever suffering I may face, and may Your love within me be infectious to everyone I meet.

The Holy Spirit takes many forms. As wind or breath, the Holy Spirit invisibly but powerfully enters your world (Acts 2:2). As a dove, the Holy Spirit provides you with gentleness and peace (Luke 3:22). As water, the Holy Spirit cleanses and washes (John 7:37–39). As a cloud, the Holy Spirit leads you down the right road (Exodus 16:10). As dew, the Holy Spirit refreshes (Genesis 2:4–6). As fire, the Holy Spirit refines, bringing out the best in you (Isaiah 4:4). As the anointing oil, the Holy Spirit soothes and heals you (Acts 10:38). As a still, small voice, the Holy Spirit whispers to your innermost self (1 Kings 19:11–13).

Pray to the Holy Spirit today, in all His facets. Allow Him to be your power, peace, cleanser, guide, refresher, refiner, soother, and intimate adviser.

> *I tell you the truth; It is expedient for you that I go away:*
> *for if I go not away, the Comforter will not come unto*
> *you; but if I depart, I will send him unto you.*
> JOHN 16:7

As the wind is thy symbol, so forward our goings.

As the dove, so launch us heavenwards.

As water, so purify our spirits.

As a cloud, so abate our temptation.

As dew, so revive our languor.

As fire, so purge out our dross.

CHRISTINA ROSSETTI

MY PRAYER STARTER: Holy Spirit, fill me with all Your facets. Let this man reflect Your perfect attributes to everyone I meet.

The word *praise* appears 259 times in the King James Bible! In Psalms, it shows up 150 times! Psalm 150 gives the who, what, where, when, how, and why of praise. Who should give the Lord praise and thanks for all He's done? "Every thing that hath breath" (Psalm 150:6). How and with what? With the sound of a musical instrument, which could include your voice, and with dancing (Psalm 150:3–5). Where? "In his sanctuary" (Psalm 150:1), which now lies within you (1 Corinthians 3:16)! For what? "For his mighty acts. . .according to his excellent greatness" (Psalm 150:2).

This is just the beginning. As you praise God continually, your blessings will accumulate. Consider exploring what else the Bible says about praise, for the sake of you and your Lord Jesus Christ.

For here have we no continuing city, but we seek one to come. By [Jesus] therefore let us offer the sacrifice of praise to God continually, that is, the fruit of our lips giving thanks to his name.
HEBREWS 13:14–15

O God our Father, we would thank thee for all the bright things of life. Help us to see them, and to count them, and to remember them, that our lives may flow in ceaseless praise; for the sake of Jesus Christ our Lord.
JOHN HENRY JOWETT

MY PRAYER STARTER: Majestic Creator, Your glory exceeds all imagination. Help me continually find new ways to praise You.

There are some things you just can't do on your own. And one of those things is managing yourself. You must admit that you are the clay and *God* is the potter. You are the work of His hand. So give yourself up to Him. Let Him take you over completely. God will mold you into the man He wants you to be, someone who is splendid in His eyes. Then you will be empowered to do His good work.

If a man therefore purge himself from these [dishonorable things], he shall be a vessel unto honour, sanctified, and meet for the master's use, and prepared unto every good work.

2 TIMOTHY 2:21

Here, Lord, I abandon myself to Thee. I have tried in every way I could think of to manage myself, and to make myself what I know I ought to be, but have always failed. Now I give it up to Thee. Do Thou take entire possession of me. Work in me all the good pleasure of Thy will. Mold and fashion me into such a vessel as seemeth good to Thee. I leave myself in Thy hands, and I believe Thou wilt, according to Thy promise, make me into a vessel unto Thy own honor, "sanctified, and meet for the Master's use, and prepared unto every good work."

HANNAH WHITALL SMITH

MY PRAYER STARTER: Almighty God, let me never interfere with Your sculpting. Chip away anything that comes between You and me, no matter how much it might mean to me.

At times, you may feel as if the vision you had for your life is fading. You don't understand why certain things have happened. You're uncertain of the way forward.

Pray for God to help you continue trusting Him. Allow Him to take you by the hand as a loving father would a small child. He'll give you confident hope to quiet your heart and mind.

> *Behold, what manner of love the Father hath bestowed*
> *upon us, that we should be called the sons of God.*
>
> 1 JOHN 3:1

Grant unto us, Almighty God, that when our vision fails, and our understanding is darkened; when the ways of life seem hard, and the brightness of life is gone—to us grant the wisdom that deepens faith when the sight is dim, and enlarges trust when the understanding is not clear. And whensoever Thy ways in nature or in the soul are hard to be understood, then may our quiet confidence, our patient trust, our loving faith in Thee be great, and as children knowing that they are loved, cared for, guarded, kept, may we with a quiet mind at all times put our trust in the unseen God. So may we face life without fear, and death without fainting; and, whatsoever may be in the life to come, give us confident hope that whatsoever is best for us both here and hereafter is Thy good pleasure and will be Thy law. Amen.
GEORGE DAWSON

MY PRAYER STARTER: Lord of wisdom, my vision is often blurred by my own limitations. Give me Your spiritual sight so that I will never stray from Your perfect plan.

God has enlightened your mind so that you can see and desire Him. Because of your love for Him, a supernatural joy has sprouted in your heart. And because you serve Him, He's toughened your will, enabling you to become a coworker in His plans for this world. But this is only the beginning!

Pray that God will allow you to know Him even *more*, to consistently see His hand working in your life, to *grow* in your sincere love for Him. And because of that love, to serve Him *more* fully. For in that greater knowledge, that increased love, that fuller service, you'll find your perfect, eternal freedom in Jesus!

And we know that we are of God. . . . And we know that the
Son of God is come, and hath given us an understanding, that we
may know him that is true, and we are in him that is true, even
in his Son Jesus Christ. This is the true God, and eternal life.

1 JOHN 5:19–20

Eternal God, who are the light of the minds that know you,
the joy of the hearts that love you, and the strength of the
wills that serve you; grant us so to know you, that we may
truly love you, and so to love you that we may fully serve you,
whom to serve is perfect freedom, in Jesus Christ our Lord.
SAINT AUGUSTINE

MY PRAYER STARTER: Loving Father, I love You and want to serve You with all my being. Help me to never stop kindling the fire of my love until I reach my eternal home with You.

As you're on your Christian walk, working at pleasing God and becoming more like Jesus, you'll need a few supplies—namely, the ability to understand, discern, seek, find, know, meditate upon, hear, see, and proclaim God.

To begin, go to God with today's prayers. Ask Him for all you need—intellect, reason, diligence, wisdom, a spirit, a heart, ears, eyes, a tongue, a way of life, patience, perseverance, and more. He'll grant all your requests to continue His—and your—good work.

I thank my God. . .always in every prayer of mine for you all making request with joy, for your fellowship in the gospel from the first day until now; being confident of this very thing, that he which hath begun a good work in you will perform it until the day of Jesus Christ.

PHILIPPIANS 1:3–6

Gracious and Holy Father, Please give me: intellect to understand you, reason to discern you, diligence to seek you, wisdom to find you, a spirit to know you, a heart to meditate upon you, ears to hear you, eyes to see you, a tongue to proclaim you, a way of life pleasing to you, patience to wait for you and perseverance to look for you. Grant me a perfect end, your holy presence, a blessed resurrection and life everlasting.

SAINT BENEDICT OF NURSIA

MY PRAYER STARTER: Lord, following You takes many supplies that only You can give. Please open my heart to receive them, and give me wisdom to put them to good use.

Jesus was all about love. He showed God's love by dying for you before you even knew Him. He loved you then and He loves you now. His great plea was for you to love God with all your being and to love others as you love yourself. Jesus knew that this world needs more love, first and foremost for Him. All other love flows from that Source. So keep praying that you'll love Jesus more. Soon, you'll be so full of the King of love that fear will have no room to reside.

God is love; and he that dwelleth in love dwelleth in God, and God in him. . . . There is no fear in love; but perfect love casteth out fear.
1 JOHN 4:16, 18

Lord Jesus Christ, that we may be able rightly to pray Thee for all things, we pray first for one: help us to love Thee much, increase love and inflame it. Oh, this is a prayer Thou wilt surely hear, Thou who indeed art not love of such a sort—so cruel a sort—that Thou art only the object, indifferent to whether any one loves Thee or not; Thou indeed art not love of such a sort—in wrath—that Thou art only judgment, jealous of who loves Thee and who does not. Oh, no, such Thou art not; Thou wouldst thus only inspire fear and dread, it would then be terrible "to come to Thee," frightful "to abide with Thee," and Thou wouldst not be the perfect love which castest out fear. No, compassionate, or loving, or in love, Thou art love of such a sort that Thou Thyself dost woo forth the love which loves Thee, dost foster it to love Thee much.
SØREN KIERKEGAARD

MY PRAYER STARTER: Father, may every ounce of my love be directed toward You and, by extension, toward everyone I meet.

When things get desperate, all you need is a short prayer: "Lord, hold me up! Hold me, Lord, by my right hand!" That's today's classic prayer—and it's a good one.

Today's verses reveal how well God backs up this eleven-word plea. He promises you *twice* that you need not fear. He's God. He's with you. He'll give you all the strength you need. *Twice,* He says He'll help. *Twice,* He says He'll hold your right hand. And *three* times, God promises that all those opposing people, things, and situations will come to naught!

So take the verses below to heart. Then memorize this eleven-word prayer. It's packed with all the power you need—and more!

Fear thou not; for I am with thee: be not dismayed; for I am thy God: I will strengthen thee; yea, I will help thee; yea, I will uphold thee with the right hand of my righteousness. Behold, all they that were incensed against thee shall be ashamed and confounded: they shall be as nothing; and they that strive with thee shall perish. Thou shalt seek them, and shalt not find them, even them that contended with thee: they that war against thee shall be as nothing, and as a thing of nought. For I the LORD thy God will hold thy right hand, saying unto thee, Fear not; I will help thee.

ISAIAH 41:10–13

Lord, hold me up! Hold me, Lord, by my right hand!
CHARLES SPURGEON

MY PRAYER STARTER: Mighty Lord, when the weight of the world gets too heavy for me to bear, hold me up with Your right hand. Invigorate me with Your power and strengthen my faith.

God has enormous power. He made the earth, sea, and land. He brought life and light to all creatures. He can do anything! Do you need help? Ask God. Pray that He would save those in trouble, have mercy on the fallen, reveal Himself to the needy, heal believers and nonbelievers alike, bring in sheep that have wandered, lift those with no strength, and give ease to the brokenhearted. When you pray, God will do all that. Why? Because *all* are His sheep, in His fold, under the care, protection, and guidance of Jesus Christ the Shepherd. They're in His good hands—as are you.

> *The sea is his, and he made it: and his hands formed the dry*
> *land. O come, let us worship and bow down: let us kneel*
> *before the LORD our maker. For he is our God; and we are*
> *the people of his pasture, and the sheep of his hand.*
>
> PSALM 95:5–7

We beseech Thee, Lord and Master, to be our help and succor. Save those who are in tribulation; have mercy on the lonely; lift up the fallen; show Thyself unto the needy; heal the ungodly; convert the wanderers of Thy people; feed the hungry; raise up the weak; comfort the faint-hearted. Let all the peoples know that Thou art God alone, and Jesus Christ is Thy Son, and we are Thy people and the sheep of Thy pasture; for the sake of Christ Jesus. Amen.
SAINT CLEMENT OF ROME

MY PRAYER STARTER: Lord, Good Shepherd, protect Your sheep. Deliver us from the wolves of this world, and guide us into Your peaceful green pastures.

Lies. Some are casual, some half truths, some "little white lies." But they're basically the same. One little deception leads to another, then to another, then to a whole web of them.

It began in the garden of Eden. When the serpent asked Eve, "Did God actually say. . . ?" Eve added her own "edited" version of God's instructions. Then the serpent responded, "Ye shall not surely die" (Genesis 3:4)—a half truth, at best. Lie-believing Eve not only died but opened death's door to all.

God never wants His people to hear or utter lies. That's why He sent the Holy Spirit to speak and lead you into truth.

Lie not one to another, seeing that ye have put off the old man with his deeds; and have put on the new man, which is renewed in knowledge after the image of him that created him.
COLOSSIANS 3:9–10

Almighty God, who hast sent the Spirit of truth unto us to guide us into all truth, so rule our lives by thy power, that we may be truthful in word, deed, and thought. O keep us, most merciful Saviour, with thy gracious protection, that no fear or hope may ever make us false in act or speech. Cast out from us whatsoever loveth or maketh a lie, and bring us all to the perfect freedom of thy truth; through Jesus Christ thy Son our Lord.
BROOKE FOSS WESTCOTT

MY PRAYER STARTER: Lord of all truth, give me the wisdom to recognize lies when I hear them. Help me test everything I see with the truth in Your Word.

Your vision of the world affects your own world—both inner and outer. Pray that you and others will have a God perspective. It will change the world.

Fear not. . .thou art mine.
ISAIAH 43:1

O Thou, who art the ever-blessed God. . . , speak, we beseech Thee, to this Thy servant, for whom we pray. Take him by the hand and say unto him, "Fear not; for I am with thee. I have called thee by my name; thou art mine." Put such a spirit of trust within him that all fear and foreboding shall be cast out. . . . Let quietness and confidence be his strength. Reveal to him the vision of a universe guided and governed by Thy wise and loving care. . . . Lift up his whole being into communion with Thy life and thought. Let him ever remember that Thou dost not give to any the spirit of fearfulness, but a spirit of power and love and self-mastery. In this faith, grant, O Lord, that he may summon the energies of his soul against the miseries that cast him down. Give him courage, confidence, an untroubled heart, and a love that loves all creatures, great and small, for Thy love's sake. Amen.
SAMUEL MCCOMB

MY PRAYER STARTER: Father, let me look through Your eyes, seeing humanity with the same degree of love and compassion that You do.

God sees you. Your entire being. You are in His spotlight. You are His loved one, His chosen one, His special lamb. He's made you for His pleasure. And although He knows and sees your past and future in this moment, He wants you to take your eyes off yourself and the world around you and turn them toward Him. When you return to God's rest, you're saved from worries, fears, agitations, misgivings, misperceptions, and so much more.

Return to God. Rest in Him. Entrust yourself to His care, protection, and guidance. Put your confidence, not in the world and what it might provide you, but in God alone. He'll quiet your entire being and grant all the strength and calm you need to truly rest in Him.

> *For thus saith the Lord GOD, the Holy One of Israel;*
> *In returning and rest shall ye be saved; in quietness*
> *and in confidence shall be your strength.*
>
> ISAIAH 30:15

O Omnipotent God, who cares for each of us as if no one else existed and for all of us as if we were all but one! Blessed is the person who loves You. To You I entrust my whole being and all I have received from You. You made me for Yourself, and my heart is restless until it rests in You.
SAINT AUGUSTINE

MY PRAYER STARTER: All-seeing Creator, thank You for caring for me. When I am plagued with worry, help me find rest in Your love and promises.

It's easy to cling to past grievances, but it's not very profitable to either your well-being or that of others. Why? Because the burning bitterness of unforgiveness impedes your forward motion *and* your love toward others.

Jesus wants you to do what He does for you: forgive and move on—doing both in His love.

> *Let all bitterness, and wrath, and anger, and clamour,*
> *and evil speaking, be put away from you, with all malice:*
> *and be ye kind one to another, tenderhearted, forgiving one*
> *another, even as God for Christ's sake hath forgiven you.*
> EPHESIANS 4:31–32

I offer to Thee prayers for the pardon of those especially, who have in any way injured, grieved, or reproached me; or have caused me any harm or annoyance. And I offer also for all those whom I have in any way grieved, vexed, oppressed, and scandalized, by word or deed, knowingly or unknowingly; that Thou mayest equally forgive us all our sins, and all our offences against each other. Take away, O Lord, from our hearts all suspiciousness, indignation, anger, and contention, and whatever is calculated to wound charity, and to lessen brotherly love. Have mercy, O Lord, have mercy on those who seek Thy mercy; give grace to the needy; make us so to live that we may be found worthy to enjoy the fruition of Thy grace, and that we may attain to eternal life. Amen.
THOMAS À KEMPIS

MY PRAYER STARTER: Forgiving Savior, I can never thank You enough for saving me from my sins. Help me show Your forgiveness to others, even when they don't deserve it.

Worry is a dark, heavy cloud of distorted thoughts that comes between you and the Prince of Peace. It follows you around, blinding your mind to Jesus' light. It forms when you panic in a place of uncertainty, thinking you must create your own solutions. But your God is a God of certainty and wisdom. So put all your *what-ifs* into His hands, and thank Him for all the *what-ares* in your life. When you do, He'll remove all the faithless, unfounded fears that weigh you down. Pray for Jesus to beam His light upon you. Then rise up in peace and victory.

> *Humble yourselves therefore under the mighty hand*
> *of God, that he may exalt you in due time: casting*
> *all your care upon him; for he careth for you.*
> 1 PETER 5:6–7

O most loving Father, you who will us to give thanks for all things, to dread nothing but the loss of yourself, and to cast all our care on you, who care for us; preserve us from faithless fears and worldly anxieties, and grant that no clouds of this mortal life may hide from us the light of that love which is immortal, and which you have manifested unto us in your Son, Jesus Christ our Lord.
WILLIAM BRIGHT

MY PRAYER STARTER: God, Father of lights, dissolve the clouds of fear and doubt that linger in my mind. Let my soul be filled with the radiance of Your love and tranquility.

How pliable are you when it comes to God reshaping you? How yielded are you to the ministrations of the Master Craftsman who created and knew you before you were born? How much do you moan, groan, complain about, or, even worse, resist God's work? Envision how blessed your life will become when you put yourself totally in the Master's hand!

Begin a yielded life today. Allow God to remake you in His image. Pray for Him to re-create you as you lie compliant in His hands, becoming the man He wants you to be.

> *But now, O LORD, thou art our father; we are the clay,*
> *and thou our potter; and we all are the work of thy hand.*
> ISAIAH 64:8

I leave myself, Father, in thy hands; make and re-make this clay, shape it or grind it to atoms; it is thine own, it has nought to say; only let it always be subservient to thine ever-blessed designs, and let nothing in me oppose thy good pleasure for which I was created. Require, command, forbid; what wouldst Thou have me do? What not do? Exalted or abased, rejoicing or suffering, doing thy work or laid aside, I will always praise Thee alike, ever yielding up all my own will to Thine! Nothing remains for me but to adopt the language of Mary: "Be it unto me according to thy words" (Luke 1:38).
FRANÇOIS FÉNELON

MY PRAYER STARTER: Lord of my life, shape me into the design You have in mind. Take my own desires and conform them to Your own.

Imagine a know-it-all who thinks he is perfect and has all the talent in the world. He believes he's better than good and is the humblest of the humble. He's got so much "religion" and strength that he needs no help from God at all. How insufferable such a man would be! Yet it won't be long before he falls. Hard. For he's self-reliant, not God-reliant.

Don't be that man. God doesn't want you puffing yourself up in your own mind. He wants you humbly coming to Him, seeking more teaching, correction, grace, goodness, atonement, light, and strength. When you are God-reliant, you're continuing to grow, to progress in a life with Jesus Christ, helping to build God's kingdom up—not tear it down.

Pray for God to guide you closer to Him today. To help you never become so proud that you think you can handle life without His help. To humble you before Him as you stick to His path and walk forward in the way He's prepared just for you.

Pride goeth before destruction, and an haughty spirit before a fall.
PROVERBS 16:18

Suffer me never to think that I have knowledge enough to
need no teaching, wisdom enough to need no correction,
talents enough to need no grace, goodness enough to need no
progress, humility enough to need no repentance, devotion
enough to need no quickening, strength enough without
thy Spirit; lest, standing still, I fall back for evermore.
ERIC MILNER-WHITE

MY PRAYER STARTER: Mighty King, my own power and righteousness are nothing compared to Yours. Give me a humble perspective and the desire to lean on You for everything I do.

When you see the word *work*, your mind might automatically define it as what one does to earn money. But work comes in other forms, such as yardwork, housework, and even homework. God will bless whatever you put your hand to—sacred or secular—when you offer Him your efforts, talents, skills, and experience and leave the results to Him.

Pray today for God not only to use you and your work but to ensure that He and His love shine through it all. For His sake.

Let thy work appear unto thy servants, and thy glory
unto their children. And let the beauty of the LORD our
God be upon us: and establish thou the work of our hands
upon us; yea, the work of our hands establish thou it.

PSALM 90:16–17

I want to begin this day with thankfulness,
and continue it with eagerness.
I shall be busy; let me set about things in the spirit of service to you
and to my fellows, that Jesus knew in the carpenter's shop in Nazareth.
I am glad that he drew no line between work sacred and secular.
Take the skill that resides in my hands, and use it today;
Take the experience that life has given me, and use it;
Keep my eyes open, and my imagination alert,
that I may see how things look to others,
especially the unwell, the worried, the
overworked. For your love's sake. Amen.

RITA SNOWDEN

MY PRAYER STARTER: Father, may I never be plagued with laziness. Help me be one of Your productive sons, consistent in my work ethic and steady in my dedication to You.

You might shake your head at how the Israelites' lack of trust and faith in God, their murmuring and complaining, led them to forty years wandering in the wilderness. They grumbled in spite of the miracles they'd seen God work to rescue, defend, and provide for them! Yet do you not sometimes do the same? Complaining to God about what's happened in your life, wondering what He might've been thinking?

Time to turn that thinking into thankfulness. To get in line with God's will without reasoning against it. Pray that you will be content in your life, whatever God brings into it. Label each event as the best thing that could've happened!

> *For it is God which worketh in you both to will and to do of his good pleasure. Do all things without murmurings and disputings: that ye may be blameless and harmless, the sons of God, without rebuke, in the midst of a crooked and perverse nation, among whom ye shine as lights in the world.*
> PHILIPPIANS 2:13–15

Grant, gracious Father, that I may never dispute the reasonableness of thy will, but ever close with it, as the best that can happen. Prepare me always for what thy providence shall bring forth. Let me never murmur, be dejected, or impatient, under any of the troubles of this life, but ever find rest and comfort in this, this is the will of my Father, and of my God; grant this for Jesus Christ's sake. Amen.
THOMAS WILSON

MY PRAYER STARTER: Never-changing God, may I look inwardly when I read of the Israelites' unfaithfulness. If any ingratitude lies in my soul, help me replace it with thanksgiving.

The king of Syria sent his horses and chariots to attack Dothan, where the prophet Elisha was staying. The king's army surrounded the city at night. When Elisha's servant woke and saw all the horses and chariots, he panicked. But Elisha said, "Fear not: for they that be with us are more than they that be with them" (2 Kings 6:16), then prayed for God to open the servant's eyes. That's when the servant saw God's army!

When your troubles seem like steamrollers about to flatten you, pray that God would open your eyes to His heavenly help. He'll reveal a chariot that will carry you above your troubles!

> *And Elisha prayed, and said, LORD, I pray thee, open his eyes, that he may see. And the LORD opened the eyes of the young man; and he saw: and, behold, the mountain was full of horses and chariots of fire round about Elisha.*
> 2 KINGS 6:17

Lord, open our eyes that we may see, for the world all around us, as well as around the prophet, is full of [Your] horses and chariots, waiting to carry us to places of glorious victory. And when our eyes are thus opened, we shall see in all the events of life, whether great or small, whether joyful or sad, a "chariot" for our souls.
HANNAH WHITALL SMITH

MY PRAYER STARTER: Invisible Lord, may I never forget that You are always present. Reveal Your power in my darkest days, lest I allow my worries to consume my soul.

External events can be powerful enough to scatter your thoughts, disturbing your internal peace and preventing you from hearing what God is speaking into your life. During such times, when worry's voice seems louder than God's, make Isaiah 26:3 your mantra. Here, God promises that if you trust Him *and* keep your mind focused on Him, He'll keep you in a place of perfect peace.

> *Thou wilt keep him in perfect peace, whose mind*
> *is stayed on thee: because he trusteth in thee.*
>
> ISAIAH 26:3

O Lord, this is all my desire—to walk along the path of life that Thou hast appointed me, even as Jesus my Lord would walk along it, in steadfastness of faith, in meekness of spirit, in lowliness of heart, in gentleness of love. And because outward events have so much power in scattering my thoughts and disturbing the inward peace in which alone the voice of Thy Spirit is heard. . . , calm and settle my soul by that subduing power which alone can bring all thoughts and desires of the heart into captivity to Thyself. All I have is Thine; do Thou with all as seems best to Thy divine will; for I know not what is best. Let not the cares or duties of this life press on me too heavily; but lighten my burden, that I may follow Thy way in quietness, filled with thankfulness for Thy mercy, and rendering acceptable service unto Thee. Amen.

MARIA HARE

MY PRAYER STARTER: Lord, let my problems—be they poor health, financial difficulties, or family issues—become small in my eyes when I consider Your power to solve them. Keep my eyes peacefully fixed on You.

Some people picture God as an angry, laying-down-the-law father. Feeling unable to satisfy Him, their heart lurches. It reacts like a panicked bird flapping its wings, unable to settle down or find a way out. Others may see God as a mother figure. Loving and comforting, she nurses them at her breast, carries them on her hips, and bounces them up and down on her knees. With this perception of God, their heart soars, longing to be with Him.

Pray today that when you think of God, it doesn't awaken your heart like a panicked bird but stirs it like a child waking from a good night's sleep, joy on its face, ready to run into its mother's arms and be swept up into her lap, where comfort, love, and provision are found.

> *For thus saith the LORD, Behold, I will extend peace to her*
> *like a river. . .then shall ye suck, ye shall be borne upon her*
> *sides, and be dandled upon her knees. As one whom his mother*
> *comforteth, so will I comfort you. . . . And when ye see this,*
> *your heart shall rejoice, and your bones shall flourish.*
> ISAIAH 66:12–14

Father in heaven! When the thought of Thee wakes in our hearts let it not awaken like a frightened bird that flies about in dismay, but like a child waking from its sleep with a heavenly smile.
SØREN KIERKEGAARD

MY PRAYER STARTER: Father, I am Your dearly loved child. Help me find comfort and powerful love by running into Your embrace each morning I wake.

Sleep can be elusive at times. We find ourselves tossing and turning; the regrets and mistakes of yesterday, the worrisome events of the day just past, and the fears of an unknown tomorrow are ricocheting in our minds, keeping rest at bay.

When this happens, remind yourself who God is. That He has chosen you, loves you, and listens to you when you call upon Him. Look into your heart. Gather up your regrets, missteps, worries, fears, and uncertainties and put them in His hands. Find a comfortable position tonight and then relax your body from head to toe. Trust that He who never sleeps is watching over you tonight and will continue to do so throughout the coming day. He will defend and protect you. You're safe in His strong, loving arms.

But know that the LORD hath set apart him that is godly for himself:
the LORD will hear when I call unto him. . . . Commune with
your own heart upon your bed, and be still. . . . Put your trust
in the LORD. . . . I will both lay me down in peace, and sleep:
for thou, LORD, only makest me dwell in safety.

PSALM 4:3–5, 8

O Thou, whose captain I account myself. . .
To Thee I do commend my watchful soul,
Ere I let fall the windows of mine eyes:
Sleeping and waking, O! defend me still.
WILLIAM SHAKESPEARE

MY PRAYER STARTER: Comforting Spirit, thank You for Your unfailing provision. May I sleep in peace tonight, leaving the day's struggles in Your care.

You are Jesus' servant, His hands, feet, mouth, mind, and heart on earth. Your purpose is to do whatever He desires in whatever way He moves you. Yet you cannot accomplish His will in your own power. Instead, you must come to God as an empty vessel for Him to fill. So bring your heart, soul, mind, and mouth to Him. Ask God to fill them.

We preach not ourselves, but Christ Jesus the Lord; and ourselves your servants for Jesus' sake. For God, who commanded the light to shine out of darkness, hath shined in our hearts, to give the light of the knowledge of the glory of God in the face of Jesus Christ. But we have this treasure in earthen vessels, that the excellency of the power may be of God, and not of us.

2 CORINTHIANS 4:5–7

Use me then, my Saviour, for whatever purpose, and in whatever way, Thou mayest require. Here is my poor heart, an empty vessel; fill it with Thy grace. Here is my sinful and troubled soul; quicken it and refresh it with Thy love. Take my heart for Thine abode; my mouth to spread abroad the glory of Thy name; my love and all my powers, for the advancement of believing people; and never suffer the steadfastness and confidence of my faith to abate—that so at all times I may be enabled from the heart to say, "Jesus needs me, and I Him."

D. L. MOODY

MY PRAYER STARTER: Lord, I come to You as an empty cup, having poured out my own desires in hopes that You'll fill me with Your own. Use me as an instrument to advance Your kingdom.

Whether or not you have children of your own, you have an influencing effect on their lives. The apostle Timothy, son of a pagan Greek father and a pious Jewish mother, was raised Jewish. Both his mother and grandmother laid his spiritual groundwork. Then, after hearing Paul preach, Timothy became a Christian—making Paul his spiritual father.

Pray that God would bless His children. That their overseers—parents, grandparents, or guardians—would care for and raise them in Jesus' love and wisdom. That their households would reflect God's kingdom. And while you're at it, ask God to open your heart to how you might present God in a child's life and so become a spiritual father yourself!

> *To Timothy, my dearly beloved son. . . . I thank God. . .when*
> *I call to remembrance the unfeigned faith that is in thee,*
> *which dwelt first in thy grandmother Lois, and thy mother*
> *Eunice; and I am persuaded that in thee also.*
> 2 TIMOTHY 1:2–3, 5

Heavenly Father, from whom all fatherhood in heaven and earth is named, bless, we beg you, all children, and give to their parents and to all in whose charge they may be, your Spirit of wisdom and love; so that the home in which they grow up may be to them an image of your kingdom, and the care of their parents a likeness of your love; through Jesus Christ our Lord.
LESLIE HUNTER

MY PRAYER STARTER: Heavenly Father, may I be a spiritual father to the children I meet. May Your attributes overflow into my words and actions, exemplifying Your grace and love.

Imagine being one of the two disciples who journeyed to Emmaus on the day the disciples discovered Jesus' empty tomb. While you're talking about the day's events, Jesus draws near. But you don't recognize Him. You tell Him the story of Jesus. Then He opens the Word to you, explaining why things had to happen this way. Suddenly, you realize who He truly is!

Pray that Jesus would open your eyes to His message as you walk by His side. That His words would burn within your heart as you listen. That you would journey on in the strength of His presence and His amazing truth all the way to the end of your road, where you'll see Him again in all His glory!

> *And their eyes were opened, and they knew him; and [Jesus]*
> *vanished out of their sight. And they said one to another,*
> *Did not our heart burn within us, while he talked with us*
> *by the way, and while he opened to us the scriptures?*
>
> LUKE 24:31–32

Make our hearts to burn within us, O Christ, as we walk with Thee in the way and listen to Thy words; that we may go in the strength of Thy presence and Thy truth all our journey through, and at its end behold Thee, in the glory of the Eternal Trinity, God for ever and ever.
ERIC MILNER-WHITE

MY PRAYER STARTER: Ever-present Savior, I know that You are here, constantly guiding me home. May I quiet my soul, tuning out all distractions, to hear Your voice and receive Your strength.

When you're distraught, in need of forgiveness, in the dark, sick, sorrowful in heart and soul, burdened, or weary of everything, stretch out your hands toward God. When you do, you'll find the hope you desperately need—God's eternal hope that bestows courage, mercy, strength, and love.

If thou prepare thine heart, and stretch out thine hands toward him. . . . Thou shalt be secure, because there is hope; yea, thou shalt dig about thee, and thou shalt take thy rest in safety.

JOB 11:13, 18

Grant unto us, Almighty God, in all time of sore distress, the comfort of the forgiveness of our sins. In time of darkness give us blessed hope, in time of sickness of body give us quiet courage; and when the heart is bowed down, and the soul is very heavy, and life is a burden, and pleasure a weariness, and the sun is too bright, and life too mirthful, then may that Spirit, the Spirit of the Comforter, come upon us, and after our darkness may there be the clear shining of the heavenly light; that so, being uplifted again by Thy mercy, we may pass on through this our mortal life with quiet courage, patient hope, and unshaken trust, hoping through Thy loving-kindness and tender mercy to be delivered from death into the large life of the eternal years. Hear us of Thy mercy, through Jesus Christ our Lord. Amen.

GEORGE DAWSON

MY PRAYER STARTER: Sustaining Creator, You are my everything. Let me never trust anything in this world or fail to thank You for Your provision.

It's tempting to look to ourselves or others to help us. Yet humans are fallible, having limited power, strength, and resources. So if we trust in people or material things to save us, disappointment and heartache are bound to follow. But when we trust Jesus to deliver us, we find a myriad of blessings. He has all the power in the world. As the King of creation, Jesus can provide unlimited relief, renewal, strength, and resources.

So be wise. Determine to put your wholehearted confidence in Jesus. He, your arm of strength, is right here beside you, waiting for you to turn to Him. And watch your life start to bloom!

> *Thus saith the LORD; Cursed be the man that trusteth in man, and maketh flesh his arm, and whose heart departeth from the LORD. For he shall be like the heath in the desert, and shall not see when good cometh. . . . Blessed is the man that trusteth in the LORD, and whose hope the LORD is. For he shall be as a tree planted by the waters, and that spreadeth out her roots by the river, and shall not see when heat cometh, but her leaf shall be green; and shall not be careful in the year of drought, neither shall cease from yielding fruit.*
>
> JEREMIAH 17:5–8

Dear Jesus. . .how foolish of me to have called
for human help when You are here.
CORRIE TEN BOOM

MY PRAYER STARTER: Lord, Provider of salvation, thank You for giving my life purpose. Let me never seek others for the spiritual peace and protection that only You can give.

When Jesus walked this earth, He experienced grief, rejection, sorrow, hatred, weakness, and trouble. He did it to save you. To ensure you would know that everything you've faced—and are facing now—can be overcome. For although Jesus had more than His fair share of trouble, He had something else: a close and abiding relationship with God. This connection to Abba God gave Jesus all He needed: joy, acceptance, happiness, love, power, and peace. And because you know Jesus, you too have access to these blessings.

So ask God for His strength. Pray He would bestow upon you all the love and joy your relationship with Jesus provides. Ask Him to lead you through the troubles of this life. Know that you can endure anything with God Almighty in your corner, Jesus the Invincible at your side, and the Holy Spirit of comfort within.

He is despised and rejected of men; a man of sorrows, and acquainted with grief: and we hid as it were our faces from him; he was despised, and we esteemed him not. Surely he hath borne our griefs, and carried our sorrows.

ISAIAH 53:3–4

Almighty God, grant unto us Thy love, that we may greatly rejoice; that we, knowing trouble, and acquainted with grief, may, through the goodly deliverance of faith and hope, come to the large joy of the peace that passeth all understanding. Amen.
GEORGE DAWSON

MY PRAYER STARTER: Compassionate Savior, thank You for enduring the fires of temptation and the cross for my salvation. Give me Your spiritual resilience so that I may endure as well.

You may not know what today will bring. And that's okay. No one does. Except for God, of course. He's planned everything. So instead of giving in to uncertainty and fear, trust in God. Be confident that He—who promises to be with and support you—will give you the strength and courage to stride into today. When you do, you'll find yourself automatically following His lead.

> *Be strong and of a good courage, fear not, nor be afraid*
> *of them: for the LORD thy God, he it is that doth go*
> *with thee; he will not fail thee, nor forsake thee.*
> DEUTERONOMY 31:6

Eternal God, who commits to us the swift and solemn trust of life: since we know not what a day may bring forth, but only that the hour for serving You is always present, may we wake to Your instant claims, not waiting for tomorrow, but yielding today. Lay to rest the resistance of our passion, indolence, or fear. Consecrate the way our feet may go, and the humblest work will shine, and the roughest places be made plain. Lift us above unrighteous anger and mistrust into faith and hope and charity, through steady reliance on You. So may we be modest in our time of wealth, patient under disappointment, ready for danger, serene in death. In all things, draw us to Yourself that Your lost image may be traced again, and we may be at one with You.
JAMES MARTINEAU

MY PRAYER STARTER: Sovereign Lord, You know the strength I'll need to get through today. Prepare me as I wake each morning, granting me sufficient faith to stay on Your path.

Need some wisdom? Seek God and His Word, and you'll get it! That's what King Asa did. He sought God, found Him, got wisdom, and then did things—like tearing down idols—to please Him.

One day, Zerah, the Ethiopian, came with an army of a million men to war against Asa's army of only 580,000. So Asa prayed to God. As a result, not only did Asa and his people gain the strength to defeat the million-man army, but they "carried away very much spoil" (2 Chronicles 14:13).

Need wisdom? Seek God, and you'll get even more than you asked for!

> *And Asa cried unto the LORD his God, and said, LORD, it is*
> *nothing with thee to help, whether with many, or with them*
> *that have no power: help us, O LORD our God; for we rest*
> *on thee, and in thy name we go against this multitude.*
> *O LORD, thou art our God; let no man prevail against thee.*
> 2 CHRONICLES 14:11

Strengthen me, O God, by the grace of Thy Holy Spirit; grant me to be strengthened with might in the inner man, and to empty my heart of all useless care and anguish. O Lord, grant me heavenly wisdom, that I may learn above all things to seek and to find Thee, above all things to relish and to love Thee, and to think of all other things as being, what indeed they are, at the disposal of Thy wisdom. Amen.
THOMAS À KEMPIS

MY PRAYER STARTER: God, I am a finite man in a flawed world. So when I'm faced with impossible odds, fill my mind with Your wisdom.

When we find ourselves ensconced in our own little world, our vision can become skewed and God's presence blurry. That's when it's time for an eye/I exam. Examine the Creator's creation. Look at God's people and animals. Raise your eyes to His skies, stars, trees—all the nature that surrounds you. Ask Jesus to fill you with the Spirit so that you can see God in everything. When you do, your actions will become more aligned to God and His will for all His creation.

But ask now the beasts, and they shall teach thee; and the fowls of the air, and they shall tell thee: or speak to the earth, and it shall teach thee: and the fishes of the sea shall declare unto thee. Who knoweth not in all these that the hand of the LORD hath wrought this? In whose hand is the soul of every living thing, and the breath of all mankind.

JOB 12:7–10

Fulfil us, Lord Jesus, with the grace of thy Holy Spirit, that everything we see may represent to us the presence, the excellency, and the power of God, and our conversation with the creatures lead us unto the Creator; that so our actions may be done more frequently with an eye to God's presence, by our often seeing him in the glass of creation; who with thee and the Holy Spirit liveth and reigneth, ever one God, world without end. Amen.

JEREMY TAYLOR

MY PRAYER STARTER: All-encompassing Creator, I am in awe of Your beautiful artwork that surrounds me. Remove my focus from myself and point it toward You.

It's one thing to rise—to roll out of bed and into your day. It's another thing to rise and *shine*—to be aware of God's presence, stirred by the Holy Spirit, and empowered by Jesus' light within. For when you awaken to the awareness of the Holy Three, you can have a vital heart-to-heart talk with God before you speak to anyone else. As you gain strength, you'll not only face the day but truly enjoy it—no matter what. Then you'll truly rise and shine—and the Son of righteousness with you, with healing in His wings, causing you to leap into your day and dance to an inner song! So awaken with full awareness of the Trinity, and Jesus Christ will give you all the light you need for today's path.

> *But all things that are reproved are made manifest by*
> *the light: for whatsoever doth make manifest is light.*
> *Wherefore he saith, Awake thou that sleepest, and arise*
> *from the dead, and Christ shall give thee light.*
> EPHESIANS 5:13–14

O Lord, when I awake and day begins,
waken me to Thy Presence;
waken me to Thine indwelling;
waken me to inward sight of Thee,
and speech with Thee,
and strength from Thee;
that all my earthly walk may waken into song
and my spirit leap up to Thee all day, all ways.
ERIC MILNER-WHITE

MY PRAYER STARTER: Father, whenever I open my physical eyes in the morning, let my spiritual eyes open as well. Make me deeply aware of Your presence, and light the way ahead of me.

It's amazing how God created you, fashioning you into something He desired. How He breathed the breath of life into you and gave you the power to rise out of darkness and into His light. How He made you for a specific reason, purpose, and function to live in this moment. Imagine—God sacrificed His Son for you thousands of years ago so that you could commune with Him right now. And when you became a believer, He sent the Holy Spirit to live within you, guiding you and translating your prayers. All this is hard to grasp. God is so much higher than you, yet He still resides within.

It's good to remind yourself daily of God's wonder and your role in His plan for this world. Pray and praise Him. Thank Him for giving you life, reason, knowledge, good desires, and all else. For without Him, you'd be nothing!

For my thoughts are not your thoughts, neither are your ways my ways, saith the LORD. For as the heavens are higher than the earth, so are my ways higher than your ways, and my thoughts than your thoughts.

ISAIAH 55:8–9

God is what thought cannot better; God is whom thought cannot reach; God no thinking can even conceive. Without God, men can have no being, no reason, no knowledge, no good desire, naught. Thou, O God, art what thou art, transcending all.

ERIC MILNER-WHITE

MY PRAYER STARTER: Eternal Savior, thank You for Your unparalleled love. You died for me, and You have a specific purpose for my life; help me love and serve You better each day.

All your strength lies in God's Spirit within you. Jesus says you have all the power you need to live. Nothing can hurt you. Pray for that strength, believing it's yours. And it will be.

> *Behold, I give unto you power to tread on serpents and scorpions, and over all the power of the enemy: and nothing shall by any means hurt you. Notwithstanding in this rejoice not, that the spirits are subject unto you; but rather rejoice, because your names are written in heaven.*
>
> LUKE 10:19–20

O Thou divine Spirit, let me find my strength in Thee. I need Thee, that I may be strong everywhere. I long to be independent of all circumstances, alike of the cloud and of the sunshine. I want a power to save me from sinking in despondency, and to rescue me from soaring in pride. I want both a pillar of fire and a pillar of cloud; a refuge from the night of adversity, and a shield from the day of prosperity. I can find them in Thee. Thou hast proved Thy power over the night and over the day. Come into my heart, and Thy power shall be my power. I shall be victorious over all circumstances, at home in all scenes, restful in all fortunes. I shall have power to tread on scorpions, and they shall do me no hurt; the world shall be mine when Thy Spirit is in me. Amen.

GEORGE MATHESON

MY PRAYER STARTER: All-powerful God, thank You for Your comforting Spirit within me. Let me be receptive to His leading, unafraid of where He might take me.

When Jesus heard Lazarus was dying, "he abode two days still in the same place where he was" (John 11:6). *Then* He walked to Bethany and found that Lazarus had been dead for four days (John 11:17)! Of course, Jesus knew He'd raise Lazarus from the dead. It was all so people would see God's glory.

Jesus' unwavering trust in God is displayed throughout the New Testament. He knew and trusted God's plan. That's why He never rushed.

You trust in God. You believe He's working everything out for the greater good. And while reading His Word, you glean knowledge of His plan. Like Jesus, you don't need to stress. Ask God to slow you down so that you won't trip. Realize there's no need to hurry—you're already living in eternity. Instead of stressing, take time to know God, enjoy His gifts, and get better acquainted with others along your way.

> *Also, that the soul be without knowledge, it is not*
> *good; and he that hasteth with his feet sinneth.*
> PROVERBS 19:2

In the name of Jesus Christ who was never in a hurry, we pray, O God, that You will slow us down, for we know that we live too fast. With all eternity before us, make us take time to live—time to get acquainted with You, time to enjoy Your blessing, and time to know each other.
PETER MARSHALL

MY PRAYER STARTER: God, Your plan is a mystery to me sometimes. When I can't see the road ahead, illuminate it one step at a time and grant me the faith to move forward.

It's through God's love for you that you've gained Jesus Christ. It's through Him that you've gained the Holy Spirit. Within you, you have unconquerable divine strength that leads you down the path of godliness. You have the promise-filled Word that helps you escape this world's darkness and see the reality of God in your life. You are able to take on the divine nature, to become more and more like Jesus, who is above everything in this world. In Him alone you have all you need to be content—and so much more!

Pray each day that God would give you what you require—*Himself.* By doing so, you will never be in need.

According as his divine power hath given unto us all things that pertain unto life and godliness, through the knowledge of him that hath called us to glory and virtue: whereby are given unto us exceeding great and precious promises: that by these ye might be partakers of the divine nature, having escaped the corruption that is in the world through lust.

2 PETER 1:3–4

God, of your goodness, give me yourself; for you are sufficient for me. I cannot properly ask anything less, to be worthy of you. If I were to ask less, I should always be in want. In you alone do I have all.
JULIAN OF NORWICH

MY PRAYER STARTER: Lord, my eternal Guide, I am nothing without You. Give me Your Spirit and help me trust in Your promises for strength and contentment.

Today's evening prayer is a starting point for thanking God for the myriad of people in your life. As you pray, start naming names!

> *[I] cease not to give thanks for you, making*
> *mention of you in my prayers.*
> EPHESIANS 1:16

Eternal and ever-blessed God, we give thee thanks, as the
day comes to an end, for those who mean so much to us,
and without whom life could never be the same.
We thank thee for those to whom we can go at
any time and never feel a nuisance. . . .
We thank thee for those with whom we can talk, and
keep nothing back, knowing that they will not laugh
at our dreams or mock at our failures. . . .
We thank thee for those who by their warning counsel
and their rebuke have kept us from mistakes we might
have made, and sins we might have committed.
And above all we thank thee for Jesus, the pattern of our
lives, the Lord of our hearts, and the Saviour of our souls.
WILLIAM BARCLAY

MY PRAYER STARTER: Lord, thank You for the friends You've given to me.
Bless them with Your peace and aid them on their journey with You.

When you need a little pick-me-up, take a deep breath, close your eyes, and go to Jesus. Imagine His face smiling upon you. Feel His Spirit giving you the energy you desire. Then be as the lame man who, after being healed in Jesus' name, found his feet strengthened and "leaping up stood, and walked" (Acts 3:8). Dance as David did as he joyously brought home the ark, the presence of God. Sing and be glad, knowing the joy of the Lord is your strength. Pray for that joy to be yours today!

> *When the LORD turned again the captivity of Zion, we were like them that dream. Then was our mouth filled with laughter, and our tongue with singing: then said they among the heathen, The LORD hath done great things for them. The LORD hath done great things for us; whereof we are glad.*
>
> PSALM 126:1–3

Come and help us, Lord Jesus. A vision of your face will brighten us; but to feel your Spirit touching us will make us vigorous. Oh! for the leaping and walking of the man born lame. May we today dance with holy joy, like David before the ark of God. May a holy exhilaration take possession of every part of us; may we be glad in the Lord; may our mouth be filled with laughter, and our tongue with singing, "for the Lord hath done great things for us whereof we are glad."
CHARLES SPURGEON

MY PRAYER STARTER: God of comfort, to keep walking on this earth, I sometimes need a taste of heaven. Flood my soul with the joy of Your salvation.

We naturally tend to be self-focused. We've got our own ideas, plans, possessions, and goals. So when we're presented with others' needs, we feel put out—even when it's just for a few minutes. But God wants us to be the opposite, willingly and eagerly. He wants us less self-focused and more others-focused. He wants us to be like Jesus!

So when you put yourself aside to help others, pray for Jesus to give you patience, fortitude, and—most importantly—grace. To give others first priority—even if it means canceling your plans or inconveniencing yourself. For when you put others before yourself, you are putting Jesus first. Whatever you do for them, you are actually doing for Him—the One who sacrificed all for you!

Let nothing be done through strife or vainglory; but in lowliness of mind let each esteem other better than themselves. Look not every man on his own things, but every man also on the things of others.
PHILIPPIANS 2:3–4

Give us patience and fortitude to put self aside for you in the most unlikely people: to know that every man's and any man's suffering is our own first business, for which we must be willing to go out of our way and to leave our own interests.
CARYLL HOUSELANDER

MY PRAYER STARTER: Compassionate Lord, may I never focus on my own desires so much that I neglect the needs of others. Let my actions reflect the self-sacrificial love You showed to me.

You're a work in progress. So don't be discouraged when things aren't going your way. Perhaps God is putting challenges in your path to test and teach you, to exercise your faith. Consider them as opportunities to change your perspective, to take another tack, to align yourself with God's efforts instead of resisting them.

In George MacDonald's *Warlock o'Glenwarlock*, a student asks his teacher how to make the best of this life. The teacher says, "Simply by falling in with God's design in the making of you. That design must be worked out—cannot be worked out without you. You must walk in the front of things with the will of God—not be dragged. . .behind him!" Then he advises the student to pray today's classic prayer.

Why not do the same? Trade discouragement for design! Run to God, as a child runs to his Abba. Willingly fall in with His plan to make the best you. Ask what you can do to help!

> *[I] will be a Father unto you, and ye shall be my sons*
> *and daughters, saith the Lord Almighty.*
> 2 CORINTHIANS 6:18

O Maker of me, go on making me, and let me help Thee.
Come, oh Father, here I am: let us go on. I know my
words are those of a child, but it is Thy child that prays
to Thee. It is Thy dark I walk in, it is Thy hand I hold.
GEORGE MACDONALD

MY PRAYER STARTER: All-knowing Father, may I never be distracted by turbulent waves in the ocean of Your plan. May I walk over them with confidence, knowing You'll keep me from sinking.

King David was the apple of God's eye because he obeyed and trusted God. When God delivered him from his enemies, David called God a buckler—a small round shield held by a handle at arm's length or worn on the left arm. In other words, David held his Protector close.

Pray for a close, personal trust in God to lead you out of darkness and help fight your battles.

> *For thou art my lamp, O LORD: and the LORD will lighten my darkness. For by thee I have run through a troop: by my God have I leaped over a wall. As for God, his way is perfect; the word of the LORD is tried: he is a buckler to all them that trust in him.*
>
> 2 SAMUEL 22:29–31 (SEE PSALM 18:28–30)

It has pleased Thee to hide from us a perfect knowledge, yet Thou callest for a perfect trust in Thee. We cannot see to-morrow, we know not the way that we take, darkness hangs about our path and mystery meets us at every turn. Yet Thou hast shut us up to a final faith in goodness, justice, truth; that loving these for themselves alone, we may find the love that passeth knowledge, and look upon Thy face. O suffer us not for any terror of darkness or from any torment of mind to sin against our souls, or to fail at last of Thee. Amen.

WILLIAM EDWIN ORCHARD

MY PRAYER STARTER: Mighty God, save me from the powers of darkness and their vicious attacks. Be my shield, preserving my faith and integrity in times of despair and conflict.

Jesus is your Good Shepherd (John 10:11–18). He knows you—and you know Him. He calls you—and you discern His voice. You never lack direction, support, guidance, or wisdom. No matter where you are, Jesus will lead you every step of the way. You simply need to listen.

Put yourself in Jesus' hands. He'll breathe His desires into you, clarifying which path He wants you to choose. And as you follow each nudge of His inspiration, you'll find yourself becoming more and more like your Good Shepherd.

The LORD is my shepherd; I shall not want. He maketh me to lie down in green pastures: he leadeth me beside the still waters. He restoreth my soul: he leadeth me in the paths of righteousness for his name's sake. Yea, though I walk through the valley of the shadow of death, I will fear no evil: for thou art with me; thy rod and thy staff they comfort me.

PSALM 23:1–4

My God, I want Thy guidance and direction in all I do. Let Thy wisdom counsel me, Thy hand lead me, and Thine arm support me. I put myself into Thy hands. Breathe into my soul holy and heavenly desires. Conform me to Thine own image. Make me like my Saviour. Enable me in some measure to live here on earth as He lived, and to act in all things as He would have acted.

ASHTON OXENDEN

MY PRAYER STARTER: Lord, Shepherd of my soul, keep me in the pasture of Your presence. If I start to wander, guide me back with the staff of Your Word and Spirit.

God has placed your soul within a body and sent you on a journey. He doesn't want you to set your anchor in earthly things, but to steer straight for His kingdom. To help you stay afloat, God's Spirit speaks to yours, inspiring and guiding you until you reach your heavenly haven.

Pray that God would open your awareness to His provisions—physical and spiritual—as you journey ever closer to Him.

> *But ye are not in the flesh, but in the Spirit, if so be that the*
> *Spirit of God dwell in you. . . . And if Christ be in you, the body*
> *is dead because of sin; but the Spirit is life because of righteousness.*
> *But if the Spirit of him that raised up Jesus from the dead*
> *dwell in you, he that raised up Christ from the dead shall also*
> *quicken your mortal bodies by his Spirit that dwelleth in you.*
> ROMANS 8:9–11

O God, whose eternal providence has embarked our souls in our bodies, not to expect any port of anchorage on the sea of this world, to steer directly through it to your glorious kingdom, preserve us from the dangers that on all sides assault us, and keep our affections still fitly disposed to receive your holy inspirations, that being carried strongly forward by your Holy Spirit we may happily arrive at last in the haven of eternal salvation, through our Lord Jesus Christ.
JOHN WESLEY

MY PRAYER STARTER: Everlasting God, let me never value the meaningless things of this world over Your eternal promises. May I keep my anchor on board until I reach heaven's shore.

Some days, we may be mired in confusion, doubt, and uncertainty. We cannot see the forest for the trees, and thus find ourselves unable to move forward. But don't worry! God guides the meek. Light rises in the darkness for all God followers—including you.

Simply ask God for His wisdom, and He'll give it (James 1:5). He'll tell you what to do, nudging you in the right direction. He'll save you from making a mistake. He'll give you all the light you need when you trust in the shadow of His wings!

> *How excellent is thy lovingkindness, O God! therefore the*
> *children of men put their trust under the shadow of thy*
> *wings. They shall be abundantly satisfied. . .and thou shalt*
> *make them drink of the river of thy pleasures. For with thee*
> *is the fountain of life: in thy light shall we see light.*
> PSALM 36:7–9

O God, by whom the meek are guided in judgment, and light riseth up in darkness for the godly; grant us, in all our doubts and uncertainties, the grace to ask what Thou wouldst have us to do; that the spirit of wisdom may save us from all false choices, and that in Thy light we may see light, and in Thy straight path may not stumble, through Jesus Christ our Lord.
WILLIAM BRIGHT

MY PRAYER STARTER: God of wisdom, thank You for guiding and protecting me. Help me be a man who always looks to You—and no one else—for the wisdom I need to follow Your plan.

God loves you. As a result, He sent His Son, Jesus, to save you. And you've "seen" Jesus—the personification of love! Likewise, God wants you to love others. When you do, it's obvious that God is in you—and you in Him.

Do you see how love comes full circle? How your love toward others shows the perfect completeness of God's love?

If you need more love from God so that you can love others, pray for it at every moment of your day. When God overwhelms you with His love, you will have the power to love as fully as your Shepherd of love, Jesus Christ.

Herein is love, not that we loved God, but that he loved us, and sent his Son to be the propitiation for our sins. Beloved, if God so loved us, we ought also to love one another. No man hath seen God at any time. If we love one another, God dwelleth in us, and his love is perfected in us.

1 JOHN 4:10–12

O God, Fountain of love, pour Thy love into our souls, that we may love those whom Thou lovest, with the love Thou givest us, and think and speak of them tenderly, meekly, lovingly; and so loving our brethren and sisters for Thy sake, may grow in Thy love, and dwelling in love may dwell in Thee; for Jesus Christ's sake. Amen.
EDWARD B. PUSEY

MY PRAYER STARTER: Merciful God, may I be a conductor of Your powerful love. May it flow from me like electricity to everyone I meet so that they can offer it back to You.

Others may scoff at your beliefs, perhaps even mock you. But no matter what the world says, you know you're living in the truth of God's Word. So content yourself with hearing God speak through His Word. Rest easy, knowing He has the final say-so; He will love you and lead you down the right path to Himself. Care only for God's approval. Do things His way—even if it means going against the world's ways. For God is your true treasure. He's the Light of your world, the Love of your life, the Master of your heart and soul, from here to eternity! He'll give you the strength and passion to turn from the world and to Him.

We were bold in our God to speak unto you the gospel of God with much contention. . . . But as we were allowed of God to be put in trust with the gospel, even so we speak; not as pleasing men, but God. . . . So being affectionately desirous of you, we were willing to have imparted unto you, not the gospel of God only, but also our own souls, because ye were dear unto us.

1 THESSALONIANS 2:2, 4, 8

O Lord God, grant us always, whatever the world may say, to content ourselves with what thou wilt say, and to care only for thine approval, which will outweigh all words.
CHARLES GEORGE GORDON

MY PRAYER STARTER: Lord of truth, I know You have the words of eternal life. Let me never compromise my obedience to You, even when it's unpopular.

Thank God for God. When you don't have the strength to follow His instructions, He'll empower you. With His unlimited resources, He'll equip you with whatever you need to carry out His plan for your life. He'll give you the energy to keep trying, to persevere. For God not only works *on* you, He works *in* you, energizing you with the same power He used to raise Jesus from the dead! Even more amazing is that He'll give you all the peace you need as you go through this process of hearing, obeying, and doing. Oh, what a God you have! There is no greater help available to you than that of the Holy Three.

Now the God of peace, that brought again from the dead our Lord Jesus, that great shepherd of the sheep, through the blood of the everlasting covenant, make you perfect in every good work to do his will, working in you that which is wellpleasing in his sight, through Jesus Christ; to whom be glory for ever and ever. Amen.

HEBREWS 13:20–21

From this moment on I promise that I'll try to do whatever You tell me for the rest of my life, insofar as You'll make it clear to me what Your wishes are. I'm weak and many times I'll probably want to renege on this. But Lord, You'll have to help me with that too.

CATHERINE MARSHALL

MY PRAYER STARTER: God, I know that Your strength knows no limits. Just as You raised Jesus from the dead, resurrect my soul from apathy and inaction. Invigorate me with Your Spirit.

Boldly is the only form of the word *bold* that appears in the Gospels in the King James Version. And it does so only twice. One instance refers to how Jesus spoke (John 7:26). The other is in Mark 15:43—"Joseph of Arimathaea. . .went in boldly unto Pilate, and craved the body of Jesus." All the other New Testament forms of *bold* appear *after* Jesus' followers received the Holy Spirit.

Like other followers of Jesus, you have been given the Holy Spirit, your Comforter and Interpreter. And because Jesus is your high priest, you can boldly go to God in prayer so that you'll have what you need for every task—menial or great.

> *Let us therefore come boldly unto the throne of grace, that we may obtain mercy, and find grace to help in time of need.*
> HEBREWS 4:16

Our Lord, our Guide even unto death, grant us, we pray Thee, grace to follow Thee whithersoever Thou goest. In little daily duties to which Thou callest us, bow down our wills to simple obedience, patience under pain or provocation, strict truthfulness of word and manner, humility, kindness: in great acts of duty or perfection if Thou shouldest call us to them, uplift us to self-sacrifice, heroic courage, laying down of life for Thy Truth's sake or for a brother. Amen.
CHRISTINA ROSSETTI

MY PRAYER STARTER: Ever-listening Father, thank You for listening to my prayers. May I never be ashamed to pray to You; rather, may I approach You with an attitude of boldness and praise.

Jesus gave you two rules: (1) love God with all your heart, soul, and mind, and (2) love others as yourself. To fulfill that second rule, you must be clothed in mercy, kindness, humility, gentleness, patience, forbearance, and forgiveness. And above all those things, you're to put on love—all because of what Jesus Christ did for you.

You should pray for that "outfit" every day. The more you clothe yourself with those qualities, the more friends you'll make, the more like Jesus you'll become, and the better the world will be! Make it your prayer today.

Put on therefore, as the elect of God, holy and beloved, bowels of mercies, kindness, humbleness of mind, meekness, longsuffering; forbearing one another, and forgiving one another, if any man have a quarrel against any: even as Christ forgave you, so also do ye. And above all these things put on charity, which is the bond of perfectness.
COLOSSIANS 3:12–14

Almighty and most merciful Father, who has given us a new commandment that we should love one another, give us also grace that we may fulfil it. Make us gentle, courteous, and forbearing. Direct our lives so that we may look each to the good of others in word and deed. And hallow all our friendships by the blessing of thy spirit, for his sake, who loveth us and gave himself for us, Jesus Christ our Lord. Amen.
BROOKE FOSS WESTCOTT

MY PRAYER STARTER: Loving Savior, clothe me with Your love. Let it be the first thing people see when they look at me. Make me more like You.

Let's face it: every man is tempted at times—including you. But you don't have to give in to the things that threaten to come between you and God. God promises He won't let you be tempted more than you're able to handle. And when temptation comes, God will give you an escape route.

Pray that God would enable you to follow Him—to love, trust, and delight in Him—so that if any temptation *does* come your way, it will draw you closer to Him!

> *There hath no temptation taken you but such as is common*
> *to man: but God is faithful, who will not suffer you to be*
> *tempted above that ye are able; but will with the temptation*
> *also make a way to escape, that ye may be able to bear it.*
>
> 1 CORINTHIANS 10:13

Oh, teach us to know you, our God, and enable us to do your will as we ought to do. Give us hearts to love you, to trust and delight in you. That no temptations may draw us, nor any tribulations drive us from you; but that all your dispensations to us, and all your dealings with us, may be the messengers of your love to our souls, to bring us still nearer to your blessed self, and to make us still fitter for your heavenly kingdom.

BENJAMIN JENKS

MY PRAYER STARTER: Father, as Your son, I don't want to do anything against Your plan. When I am tempted to step out of line, give me strength to endure.

Because you trust God, He lives in your heart. That's the first amazing benefit. The next is that you can run to God, to the "secret place of the most High" (Psalm 91:1), and dwell there with Him. You get to hang out in God's presence. You can be in that place where God reigns, abiding "under the shadow of the Almighty" (v. 1), away from the heat of the day. When you claim God as your refuge and your fortress, when you declare to yourself, to God, and to the world that you rely on *Him*—that He has all your confidence—you gain everything: protection, provision, rest, healing, shielding, security, blessings, angelic assistance, power, long life, and God's ear. Pray that you learn how to abide in God 24-7.

He that dwelleth in the secret place of the most High shall abide under the shadow of the Almighty. I will say of the LORD, He is my refuge and my fortress: my God; in him will I trust.

PSALM 91:1–2

Infinite One who fills the universe with Your unsearchable presence, and has a dwelling-place in every heart that trusts in You: I come now in a spirit of thanksgiving, and I would commune with You in prayer that I may learn to live in Your constant presence. Indeed, may I learn to pray as I ought in spirit and in truth.

JAMES MARTINEAU

MY PRAYER STARTER: Lord, Author of my salvation, thank You for the many undeserved gifts You've given me. May I always run to You for everything, no matter how small.

God's Spirit hovered over the deep, dark waters. Then God spoke, and light was formed, bringing color. In its wake came land, sea, sky, and creatures.

God is the Master Craftsman. And all He's made is good. But do you *see* it?

Pray that God would open your eyes today to the beauty of His creation. That you would notice each leaf, snowflake, or animal that dwells in your midst. That you would take note of the sun, stars, and moon that light up your little piece of heaven. That you would see everyone you encounter as a reflection of God's light and love. That He would give you the mind and heart to rejoice in all you see—to celebrate His world.

In the beginning God created the heaven and the earth. And the earth was without form, and void; and darkness was upon the face of the deep. And the Spirit of God moved upon the face of the waters. And God said, Let there be light: and there was light. And God saw the light, that it was good: and God divided the light from the darkness.

GENESIS 1:1–4

Creator Spirit, who broodest everlastingly over the lands and waters of the earth, enduing them with forms and colours which no human skill can copy, give me today, I beseech Thee, the mind and heart to rejoice in Thy creation.

JOHN BAILLIE

MY PRAYER STARTER: Awesome Creator, Your universe is breathtaking in its expansiveness and beauty. Whenever I peer into the cosmos, remind me of Your power that created it all.

From the time you were hidden in your mother's womb to the moment you're reading these lines to the day you enter heaven, Jesus Christ is with you. Live for Him and love Him from beginning to end.

> *My reward is with me, to give every man according as his*
> *work shall be. I am Alpha and Omega, the beginning and*
> *the end, the first and the last. . . . I Jesus have sent mine*
> *angel to testify unto you these things in the churches.*
>
> REVELATION 22:12–13, 16

May Christ-Omega keep me always young "to the greater glory
    of God." For old age comes from him, old age leads on to
    him, and old age will touch me only in so far as he wills.
    To be "young" means to be hopeful, energetic,
    smiling—and clear-sighted.

May I accept death in whatever guise it may come to me in Christ-
    Omega, that is within the process of the development of life. . . .
    Jesus-Omega, grant me to serve you, to proclaim you, to
    glorify you, to make you manifest, to the very end, through
    all the time that remains to me of life, and above all through
    my death. Desperately, Lord Jesus, I commit to your care
    my last active years, and my death: do not let them impair
    or spoil my work I have so dreamed of achieving for you.

TEILHARD DE CHARDIN

MY PRAYER STARTER: Lord, Author of life itself, I present my life as a blank page. Let me always give You the pen, allowing You to write whatever story You desire.

Jesus has immeasurable love and compassion for you, and He demonstrated it by showing you how God wants you to live—how you should love Him, yourself, and others.

Nothing can separate you from the love personified by Jesus. Revel in His love today. Allow it to envelop you, to permeate your life. Let it absorb your entire being until there's no room for fear, doubts, misgivings, worries, anger, or envy. Permit that love to lift you into His arms. There's no better place to be.

> *Who shall separate us from the love of Christ? shall tribulation, or distress, or persecution, or famine, or nakedness, or peril, or sword? . . . Nay, in all these things we are more than conquerors through him that loved us. For I am persuaded, that neither death, nor life, nor angels, nor principalities, nor powers, nor things present, nor things to come, nor height, nor depth, nor any other creature, shall be able to separate us from the love of God, which is in Christ Jesus our Lord.*
>
> ROMANS 8:35, 37–39

Lord Jesus, may the sweet burning ardour of your love so absorb my soul entirely and make it a stranger to all that is not you or for you.
SAINT FRANCIS OF ASSISI

MY PRAYER STARTER: Loving God, thank You for taking me into Your care as a father does his son. Even when nothing in the world seems safe, may I always find comforting solace in Your arms.

As believers in God, we're pilgrims upon this earth, strangers in this universe (1 Peter 2:11). Yet we're comforted by the fact that God not only becomes our sheltering home here but provides one for us in heaven. When our bodies pass away, we'll have a room in the eternal heavenly house of God (2 Corinthians 5:1).

While we're walking the earth as Jesus did, we can find inspiration in that great cloud of witnesses who've gone before (Hebrews 12:1). As we read the stories in the Old and New Testaments, we gain fresh hope, renewed by the courage of fellow sojourners who overcame the things of this world.

Read about and consider the godly who've gone before. Feel the power of their stories. Let it refresh even your most tiresome tasks. Then praise God for our fellow pilgrims and for Him, our true home.

> *For whatsoever things were written aforetime were*
> *written for our learning, that we through patience*
> *and comfort of the scriptures might have hope.*
> ROMANS 15:4

Dear God, we are as strangers in Your wondrous universe, yet as children at home within Your shelter. You inspire joyful confidence in You. Enlightener of true seers and prophets, You are our Strength. May their faith and spirit rest upon all our life, refreshing the weariest task. In life and in death, You are the steadfast light of our hearts; You are our portion forever.
JAMES MARTINEAU

MY PRAYER STARTER: Never-changing God, You are the same now as You were in the days of the saints long before me. May I learn from their examples as I follow You.

Before you can be willing for God to have His way with you, you must first show Him that you're willing to be made willing.

Perhaps you have misgivings or fears about God having His way with you. If so, get to know Him better. He's already given you a heart to do so? (Jeremiah 24:7). Once you know Him well, all mistrust and fears will fade away. To grow your trust in God and your knowledge of Him, dig into His Word, seeking Him with your whole heart and hiding His wondrous, eye-opening Word there (Psalm 119:10–11, 18).

Today, let God know you're willing to be willing. Then *be* willing.

> *Come, and let us return unto the LORD: for he hath torn, and*
> *he will heal us; he hath smitten, and he will bind us up. After*
> *two days will he revive us: in the third day he will raise us up,*
> *and we shall live in his sight. Then shall we know, if we follow*
> *on to know the LORD. . . . For I desired mercy, and not sacrifice;*
> *and the knowledge of God more than burnt offerings.*

HOSEA 6:1–3, 6

Lord, I am not yet willing for thee to have thy way
with me, but I am willing to be made willing.

F. B. MEYER

MY PRAYER STARTER: Trustworthy Lord, I am sometimes hesitant in following Your plan. Erase my misgivings and replace them with a willingness to heed Your call, wherever it takes me.

When you need a vision for your life, go to God. He's the One who opens your eyes and ears and enters your heart. He's the life and strength of souls who love and seek Him. God enlightens and expands your mind; He lifts your heart's vision so that your thoughts and spirit can wing their way to His wisdom.

God's Spirit will lead you into all the knowledge you need to be a heavenly kingdom dweller on earth. As a man with the mind of Jesus Christ, soar to God today and elevate the vantage point of your heart.

> *But as it is written, Eye hath not seen, nor ear heard, neither*
> *have entered into the heart of man, the things which God hath*
> *prepared for them that love him. But God hath revealed them unto*
> *us by his Spirit: for the Spirit searcheth all things, yea, the deep*
> *things of God. . . . For who hath known the mind of the Lord,*
> *that he may instruct him? But we have the mind of Christ.*
>
> 1 CORINTHIANS 2:9–10, 16

O God, light of the minds that see you, life of the souls that love you, and strength of the souls that seek you, enlarge our minds and raise the vision of our hearts, that, with swift wings of thought, our spirits may reach you, the eternal wisdom, you who live from everlasting to everlasting; through Jesus Christ our Lord. Amen.
SAINT AUGUSTINE

MY PRAYER STARTER: Heavenly Father, elevate my thoughts far above the petty concerns of this life. Widen my field of vision, showing me the truth found in Your Word.

Jesus is in everything. He "is the image of the invisible God" (Colossians 1:15). Through Him everything—visible and invisible, in heaven and on earth—was made. Jesus holds all created things together, including you!

As a result, there is nothing for you to fear. Your heart can take courage in His words: "Be of good cheer; it is I; be not afraid" (Matthew 14:27).

So pray today that God would help you understand that Jesus is in everything that comes your way. That nothing will touch you that hasn't first gone through Him.

Jesus will reveal Himself to you in all things, all ways, and all your days. You only need to look for His smiling face.

> *[Jesus Christ] is the image of the invisible God, the firstborn of every creature: for by him were all things created, that are in heaven, and that are in earth, visible and invisible, whether they be thrones, or dominions, or principalities, or powers: all things were created by him, and for him: and he is before all things, and by him all things consist.*
> COLOSSIANS 1:15–17

Lord, purge our eyes to see
Within the seed a tree,
Within the glowing egg a bird,
Within the shroud a butterfly.
Till, taught by such we see
Beyond all creatures, Thee
And hearken to Thy tender word
And hear its "Fear not; it is I."
CHRISTINA ROSSETTI

MY PRAYER STARTER: Sovereign Lord, I am sometimes baffled by the bad things that happen. Help me believe that You are behind the scenes, directing each event for the greater good.

Someone else's burden has been laid upon your heart. But you're not sure what to pray for. You've heard the person's troubles and wishes—to be healed, find a job, be more joyful or less stressed, etc. But you're not sure what *God's* will is for this individual.

That's why today's classic prayer is so powerful: it outlines the individual's issue but leaves the solution up to the Spirit. And it goes even further by asking the Spirit to "pray in me the prayer Thou art praying"—all so that God's will would be done in Jesus' name. Use this prayer today and experience its power.

> *Likewise the Spirit also helpeth our infirmities: for we know not what we should pray for as we ought: but the Spirit itself maketh intercession for us with groanings which cannot be uttered. And he that searcheth the hearts knoweth what is the mind of the Spirit, because he maketh intercession for the saints according to the will of God.*
>
> ROMANS 8:26–27

Blessed Holy Spirit, Thou knowest this man, and what the lacking thing is in him. There is trouble there. Thou knowest this sick woman, and what the difficulty is there. This problem, and what the hindrance is in it. Blessed Spirit, pray in me the prayer Thou art praying for this man, and this thing, and this one. The prayer Thou art praying, I pray that, in Jesus' name. Thy will be done here under these circumstances.

S. D. GORDON

MY PRAYER STARTER: All-seeing God, I can't always know what's best for someone. Fill me with compassion when I pray for others, but let me always place the outcome in Your hands.

No matter where God has placed you or where He sends you, know He's always with you. You're in His hands. And Jesus says that no person or thing will be able to snatch you away (John 10:28–29)! That eternal tie between you, God, Jesus, and the Spirit can never be severed.

Also, God promises to give you strength to bear any burden laid upon you: "Cast thy burden upon the LORD, and he shall sustain thee" (Psalm 55:22).

Pray today for willingness to go where God sends, knowing He'll stick with you. Pray that He'll sustain you and give you the muscle to carry any burden—and He will. Let Him sever all ties, except those between Him and you. Before long, you'll be a mighty servant of God.

I am continually with thee: thou hast holden me by my right hand.
Thou shalt guide me with thy counsel, and afterward receive me
to glory. Whom have I in heaven but thee? and there is none upon
earth that I desire beside thee. My flesh and my heart faileth:
but God is the strength of my heart, and my portion for ever.

PSALM 73:23–26

Lord, send me anywhere, only go with me. Lay any burden on me, only sustain me. Sever any ties, but the ties that bind me to your heart and to your service.
DAVID LIVINGSTONE

MY PRAYER STARTER: Lord God, I cannot praise You enough for Your unbreakable faithfulness toward me. Grant me the perseverance and willpower to endure whatever struggles I face.

Amid the darkness at the beginning of creation, God spoke the first words: "Let there be light" (Genesis 1:3). Pray for that light to shine within you, bringing you the joy of the Lord.

God's light will drive away the darkness of sin and the mists of doubt, fear, and wrong thinking from your heart. It will guide your feet on the way, keeping you from stumbling.

Let there be light!

> *The sun shall be no more thy light by day; neither for brightness*
> *shall the moon give light unto thee: but the LORD shall be*
> *unto thee an everlasting light, and thy God thy glory. Thy*
> *sun shall no more go down; neither shall thy moon withdraw*
> *itself: for the LORD shall be thine everlasting light.*
> ISAIAH 60:19–20

O Thou, who art the true Sun of the world, ever rising, and never going down; who, by Thy most wholesome appearing and sight dost nourish, and gladden all things in heaven and earth; we beseech Thee mercifully to shine into our hearts, that the night and darkness of sin, and the mists of error on every side, being driven away, by the brightness of Thy shining within our hearts, we may all our life walk without stumbling, as in the day-time, and, being pure and clean from the works of darkness, may abound in all good works which Thou hast prepared for us to walk in. Amen.
ERASMUS

MY PRAYER STARTER: Almighty Creator, just as You filled the world with light in the beginning, fill me with the light of the Holy Spirit, dissolving the shadows that linger in my soul.

God is holy. And so is His Word. When the scriptures speak, God speaks (Galatians 3:8). So immerse yourself in the Word. Receive it as God's voice speaking directly into your heart. And then live by it, allowing it to direct your feet and light your pathway.

By staking your confidence in God's promises, you'll find the courage, strength, and provisions to live the life God desires you to live.

Pray for God's guidance before you read His Word. Ask Him to highlight the portions He's revealing to you, to interpret anything that's unclear. And then slowly, thoughtfully delve into the scriptures with the Spirit's guidance. It's the most important journey you can embark upon.

> *But continue thou in the things which thou hast learned and hast been assured of, knowing of whom thou hast learned them. . . . All scripture is given by inspiration of God, and is profitable for doctrine, for reproof, for correction, for instruction in righteousness: that the man of God may be perfect, thoroughly furnished unto all good works.*
> 2 TIMOTHY 3:14, 16–17

O God, whose name is holy of itself, we pray that it may be hallowed also by us. To this end help us, O blessed Father in heaven, that thy word may be taught in truth and purity, and that we, as thy children, may lead holy lives in accordance with it; through Jesus Christ, thy Son, our Lord. Amen.
MARTIN LUTHER

MY PRAYER STARTER: Lord, I am a man with flawed understanding. Send Your Spirit to assist me in my journey toward truth as I read Your Word.

Live with the hope that God, who orders the world, will also order your inner life so that you can understand the hidden wisdom He brings to light. Pray for that wisdom and hope today.

> *But we speak the wisdom of God in a mystery, even the hidden wisdom, which God ordained before the world unto our glory. . . . God hath revealed them unto us by his Spirit: for the Spirit searcheth all things, yea, the deep things of God.*
>
> 1 CORINTHIANS 2:7, 10

Almighty God, by Whose word all things work, by Whose guidance all things go, so order our inward life that we may be enabled to understand the things that we see; and by Thy guidance in the spiritual life and in charity, so order what there is disordered in our lives, so bring our minds to the truth, our consciences to the law, our eyes to the light, and our hearts to Thy true love, that amidst the seeming discords of life, we may hear the music of the heavenly will, and catch ofttimes the charms of the heavenly order. So give us hope that we may pass on through time, into the higher and better education of the eternal life to come, and that at last we may know those things that are hidden, and which now we cannot know, and learn the glorious beauty and the glorious loving of the eternal years.

GEORGE DAWSON

MY PRAYER STARTER: God of wisdom, don't let my thoughts about You become entangled and confused. Grant me clarity in my beliefs and peace in my soul.

Jesus has come to stand in your midst. His first words are "Peace be unto you." He shows you His hands and side, the wounds He suffered to save you and bring you into the fold. Your heart rejoices, for you feel His light, power, joy, and love. He says again, "Peace be unto you," and the feeling grows deeper.

And then the Holy Three arrive. Jesus says, "As my Father hath sent me, even so send I you" (John 20:21). You feel His breath upon you as you hear His words "Receive ye the Holy Ghost" (v. 22).

Breathe. Breathe in Jesus' presence, God's love, and the Holy Spirit's power.

Today, ask God to teach you how to breathe deeply in faith.

Then. . .when the doors were shut where the disciples were assembled for fear of the Jews, came Jesus and stood in the midst, and saith unto them, Peace be unto you. And when he had so said, he shewed unto them his hands and his side. Then were the disciples glad, when they saw the LORD. Then said Jesus to them again, Peace be unto you: as my Father hath sent me, even so send I you. And when he had said this, he breathed on them, and saith unto them, Receive ye the Holy Ghost.

JOHN 20:19–22

O God. . .teach me to breathe deeply in faith.
SØREN KIERKEGAARD

MY PRAYER STARTER: Lord, Giver of peace, I need Your breath every day—for faith, peace, and wisdom. Let the Holy Spirit fill me with the comforting assurance of Your presence.

God loves, encourages, strengthens, and uplifts you so that you can meet all your challenges in His power. Ask for His blessings today. Know you have received them—and be sure to pass them on to everyone you meet!

And let us consider one another to provoke unto love and to good works.
HEBREWS 10:24

O God, our heavenly Father, we Thy children come to Thy feet with our supplications. We cannot live without Thy blessings. Life is too hard for us and duty is too large. We get discouraged, and our feeble hands hang down. We come to Thee with our weakness, asking Thee for strength. Help us always to be of good cheer. Let us not be disheartened by difficulties. Let us never doubt Thy love or any of Thy promises. Give us grace to be encouragers of others, never discouragers. Let us. . .be a benediction to every one we meet, always making life easier, never harder, for those who come within our influence. Help us to be as Christ to others, that they may see something of His love in our lives and learn to love Him in us. We beseech Thee to hear us, to receive our prayer, and to forgive our sins, for Jesus Christ's sake. Amen.
J. R. MILLER

MY PRAYER STARTER: Gracious Lord, thank You for Your blessings, even the ones I haven't received yet. Give me wisdom to handle them properly and to share them with others.

Isaiah 29:13 is an eye-opener: "This people draw near me with their mouth, and with their lips do honour me, but have removed their heart far from me." Do you feel its sting?

God clearly doesn't want you to give Him lip service, to consent in your words while dissenting in your heart. He wants you to pray with your entire being—mind, soul, strength, and heart.

So before you pray today, sit back for a few moments and breathe. Think about your love for God and His love for you. Then pray the prayer below, changing the wording as needed so that your words come deep from your very core. Add on whatever your heart is speaking to you, what it wants to say to your Father God. You'll find blessings galore, prompting you to be even more faithful in prayer day after day.

> *Blessed are they that keep his testimonies, and*
> *that seek him with the whole heart.*
>
> PSALM 119:2

Assist me mercifully, O Lord, in all my supplications and prayers, that I may not draw near to thee with my lips while my heart is far from thee. Give me a hearty desire to pray, and grace to pray faithfully, that I may live under thy most mighty protection here, and praise thee hereafter; through Jesus Christ.
SABINE BARING-GOULD

MY PRAYER STARTER: God, may my prayers be the heartfelt words of a son to his father. Fill me with sincerity and love, and let my conversations with You never become routine.

Psalm 18 calls God your strength, rock, fortress, deliverer, shield, savior, and high tower. He's exactly who you need when you're caught in the riptide of affliction, being pulled under by grief. God rushes in at your cry, drawing you out of the waters and putting you on dry ground, where you can find your footing once again.

Pray. God will answer and lift you up.

> *In my distress I called upon the LORD, and cried unto my God:*
> *he heard my voice out of his temple, and my cry came before*
> *him, even into his ears. . . . He sent from above, he took me, he*
> *drew me out of many waters. . . . He brought me forth also into*
> *a large place; he delivered me, because he delighted in me.*
>
> PSALM 18:6, 16, 19

O holy and loving Father, Whose mercies are from everlasting to everlasting, we thank Thee that Thy children can flee for refuge in their afflictions to the blessed certainty of Thy love. From every grief that burdens our spirits, from the sense of solitude and loss, from the doubt and fainting of the soul in its trouble, we turn to Thee. Thou knowest our frame, Thou rememberest that we are dust. Be Thou our Strength and Deliverer; in our great need be Thou our Helper; pour Thy consolations into our hearts, and let the gospel of Thy beloved Son minister comfort and peace to our souls. Amen.
HENRY W. FOOTE

MY PRAYER STARTER: Savior, thank You for pulling me out of the swamp of sin and setting me on the rock of salvation. Whenever I feel like I'm sinking, remind me of Your promises.

Today's classic prayer shows you the peace that can settle upon you when you leave all your expectations in God's hands—when you remember that everything happens according to His good plan, one that's unimaginably better than yours. Pray and experience freedom as you leave it all up to the Master.

> *My soul, wait thou only upon God; for my expectation*
> *is from him. He only is my rock and my salvation:*
> *he is my defence; I shall not be moved.*
>
> PSALM 62:5–6

O Lord, Who hast breathed into me the breath of life, and endued me with an immortal spirit, which looks up unto Thee, and remembers it is made after Thine own image, behold with grace and favor the ardent desires which are in my heart, to recover a perfect likeness of Thee. Endue me with more contentedness in what is present, and less solicitude about what is future; with a patient mind to submit to any loss of what I have, or any disappointment of what I expect. Fill me, O Lord, with the knowledge of Thy will, in all wisdom and spiritual understanding. Fill me with goodness, and the fruits of righteousness. And fill me with all joy and peace in believing that Thou wilt never leave me nor forsake me, but make me perfect, stablish, strengthen, settle me, and be my God for ever and ever; my Guide unto death. Amen.

SIMON PATRICK

MY PRAYER STARTER: Lord, I know You are weaving the tangled threads of my life into a brilliant tapestry. Eliminate my anxious nearsightedness and replace it with faith and peace.

Love not only makes the world go round; it makes *God* go round. When you love others in your thoughts, speech, and actions, God is there.

Before praying today, think of how much love God showed when He sent His one and only Son to save you, to show you how to live and how to love. Pray God would let that same love shine on, in, and through you.

Beloved, let us love one another: for love is of God; and every one that loveth is born of God, and knoweth God. He that loveth not knoweth not God; for God is love. In this was manifested the love of God toward us, because that God sent his only begotten Son.

1 JOHN 4:7–9

O God of love, we pray thee to give us love:
Love in our thinking, love in our speaking,
Love in our doing, and love in the hidden places of our souls;
Love of our neighbours near and far;
Love of our friends, old and new;
Love of those with whom we find it hard to bear,
And love of those who find it hard to bear with us;
Love of those with whom we work,
And love of those with whom we take our ease;
Love in joy, love in sorrow;
Love in life and love in death;
That so at length we may be worthy to dwell with thee,
Who art eternal love.

WILLIAM TEMPLE

MY PRAYER STARTER: Lord God, let me be a man who reflects Your love as the moon reflects the sunlight. Let others see in me the unmistakable glow of Your compassion.

God's Word molds you into the person God wants you to be. It teaches you about God's grace, the Gospel, and Jesus—God's gift of grace to you. When you instruct others about God and His Word, you need God's grace not only to teach but to learn from those whom you teach.

Today's prayers ask God for grace to teach and learn. They ask for the Word of God to speak to you and give you the words to speak to others. They ask for God's wisdom to educate you so that He can use you to educate others.

The more you learn from God's Word, the more grace you'll gain, the more you'll live by God's promises, the more you'll find your needs fulfilled, and the more complete you'll become. Pray for the transforming power of God's Word of grace.

And now, brethren, I commend you to God, and to the word
of his grace, which is able to build you up, and to give you
an inheritance among all them which are sanctified.

ACTS 20:32

Lord Jesus, merciful and patient, grant us grace, I beg you, ever to teach in the teachable spirit; learning along with those we teach, and learning from them whenever you please. Word of God, speak to us, speak by us what you will. Wisdom of God, instruct us. . .that we and they may all be taught of God.
CHRISTINA ROSSETTI

MY PRAYER STARTER: God, I need Your grace when I study Your Word. When I share what I learn with others, may I let Your Spirit give me the words so that I will speak only Your truth.

God's light follows you everywhere you go, giving you rest whenever and wherever you need it. Secure in His presence, you need not fear at night. As you close your eyes, know He is with you, guarding you as you sleep. If you awaken during the night, He will be there to soothe your mind and heart. And when you rise to a new day, turn to His presence once again, to Jesus, your Sun, and the Spirit, your Comforter.

With the Holy Three in your midst, you'll find the strength and eagerness to face the tasks before you, the strength to tackle whatever comes, and the guidance to stay on the path of peace.

Pray today for the rest you can find in God alone.

> *The dayspring from on high hath visited us, to give light to them that sit in darkness and in the shadow of death, to guide our feet into the way of peace.*
>
> LUKE 1:78–79

Go with each of us to rest; if any awake, temper them the dark hours of watching; and when the day returns, return to us, our sun and comforter, and call us up with morning faces and with morning hearts, eager to labour, eager to be happy, if happiness should be our portion, and if the day be marked for sorrow, strong to endure it. Amen.

ROBERT LOUIS STEVENSON

MY PRAYER STARTER: Dependable Lord, even when I'm not conscious of Your presence, You are there nonetheless. Thank You for Your constant supervision.

God doesn't want just your mind. Or just your body. Or soul. Or spirit. He wants *all* of you. That means He wants your inner heart too. He wants you to give Him full possession of your very core, to open up and allow His Son to reign there so that you'll follow His every nudge down the right path.

God gave you life. So live for Him. God worked to make you. So work for His benefit. Jesus gave His life for you. So give yours to Him. Jesus promised to never leave you. So don't desert Him.

Pray today's prayers, giving the Lord your entire heart. Live wholeheartedly and unashamedly for God's glory.

> *For this cause I bow my knees unto the Father of our Lord*
> *Jesus Christ, of whom the whole family in heaven and earth*
> *is named, that he would grant you, according to the riches of*
> *his glory, to be strengthened with might by his Spirit in the*
> *inner man; that Christ may dwell in your hearts by faith.*
> EPHESIANS 3:14–17

O Lord, take full possession of my heart, raise there your throne, and command there as you do in heaven.
Being created by you, let me live for you;
being created for you, let me always act for your glory;
being redeemed by you, let me give to you what is yours;
and let my spirit cling to you alone, for your name's sake.
JOHN WESLEY

MY PRAYER STARTER: God, You gave everything to save me, so I want to give all of me back to You. If I'm unknowingly holding back anything, take that from me too. I surrender it all.

One of the great things about being a God follower is that whether you're alive or dead, Jesus Christ is with you. He's "Lord both of the dead and living" (Romans 14:9)! So while you're here, God the Father will support, strengthen, and energize you to keep you walking His way. And then, when your work here is done, Jesus will meet you at the gates of heaven, where God the Father already has a place prepared for you—one that's safe, where you can rest in peace at last.

So don't worry. Keep following God. Pray for His help while you're in the sun today and for His heavenly haven when your earthly days are done!

And I heard a voice from heaven saying unto me, Write, Blessed are the dead which die in the Lord from henceforth: Yea, saith the Spirit, that they may rest from their labours; and their works do follow them.

REVELATION 14:13

O Father, support me all the day long of this troublous life, until the shadows lengthen, and the evening comes, and the busy world is hushed, and the fever of life is over, and my work is done. Then, dear Father, in Thy mercy grant me a safe lodging, a holy rest, and a peace at the last; through Jesus Christ, Thy Son and my Lord. Amen.

JOHN HENRY NEWMAN

MY PRAYER STARTER: Reassuring Father, thank You for the never-ending strength and peace You provide me. Even more, thank You for the joys of heaven that I will one day experience.

Today's classic prayer is like a love letter God has sent to your soul. Your soul reads God's letter then pens one of its own. And God's reply brings it full circle.

God's love is a living, breathing force that goes full circle. First, God loved you, yet He lost you due to sin. So He sent His beloved Son to bring you back. You accepted His Son, who now lives within you. He in God and you in Him.

Today, let your soul speak its love to God.

> *I in them, and thou in me, that they may be made perfect*
> *in one; and that the world may know that thou hast sent*
> *me, and hast loved them, as thou hast loved me.*
>
> JOHN 17:23

AND GOD SAID TO THE SOUL:
I desired you before the world began. I desire you now as you desire me. And where the desires of two come together. The love is perfected.

HOW THE SOUL SPEAKS TO GOD:
Lord, you are my lover, my longing, My flowing stream, my sun, And I am your reflection.

HOW GOD ANSWERS THE SOUL:
It is my nature that makes me love you often, For I am love itself. It is my longing that makes me love you intensely, For I yearn to be loved from the heart. It is my eternity that makes me love you long, For I have no end.

MECHTHILD OF MAGDEBURG

MY PRAYER STARTER: God of infinite forgiveness, I am amazed by Your endless love. Let our relationship be entirely mutual—let me love You as You have loved me.

There's power in thanking God. When the ark of God was first brought into King Solomon's temple, the people lifted their voices in thanksgiving and praise to God, and the Lord's presence filled the meeting place!

Today's classic prayer begins with thanksgiving, which is followed by pleas that admit humanity's imperfections. Yet you'll find it to be a power-filled and perfect prayer.

It came even to pass, as the trumpeters and singers were as one,
to make one sound to be heard in praising and thanking the LORD;
and when they lifted up their voice. . .and praised the LORD,
saying, For he is good; for his mercy endureth for ever: that then
the house was filled with a cloud, even the house of the LORD.

2 CHRONICLES 5:13

Lord, behold us here assembled. We thank Thee for this place in which we dwell; for the love that unites us; for the peace accorded us this day; for the hope with which we expect the morrow; for the health, the work, the food, and the bright skies, that make our lives delightful; for our friends in all parts of the earth. Let peace abound in our community. Purge out of every heart the lurking grudge. Give us grace and strength to forbear and to persevere. Offenders, give us the grace to forgive offenders. Forgetful ourselves, help us to bear cheerfully the forgetfulness of others. Give us courage and gaiety and the quiet mind.
ROBERT LOUIS STEVENSON

MY PRAYER STARTER: God, thank You for allowing me to worship You, even though I am a flawed man. Just as You have forgiven me, give me the grace to forgive others for their faults.

God has formed you into the man you are now, the one reading these words. He has certain tasks He wants you to perform. He has a mission for you—to live as an example to this generation, shed your light, love and forgive all, and resemble Jesus.

But God needs some help. He needs you to be willing. You must be pliant, ready to bend to His will. That means ignoring your own desires. Conquering fear. Refusing a worldly mindset. God wants you to give Him total control. To refer all things to the wisdom of the Holy Spirit within. To be humble and obedient. To acknowledge that Jesus Christ rules your heart—and to let Him do it!

That's what today's four-word classic prayer is all about: being humble and obedient, surrendering yourself to God's will. Having that mind of Jesus Christ in you. And in so doing, grasping the courage, peace, strength, and power that accompany it!

*Let this mind be in you, which was also in Christ Jesus: who, being
in the form of God, thought it not robbery to be equal with God:
but made himself of no reputation, and took upon him the form of
a servant, and was made in the likeness of men: and being found
in fashion as a man, he humbled himself, and became obedient.*

PHILIPPIANS 2:5–8

Oh, Lord, bend me!
EVAN ROBERTS

MY PRAYER STARTER: Supreme Lord, make me totally submitted to You. Fit me into Your mold, trimming away any excess pride, selfishness, or cowardice.

Consider how often God has been with you when the going got hard, how much He's brought you through. He was with you amid the fire and flood. He dammed the tsunami of troubles in your life. When earthly burdens were weighing you down, He lifted you up. When you were as helpless as a baby, unable to find your feet, God—your rock and foundation, refuge and strength, fortress and protector—stayed with you. What a God! Praise Him!

When thou passest through the waters, I will be with thee; and through the rivers, they shall not overflow thee: when thou walkest through the fire, thou shalt not be burned; neither shall the flame kindle upon thee.

ISAIAH 43:2

It is in my heart to praise thee, O my God;
Let me never forget thee,
what thou has been to me. . . .
When my way was through the sea,
and when I passed under the mountains
there was thou present with me. . . .
When I was one altogether helpless,
when tribulation and anguish was upon me
day and night, and the earth was without foundation. . . .
Thou was with me and the Rock of thy Presence.

JAMES NAYLER

MY PRAYER STARTER: Almighty Sustainer, You've brought me through every difficulty I've ever had. Thank You for being my reliable refuge, and may I always turn to You in every situation.

Be assured that God has a plan. That He loves you and knows what's best. That's where you'll find the strength to wait on Him for guidance. Today, pray for patience, then believe you've received it. Experience the immediate calm that follows.

> *Walk worthy of the Lord unto all pleasing, being fruitful in every good work, and increasing in the knowledge of God; strengthened with all might, according to his glorious power, unto all patience and longsuffering with joyfulness; giving thanks unto the Father.*
> COLOSSIANS 1:10–12

O my God, Thou and Thou alone art all-wise and all-knowing! I believe that Thou knowest just what is best for me. I believe that Thou lovest me better than I love myself, that Thou art all-wise in Thy Providence and all-powerful in Thy protection. I thank Thee, with all my heart, that Thou hast taken me out of my own keeping, and hast bidden me to put myself in Thy hands. I can ask nothing better than this, to be Thy care, not my own. O my Lord, through Thy grace, I will follow Thee whithersoever Thou goest, and will not lead the way. I will wait on Thee for Thy guidance, and, on obtaining it, I will act in simplicity and without fear. And I promise that I will not be impatient, if at any time I am kept by Thee in darkness and perplexity; nor will I complain or fret if I come into any misfortune or anxiety. Amen.
JOHN HENRY NEWMAN

MY PRAYER STARTER: Lord, I can be an impatient man at times. Teach me patience and give me the strength to endure so that I can be an effective godly example to others.

When those you care about are rocked by illness, weakness, or anxiety, lift them to Jesus. If fear or sadness threatens to drag them into the depths of the sea, pray for Him to rescue them. Ask that they would turn to Him who has power over the wind and waves. May God then loosen their fears and strengthen their faith, leaving them awed by Jesus' love.

There arose a great tempest in the sea, insomuch that the ship was covered with the waves: but he was asleep. And his disciples came to him, and awoke him, saying, Lord, save us: we perish. And he saith unto them, Why are ye fearful, O ye of little faith? Then he arose, and rebuked the winds and the sea; and there was a great calm. But the men marvelled, saying, What manner of man is this, that even the winds and the sea obey him!

MATTHEW 8:24–27

Lord of great compassion, we pray to you for those who are nervously ill, and too weak and anxious to lift themselves above the fear and sadness that threaten to overwhelm them. Do you yourself, O Lord, lift them up and deliver them, as you delivered your disciples in the storm at sea, strengthening their faith and banishing their fear. Turning to you, O Lord, may they find you, and finding you may they find also all you have laid up for them within the fortress of your love.

ELIZABETH GOUDGE

MY PRAYER STARTER: Father, many of my friends are struggling with their health, mind, and faith. Give them peace, assuring them of Your presence and calming them with Your love.

Running for his life, the prophet Elijah fled into the wilderness. He was stressed and strained, ready to give up and die. But God had other ideas. First, He allowed Elijah to get some much-needed rest and renewal. Then God told him to stand on the mountain before Him, where He would pass by. After a mighty wind, earthquake, and fire, God spoke to Elijah in a still, small voice.

When you find yourself on the run, stressing, straining, and striving, go to God. Turn your ear to His voice. When He speaks, let His words give you the tranquility you need.

And, behold, the LORD passed by, and a great and strong wind rent the mountains, and brake in pieces the rocks before the LORD; but the LORD was not in the wind: and after the wind an earthquake; but the LORD was not in the earthquake: and after the earthquake a fire; but the LORD was not in the fire: and after the fire a still small voice.

1 KINGS 19:11–12

Drop Thy still dews of quietness, of our desire
Till all our strivings cease; Thy coolness and Thy balm;
Take from our souls Let sense be dumb,
the strain and stress, let flesh retire;
And let our ordered lives confess Speak through the earthquake,
The beauty of Thy peace. wind and fire,
Breathe through the heats O still, small voice of calm!
JOHN GREENLEAF WHITTIER

MY PRAYER STARTER: Father, amid the bombastic hustle of life, let me hear Your still, small whisper. Your voice is the only voice that matters.

According to *Strong's Bible Concordance*, the Hebrew word for *waiteth* in Psalm 62:1 implies "a state of silent stillness with quiet and trust." The word *wait* in verse 5 means "to hold peace, quiet yourself, rest, be still and silent." Most of us need to learn how to wait before God in that way—to just *be* with Him, communing in silence.

Make your primary goal today to wait quietly before God. Allow His Spirit to revitalize your own from the deepest place within. Begin by asking God to teach you how to find your silent refuge in Him. Then sit quietly. . .and wait. Trust Him to lead you where He is.

> *Truly my soul waiteth upon God. . . . My soul, wait thou only upon*
> *God. . . . Trust in him at all times. . . : God is a refuge for us.*
> PSALM 62:1, 5, 8

Teach us, O Spirit of God, that silent language which says all things. Teach our souls to remain silent in thy presence: that we may adore thee in the depths of our being and await all things from thee, whilst asking of thee nothing but the accomplishment of thy will. Teach us to remain quiet under thy action and produce in our soul that deep and simple prayer which says nothing and expresses everything, which specifies nothing and includes everything.

JEAN NICHOLAS GROU

MY PRAYER STARTER: God of peace, You are my only source of peace in this life. Whenever I am busy, give me the wisdom each day to slow down enough to talk quietly with You.

In times of spiritual dryness, you may find yourself unwilling or unable to pray. Praying brings you neither comfort nor joy. Yet by *not* praying, you're stopping up the very source of power and renewal you so desperately need.

So whether you want to or not, go to God. Ask Him to give you a heart longing for His presence, a spirit that finds solace in Him alone. Ask God to bring past blessings, present wonders, and future good to your mind. Pray for Him to rekindle your soul.

Renew a right spirit within me.
PSALM 51:10

Gracious Father, who givest the hunger of desire, and satisfies our hunger with good things; quicken the heart of Thy servant who mourns because he cannot speak to Thee, nor hear Thee speak to him. Refresh, we beseech Thee, the dulness and dryness of his inner life. Grant him perseverance that he may never abandon the effort to pray, even though it brings for a time no comfort or joy. Enlarge his soul's desires that he may be drawn to Thee. Send forth Thy Spirit into his heart to help his infirmities; to give him freedom of utterance, and warmth of feeling. Let him muse upon Thy goodness; upon the blessings with which Thou hast strewn his path; upon the mystery of the world, and the shame of sin, and the sadness of death—until the fire kindles and the heart melts in prayer and praise and supplication.
SAMUEL MCCOMB

MY PRAYER STARTER: God, Hearer of my cries, I sometimes feel as if my prayers are futile. During these moments, give me the fortitude to keep praying, knowing that my joy will soon return.

The wonders of the sky and earth are just poor reflections of the new heaven and earth that await you. A place where you will dwell in peace. Where the only light will be that of Jesus Christ. Where there will be no noise or silence but the music of angels. Where there will be no fear or hope but all things shared. Where there will be no beginning or end but a glorious eternity in a heavenly world.

Today, pray for God to bring you there on that glorious day—but first, to keep that vision in your mind, spirit, and heart as you face these present hours.

> *And the city had no need of the sun, neither of the moon,*
> *to shine in it: for the glory of God did lighten it, and the*
> *Lamb is the light thereof. . . . And the gates of it shall not*
> *be shut at all by day: for there shall be no night there.*
>
> REVELATION 21:23, 25

Bring us, O Lord God, at our last awakening into the house and gate of heaven to enter into that gate and dwell in that house, where there shall be no darkness nor dazzling, but one equal light; no noise nor silence, but one equal music; no fears nor hopes, but one equal possession; no ends nor beginnings, but one equal eternity; in the habitations of thy glory and dominion, world without end.

JOHN DONNE

MY PRAYER STARTER: Lord of heaven, may I never focus so much on this world that I forget the one for which I was made. Remind me constantly of Your infinite peace and joy that awaits.

God planted within your heart a desire to follow His path for your life. But sometimes that path has fallen short of your expectations. When this happens, pray for God to keep you on His path, regardless of where you think you should be by now. To keep your feet steady as you walk in His better way, wherever it may lead. To give you the wisdom to follow Him cheerfully. To strengthen your spiritual muscle while you labor for Him.

Now our Lord Jesus Christ himself, and God, even our Father, which hath loved us, and hath given us everlasting consolation and good hope through grace, comfort your hearts, and stablish you in every good word and work.
2 THESSALONIANS 2:16–17

O God, who hast in mercy taught us how good it is to follow the holy desires which Thou manifoldly puttest into our hearts, and how bitter is the grief of falling short of whatever beauty our minds behold, strengthen us, we beseech Thee, to walk steadfastly throughout life in the better path which our hearts once chose; and give us the wisdom to tread it prudently in Thy fear, as well as cheerfully in Thy love; so that, having been faithful to Thee all the days of our life here, we may be able hopefully to resign ourselves into Thy hands hereafter. Amen.
ROWLAND WILLIAMS

MY PRAYER STARTER: Lord God, even when Your path is temporarily disappointing to me, remind me of the bigger picture so that I'll have the willpower to keep following You.

Parents aren't perfect. Yet even they won't give their son a stone when he asks for bread. So if imperfect parents know how to give good gifts upon request, imagine how much better the gifts from your Father God will be—regardless of how imperfect you are. But you need to ask. Do so today, expecting God to give.

> *What man is there of you, whom if his son ask bread, will*
> *he give him a stone? Or if he ask a fish, will he give him a*
> *serpent? If ye then, being evil, know how to give good gifts*
> *unto your children, how much more shall your Father which*
> *is in heaven give good things to them that ask him?*
> MATTHEW 7:9–11

O my Lord! How can one ask you for favors who has served you so ill and has hardly been able to keep what you have already given? How can you have any confidence in one who has so often betrayed you? What, then, shall I do, comfort of the comfortless, and help of all who seek help from you? Can it be better to keep silence about my necessities, hoping that you will relieve them? No, indeed; for you, my Lord and my joy, knowing how many they must be and how it will alleviate them if we speak to you of them, do bid us pray to you and say that you will not fail to give.
SAINT TERESA OF ÁVILA

MY PRAYER STARTER: Gracious Father, thank You for welcoming my requests. Despite my imperfections, You still call me Your son, and I know I can come to You for anything.

God wants to be with you when you plan your day. Then He wants you to consult Him every step of the way. This may sound restricting, but once you start asking Him, "What do You think, Lord?" at every turn, you'll find real freedom! When you do everything according to *His* desire, all *your* desires—and more—will be met.

So trust in God. Ask Him for advice about everything—what to eat, what job to take, and even whom to love! Rely on God's wisdom instead of your own intuition. Seek Him in all your situations and endeavors. Then you'll be walking on His path, without fear of stumbling or walking into a trap. God's way is the right way.

> *Trust in the LORD with all thine heart; and lean not unto thine*
> *own understanding. In all thy ways acknowledge him, and*
> *he shall direct thy paths. . . . Then shalt thou walk in thy way*
> *safely, and thy foot shall not stumble. . . . For the LORD shall*
> *be thy confidence, and shall keep thy foot from being taken.*
> PROVERBS 3:5–6, 23, 26

Lord, enable me to regulate this day so as to please You!
Give me spiritual insight to discover what is Your will in
all the relations of my life. Guide me as to my pursuits,
my friendships, my reading, . . .my Christian work.
HANNAH WHITALL SMITH

MY PRAYER STARTER: Lord, I want to follow You in every decision I make, not just the big ones. May turning to You for help become second nature to me, not just a last resort.

Today's classic prayer will put a smile on your face and joy in your heart. It was obviously written by someone who found happiness no matter what came around life's corner.

The key to such a merry heart and joy-filled spirit lies in knowing God. For with that knowledge grows trust in God, utter confidence that He will work all things out for your good.

A merry heart maketh a cheerful countenance: but by sorrow of the heart the spirit is broken. . . . A merry heart doeth good like a medicine: but a broken spirit drieth the bones.

PROVERBS 15:13; 17:22

Give us, Lord, a bit o' sun
a bit o' work and a bit o' fun;
give us all, in the struggle
and splutter,
our daily bread and a bit o' butter.
Give us health, our keep to make
an' a bit to spare for
poor folks' sake;
give us sense, for we're
some of us duffers,
an' a heart to feel for
all that suffers.

Give us, too, a bit o' song,
an' a tale, an' a book
to help us along,
an' give us our share o'
sorrow's lesson
that we may see how
grief's a blessing.
Give us, Lord, a chance to be
our goodly best—brave,
wise and free;
our goodly best for
ourselves and others
'til all men learn to live as brothers.

OLD ENGLISH PRAYER

MY PRAYER STARTER: Lord, let my thanksgiving to You be like an ever-swelling spring of joy in my soul. Let all my happiness and contentment find their source in You.

So often we go through life unconscious of our innermost feelings and thoughts. Yet for our spiritual health, God wants us to examine ourselves, using Jesus' light to delve into the depths of our hearts and minds to search for anything that might tempt us to do something dishonorable.

With God's help and power, give yourself a spiritual exam today. Ask Jesus Christ, who lives within, to clear out whatever might be standing in His way.

> *For though he was crucified through weakness, yet he liveth by the power of God. For we also are weak in him, but we shall live with him by the power of God. . . . Examine yourselves, whether ye be in the faith; prove your own selves. Know ye not your own selves, how that Jesus Christ is in you?*
>
> 2 CORINTHIANS 13:4–5

Almighty God, and most merciful Father, give us, we beseech Thee, that grace that we may duly examine the inmost of our hearts, and our most secret thoughts, how we stand before Thee; and that we may henceforward never be drawn to do anything that may dishonor Thy name: but may persevere in all good purposes, and in Thy Holy service, unto our life's end; and grant that we may now this present day, seeing it is as good as nothing that we have done hitherto, perfectly begin to walk before Thee, as becometh those that are called to an inheritance of light in Christ.

GEORGE HICKES

MY PRAYER STARTER: God, Searcher of my soul, grant me the spiritual eyesight to spot any impure motives behind my actions. Help me purge whatever blemishes I might see.

You're here to serve God in this generation. Not to hide your talents in fear but to use them in the service of your Lord. Pray for God to equip you for His missions so that at the end of the day, He will call you His good and faithful servant!

> *His lord said unto him, Well done, good and faithful servant;*
> *thou hast been faithful over a few things, I will make thee*
> *ruler over many things: enter thou into the joy of thy lord.*

MATTHEW 25:23

O eternal God, Who has created me to do the work of God after the manner of men, and to serve Thee in this generation, and according to my capacities; give me Thy grace that I may be a prudent spender of my time, so as I may best prevent or resist all temptation, and be profitable to the Christian commonwealth; and, by discharging all my duty, may glorify Thy name. Take from me all slothfulness, and give me a diligent and an active spirit, and wisdom to choose my employment; that I may do works proportionable to my person, and to the dignity of a Christian, and may fill up all the spaces of my time with actions of religion and charity; improving my talent intrusted to me by Thee, my Lord, that I may enter into the joy of the Lord, to partake of Thy eternal felicities, even for Thy mercy's sake. Amen.

JEREMY TAYLOR

MY PRAYER STARTER: God, thank You for equipping me with a set of talents. Help me use them to advance Your kingdom and point others to Your greatness.

Day by day, moment by moment, bit by bit, the Spirit of the Lord is re-creating you, transforming you into that perfect image of God that was marred through the fall. God knew you were coming, and He *chose* you to become like Jesus Christ: "For whom he did foreknow, he also did predestinate to be conformed to the image of his Son, that he might be the firstborn among many brethren" (Romans 8:29).

To take on this image of Jesus Christ within you, you must be pliable, amenable to His ministrations. That means replacing your desires with His. Letting the Lord of lords have full sway. Seeking Him first above all things. Getting to know Him better by reading and studying the Word and spending time in His presence. Lessening yourself so that He can be more.

Today, pray from the bottom of *your* heart for Jesus to conform you to *His* heart. Believe He's doing so right now. And the next time you pass a mirror, you may be pleasantly surprised by what you see.

> *Now the Lord is that Spirit: and where the Spirit of the Lord*
> *is, there is liberty. But we all, with open face beholding as in*
> *a glass the glory of the Lord, are changed into the same image*
> *from glory to glory, even as by the Spirit of the Lord.*
> 2 CORINTHIANS 3:17–18

Lord, make me according to thy heart.
BROTHER LAWRENCE

MY PRAYER STARTER: Lord of my life, let me be like clay in Your hands. Break my stubbornness and replace it with a flexible heart that You can bend toward Your ultimate purpose.

God is always with you. You're never out of His sight. He's constantly looking out for you, empowering you to do what He's called you to do. From one task to the next, He's keeping your soul enlightened, your hands strong, and your mind alert. Take this knowledge with you throughout your days and nights as you labor for Him and others. As God directs your course, commit yourself and your desires to Him while the moment is ripe.

*For the eyes of the LORD run to and fro throughout
the whole earth, to shew himself strong in the behalf
of them whose heart is perfect toward him.*

2 CHRONICLES 16:9

Eternal and infinite One, our hours of faithful duty follow us from the past and do not perish. Stir within us that we may redeem the time. Great Giver of the task, we live day and night beneath Your constant eyes. May we be steadfast through all faintness of soul and not rest by the roadside while Your errand waits. Daily may we drive out our selfishness and delight to bear one another's burden and uphold each other's faith and hope and love. May our minds be wholly turned to finish, without undue disquiet or contention, the work we strive to do for You. O Watcher of our days and nights, we would commit them all to You.

JAMES MARTINEAU

MY PRAYER STARTER: Mighty Lord, only You can supply me with strength to fulfill the missions You give me. May I never trust in my own power, no matter how trivial the task.

Amid trouble, turn to God. He'll answer before you even call. While you're still crying out to Him, He hears you. God's heart is breaking for you. He'll bolster your faith, giving you the hope, confidence, and patience to bear whatever's happening. Remember that in His time, He *will* deliver you safely. Meanwhile, know He's holding you close.

> *And it shall come to pass, that before they call, I will*
> *answer; and while they are yet speaking, I will hear.*
> ISAIAH 65:24

When I am afflicted, I think of God. O, where shall I turn, of whom else shall I think, in my cares and sufferings, but of thee, my God! . . . Thou hast said, Before they call, I will answer, and while they yet speak, I will answer, my heart is breaking for thee, and I must have mercy upon thee: therefore, I will not prescribe the time for thee to deliver me. Strengthen my faith by thy Holy Spirit; strengthen my faith, my hope, my confidence; give me patience and strength to bear my troubles. O my Father! thou hast never forsaken any one, forsake not me; thou hast always rejoiced the afflicted, rejoice me also; thou has assisted the wretched, assist me also; when, where, and as thou wilt, that all shall be according to thy wisdom, love, goodness and mercy. Be thou at peace, O my soul.
JOHANN FRIEDRICH STARCK

MY PRAYER STARTER: Reassuring Spirit, I can't face life's chaos alone. You already know what troubles I will face tomorrow, so equip me with the necessary spiritual tools today.

After leaving home, Jacob lay down and slept. In his dream, he saw a ladder between heaven and earth and "angels of God ascending and descending on it" (Genesis 28:12). God, standing above the ladder, told Jacob, "I'm with you and will watch over you. I'll never leave you until I've done all I said I would." When Jacob awoke, he said, "God's in this place—and I didn't even know it!"

As God is with you, you are with Him. No matter where you go, remember you are still together. Keep that glorious thought forever in mind as God keeps you forever in His!

> *I am with thee, and will keep thee in all places whither thou*
> *goest, and will bring thee again into this land; for I will*
> *not leave thee, until I have done that which I have spoken*
> *to thee of. And Jacob awaked out of his sleep, and he said,*
> *Surely the LORD is in this place; and I knew it not.*
> GENESIS 28:15–16

Still, still with Thee, when purple morning breaketh,
When the bird waketh, and the shadows flee;
Fairer than morning, lovelier than daylight,
Dawns the sweet consciousness, I am with Thee. . . .
So shall it be at last, in that bright morning,
When the soul waketh and life's shadows flee;
O in that hour, fairer than daylight dawning,
Shall rise the glorious thought, I am with Thee.
HARRIET BEECHER STOWE

MY PRAYER STARTER: Lord, I am a man undeserving of Your constant love and attention. Let my focus be forever on You and Your goodness toward me.

Cry out to God if you're discouraged! The psalmists did, over and over again. But after crying out, reaffirm that God is your strength—that He will draw near and help. When you hope in Him, He pulls you through.

Why art thou cast down, O my soul? and why art thou disquieted in me? hope thou in God: for I shall yet praise him for the help of his countenance. O my God, my soul is cast down within me. . . . Yet the LORD will command his lovingkindness in the daytime, and in the night his song shall be with me, and my prayer unto the God of my life.

PSALM 42:5–6, 8

O God, my God, I am all weakness, but Thou art my Strength; I am ever anew bowed down by any trial, but Thou canst and willest to lift me up. Let me not fail, O God, my Strength; let me not be discouraged, O God, my Hope. Draw me each day, if it be but a little nearer to Thee; make me, each day, if it be but a little less unlike Thee; let me do or bear each day something for love of Thee, whereby I may be fitter for Thee. Let no day pass without my having done something pleasing unto Thee. Thus alone would I live, that I may live more unto Thee; thus would I die, longing to love Thee more. Amen.

EDWARD B. PUSEY

MY PRAYER STARTER: Comforting Father, I need Your empowering Spirit to flow through me. With Your strength, I can do any task You ask me to do. All I need is the faith to begin.

Today's classic prayer is a prayer for modern times. Although written over one hundred years ago, its pleas seem to meet every contingency, every emergency a man may face. The prayer acknowledges God as the Helper of the helpless, asking Him to bring home the wanderers, heal the sick, free the captives, care for the old, comfort the weak, and liberate souls.

The world needs you to pray this prayer today.

Hear me when I call, O God of my righteousness: thou hast enlarged me when I was in distress; have mercy upon me, and hear my prayer.

PSALM 4:1

Grant us peace, and establish Thy truth in us. . . .
Remember every faithful soul in trial; and comfort,
if it be possible, every one in sorrow and distress.
O Helper of the helpless, bring the wanderer home, and
give health to the sick, and deliverance to the captive.
Sustain the aged, comfort the weak-hearted, set free those
whose souls are bound in misery and iron; remember all those
that are in affliction, necessity, and emergency everywhere.
Let us dwell with Thee in peace, as children of light;
and in Thy light, Lord, let us see the light.
Direct, O Lord, in peace, the close of our life. . . .
Gather us when Thou wilt, into the abodes of Thy
chosen; without shame, or stain, or sin. Amen.

ROWLAND WILLIAMS

MY PRAYER STARTER: Lord of all the earth, there are millions of souls who desperately need Your comfort, protection, and salvation. Provide for each of them and turn their eyes toward You.

DAY 159

God is clearly and consistently giving you clues that He exists—that He's here. Open your eyes and see the evidence of God's work in your life. Allow that proof to boost your faith. Let it enhance your belief that His goodness does still exist. And you, as His follower and servant, are an extension of that goodness, a conduit of His light.

Pray, praise, and shine on.

> *Let your light so shine before men, that they may see your good works, and glorify your Father which is in heaven.*
> MATTHEW 5:16

How easy it is for me to live with you, Lord!
How easy it is for me to believe in You!
When my mind is distraught and my reason fails,
When the cleverest people do not see further
than this evening what must be done tomorrow
You grant me the clear confidence
that You exist, and that You will take care,
that not all the ways of goodness are stopped.
At the height of earthly fame I gaze with wonder
at that path through hopelessness—
to this point, from which even I have been able to convey
to men some reflection of the light which comes from You.
ALEKSANDR SOLZHENITSYN

MY PRAYER STARTER: Lord, Creator of the cosmos, the proof of Your existence is overwhelming. Let my belief in You be so enthusiastic that it overflows onto everyone I meet.

Jesus laid down His life for you—before you even knew Him. He was born for you—before you were conceived. He began watching out for you—before you ever saw Him. He loved you—before you loved Him. Jesus has done all this—and more—so that you could get close to God. So that you could be reunited with the Father of all creation. So that you could be brought out of the darkness and led into the light. So that your missteps and debts could be forgiven, wiped clean once and for all. So you could have peace within regardless of what happens without.

Today, thank Jesus for His sacrifice on your behalf. You're in the light of the Son's kingdom now. Praise God!

Thanks unto the Father, which hath made us meet to be partakers of the inheritance of the saints in light: who hath delivered us from the power of darkness, and hath translated us into the kingdom of his dear Son: in whom we have redemption through his blood, even the forgiveness of sins. . . . Now hath he reconciled in the body of his flesh through death, to present you holy and unblameable and unreproveable in his sight: if ye continue in the faith grounded and settled, and be not moved away from the hope of the gospel.

COLOSSIANS 1:12–14, 21–23

I thank Thee, Savior, because Thou has died for me.
OLE HALLESBY

MY PRAYER STARTER: Gracious Savior, You gave everything so that I could gain Your forgiveness. May I spend my whole life praising You in return.

When you feel weakened by personal sorrow or dragged down by the world's woes, go to God, your strength. Ask Him to send His light to lead you back into the peace of His presence. There, you'll find the joy of God's hope, Jesus' love, and the Spirit's wisdom. There, music will stir your heart and a song of praise will form on your lips.

For thou art the God of my strength. . .why go I mourning because of the oppression of the enemy? O send out thy light and thy truth: let them lead me; let them bring me unto thy holy hill, and to thy tabernacles. Then will I go unto the altar of God, unto God my exceeding joy: yea, upon the harp will I praise thee, O God my God. Why art thou cast down, O my soul? and why art thou disquieted within me? hope in God: for I shall yet praise him, who is the health of my countenance, and my God.

PSALM 43:2–5

O Lord God, my soul is sorrowful, sometimes, even unto tears; sometimes also my spirit is disquieted, by reason of impending sufferings. I long after the joy of thy peace, the peace of thy children I earnestly crave. If thou give peace, if thou pour into me holy joy, the soul of thy servant shall be full of melody, and shall become devout in thy praise. Amen.

THOMAS À KEMPIS

MY PRAYER STARTER: Lord, Giver of peace, remind me of Your love when I am sorrowful. Let my life be a song of praise to You, springing from a heart of gratitude and affection.

How wonderful to become like Jesus! To share all His attributes, to reflect Him so clearly that people no longer see you but Him. Yet such a feat cannot be done in your own power—it must come through God's Spirit and voice.

Today, spend time in God's Word. Allow it to transform your mind, heart, soul, and spirit. After meditating upon the verses that have impacted your soul, commune with Jesus, taking on more and more of His persona deep within. Then pray that Jesus would mold your soul to mirror Him alone so that those you meet would see *His* grace.

> *And such trust have we through Christ to God-ward: not that*
> *we are sufficient of ourselves to think any thing as of ourselves;*
> *but our sufficiency is of God; who also hath made us able ministers*
> *of the new testament; not of the letter, but of the spirit. . . .*
> *Now the Lord is that Spirit: and where the Spirit of the Lord*
> *is, there is liberty. But we all, with open face beholding as in*
> *a glass the glory of the Lord, are changed into the same image*
> *from glory to glory, even as by the Spirit of the Lord.*
> 2 CORINTHIANS 3:4–6, 17–18

Lord, make my soul
To mirror Thee,
Thyself alone
To shine in me,
That men may see
Thy love, Thy grace,
Nor note the glass
That shows Thy face.
BLANCHE MARY KELLY

MY PRAYER STARTER: Holy God, let me be Your representative. Let my words and actions be in perfect harmony with Your own so that the world can see Your hands at work today.

When you realize the abundant compassion God has for you, you can face anything. Trust that God, the highest power, favors you above all else. Pray and take courage as you lean into His love and mercy that surround you.

> *Be merciful unto me, O God. . . . O thou most High. What time I*
> *am afraid, I will trust in thee. In God I will praise his word, in God*
> *I have put my trust; I will not fear what flesh can do unto me.*
>
> PSALM 56:1–4

Father, we pray: Bless thou this truth. Oh God, thy mercies are abundant. Are not thy mercies full and free, and have they not, oh God, found out me? We thank thee for thy mercies, thy many, abundant, full mercies. Now we pray that thou will help us to lean back upon thy mercy and trust, and not be afraid; heed sin and love righteousness, flee from iniquity and follow after godliness, but always know that in all that we do mercy is around us like the air; underneath us as the earth; above us as the stars, and we live in a merciful world and serve a merciful God; live and swim and move and have our being in the abundant mercies of the triune God. Graciously grant us, we pray thee, properly to understand this and to apply it to our hearts, and we give thee praise through Jesus Christ our Lord. Amen.

A. W. TOZER

MY PRAYER STARTER: Compassionate Creator, Your mercy is boundless and unimaginable, and I know I can rely on You to lovingly rescue me from trouble. Thank You for Your reassurance.

Do you trust God to make decisions for you? Do you believe He has your best interests at heart? Are you meek enough to accept God to do things His way and in His timing?

When you allow God to choose your path—when you believe in His love for you and submit to His way, timing, and reasonings—you'll find God's guidance and peace in every decision you make.

Today, lift up your soul to God. Bring Him your worries, issues, plans, and quandaries. Then pray today's nine-word classic prayer as you go through this day and every day, leaving all in His good hands.

Unto thee, O LORD, do I lift up my soul. O my God, I trust in thee. . . .
Lead me in thy truth, and teach me: for thou art the God of my
salvation; on thee do I wait all the day. . . . The meek will he guide
in judgment: and the meek will he teach his way. . . . What man is
he that feareth the LORD? him shall he teach in the way that he shall
choose. His soul shall dwell at ease; and his seed shall inherit the earth.

PSALM 25:1-2, 5, 9, 12-13

Dear God, you choose. I choose what you choose.

S. D. GORDON

MY PRAYER STARTER: Lord, when I am faced with an impossibly difficult fork in the road, show me the right way. I know that Your answer will be the best, so give me the faith to accept it.

God knows the things of this world can never satisfy you. That's why He offers Himself to be your all in all. That's why He offers His grace to keep you from being snared by desires that pull you away from Him.

As you pray today's prayers, you'll find yourself drawn ever closer to God's freedom and further away from the world's trappings. As God raises your heart to Him, helping you seek and desire Him above all, you'll start overflowing with His supernatural love, peace, and power.

> *And the Word was made flesh, and dwelt among us, (and we beheld his glory, the glory as of the only begotten of the Father,) full of grace and truth. . . . And of his fulness have all we received, and grace for grace. For the law was given by Moses, but grace and truth came by Jesus Christ.*
>
> JOHN 1:14, 16–17

O my God, give me thy grace so that the things of this earth and things more naturally pleasing to me, may not be as close as thou art to me. Keep thou my eyes, my ears, my heart from clinging to the things of this world. Break my bonds, raise my heart. Keep my whole being fixed on thee. Let me never lose sight of thee; and while I gaze on thee, let my love of thee grow more and more every day.

JOHN HENRY NEWMAN

MY PRAYER STARTER: Holy God, may this world's temporal pleasures always leave me feeling unsatisfied. Let me always turn to You as my source of eternal joy.

It's a credit to you and Jesus (and a benefit to others) when you follow His example. But to do so, you need help—lots of it—from Father God. You need His power to remain cheerful through disappointments, to keep trying no matter what, to stay peaceful under pressure. And that's only the beginning! Fortunately, God is on your side. Armed with today's prayers and His divine aid, you'll reach the finish line.

> *But speaking the truth in love. . .grow up into him*
> *in all things, which is the head, even Christ.*
> EPHESIANS 4:15

O God, our Father, help us all through this day so to live that
we may bring help to others, credit to ourselves and to the
name we bear, and joy to those that love us, and to you.
Cheerful when things go wrong;
Persevering when things are difficult;
Serene when things are irritating.
Enable us to be:
Helpful to those in difficulties;
Kind to those in need;
Sympathetic to those whose hearts are sore and sad. . . .
So grant that through all this day all with whom we work, and all
those whom we meet, may see in us the reflection of the master, whose
we are, and whom we seek to serve. This we ask for your love's sake.
WILLIAM BARCLAY

MY PRAYER STARTER: All-sufficient Lord, life sometimes lets me down and friends sometimes break their vows. Let me find stability—not on earth but in Your promises.

God's Word is the doorway to understanding the One who holds the entire world in His hands. It gives you the opportunity to see into the highest of minds—His ways, His love, and His plan for you. When you begin to delve into the Word, to believe and claim God's promises, you cannot help but praise the Creator and Master Planner.

Today, pray for God to enlighten your mind by the Holy Spirit's power. To give you the means and grace to understand God's Word and accept it as truth. Ask God to reveal what He wants you to know right now so that you can walk Jesus' way.

> *The entrance of thy words giveth light; it giveth understanding unto the simple. . . . Let my cry come near before thee, O LORD: give me understanding according to thy word. . . . My lips shall utter praise, when thou hast taught me thy statutes. My tongue shall speak of thy word: for all thy commandments are righteousness. Let thine hand help me; for I have chosen thy precepts.*
> PSALM 119:130, 169, 171–173

O Lord, heavenly Father, in whom is the fullness of light and wisdom, enlighten our minds by your Holy Spirit, and give us grace to receive your Word with reverence and humility, without which no one can understand your truth. For Christ's sake, amen.
JOHN CALVIN

MY PRAYER STARTER: Unfathomable God, I am a limited man, incapable of understanding Your truth on my own. Fill me with Your Spirit's wisdom so that I can better know Your mind.

When Jesus healed a deaf and mute man, the people "were beyond measure astonished, saying, He hath done all things well: he maketh both the deaf to hear, and the dumb to speak" (Mark 7:37). That may sound like ancient history, but rest assured—it's your present reality. Jesus *still* does all things well!

To obtain the supernatural calmness of surrendering all things into Jesus' hands and the patient trust that He does all things well, pray today's classic prayer—and He'll give you both!

> *For we are saved by hope. . . . We with patience wait for it. . . . The Spirit itself maketh intercession for us. . . . And he that searcheth the hearts knoweth what is the mind of the Spirit, because he maketh intercession for the saints according to the will of God. And we know that all things work together for good to them that love God.*
> ROMANS 8:24–28

O God, who makest cheerfulness the companion of strength, but apt to take wings in time of sorrow, we humbly beseech thee that if, in thy sovereign wisdom, thou sendest weakness, yet for thy mercy's sake deny us not the comfort of patience. Lay not more upon us to bear; and, since the fretfulness of our spirit is more hurtful than the heaviness of our burden, grant us that heavenly calmness which comes of owning thy hand in all things, and patience in the trust that thou doest all things well. Amen.
ROWLAND WILLIAMS

MY PRAYER STARTER: Everlasting Savior, You performed miracles during Your time on earth, and You haven't changed any. Let me believe in Your power to heal my body, mind, and spirit.

Never think you can stand alone without God. Arrogance blocks the work God can do in your life, but your need for Him makes it easy for Him to aid you in a powerful way.

Moses discovered how our need opens the door to God's power. The Egyptians had driven Moses and God's people to the edge. There was no escape. But Moses told the Israelites to calm down, to stand their ground at the edge of the Red Sea because God would fight for them. And He did—using His power and Moses' upraised hand.

Without God's strong arm, you'll fall. But with it, you'll not only stay standing but rise up and win the day!

> *[Moses said to the people,] The LORD shall fight for you, and ye shall*
> *hold your peace. . . . And the angel of God, which went before the*
> *camp of Israel, removed and went behind them; and the pillar of*
> *the cloud went from before their face, and stood behind them. . . .*
> *And Moses stretched out his hand over the sea; and the LORD caused*
> *the sea to go back by a strong east wind all that night, and made*
> *the sea dry land, and the waters were divided. And the children*
> *of Israel went into the midst of the sea upon the dry ground.*
> EXODUS 14:14, 19, 21–22

O Lord, never suffer us to think that we can
stand by ourselves, and not need thee.
JOHN DONNE

MY PRAYER STARTER: Capable Father, replace my arrogance with a constant reliance on You. Make me into a man of unflinching faith, just like Moses.

Don't just dive into a conversation. Listen. Then wait on God to lead you in what to say. Because if you don't listen, you may mishear, take offense, then speak out in anger. In the end, you'll find yourself having to extend *and* receive some forgiveness.

To improve your listening skills and quench your temper, delve into God's Word, anchoring it in your heart. It will save your soul!

Let every man be swift to hear, slow to speak, slow to wrath: for the wrath of man worketh not the righteousness of God. . . . Receive with meekness the engrafted word, which is able to save your souls.

JAMES 1:19–21

O Almighty God, give to Thy servant a meek and gentle spirit, that I may be slow to anger, and easy to mercy and forgiveness. Give me a wise and constant heart, that I may never be moved to an intemperate anger for any injury that is done or offered. Lord, let me ever be courteous, and easy to be entreated; let me never fall into a peevish or contentious spirit, but follow peace with all men; offering forgiveness, inviting them by courtesies, ready to confess my own errors, apt to make amends, and desirous to be reconciled. Let no sickness or cross accident, no employment or weariness, make me angry or ungentle and discontented, or unthankful, or uneasy to them that minister to me; but in all things make me like unto the holy Jesus. Amen.

JEREMY TAYLOR

MY PRAYER STARTER: God, I want to resemble Jesus in my patience toward others. Slow down my reaction time when people annoy me. Give me the chance to see them through Your eyes.

The moment you received Jesus Christ, the Spirit began residing within you. He was with God at the beginning of creation, hovering upon the darkness of the water. And He's with you now.

Call on the Spirit. Invite Him into this moment. Pray today's classic prayer slowly, giving yourself the opportunity to commune with Him, spirit to Spirit.

And the spirit of the LORD shall rest upon him.
ISAIAH 11:2

Come, true light. Come, life eternal. Come, hidden mystery.
Come, treasure without name. Come, reality beyond all words.
Come, person beyond all understanding. Come, rejoicing without end.
Come, light that knows no evening.
Come, unfailing expectation of the saved.
Come, raising of the fallen. Come, resurrection of the dead.
Come, all-powerful, for unceasingly you create, refashion and change all things by your will alone.
Come, invisible whom none may touch and handle.
. . . .
Come, Alone to the alone.
Come, for you are yourself the desire that is within me.
Come, my breath and my life. Come, the consolation of my humble soul.
Come, my joy, my glory, my endless delight.
SAINT SYMEON

MY PRAYER STARTER: Holy Spirit, You are my everything. Let my life be a continual, personal communion with You. Indwell my body, conforming my actions to Your perfect will.

God wants you to consider your life a blessing, not a drudgery, and to bloom where He has planted you to do His will for His glory. Every day is God's gift to you, as are your job, the tasks He puts into your hands, and the roles only you can fulfill. So enjoy your life. Take pleasure in what God's given you. Rejoice in your work. As God rewards you, reward Him back by sharing your joy with Him.

And while you're living, don't waste time looking back at what might have been. Instead, focus on the now, knowing that no matter what happens today, you'll be with God tomorrow.

Behold that which I have seen: it is good and comely for one to eat and to drink, and to enjoy the good of all his labour that he taketh under the sun all the days of his life, which God giveth him: for it is his portion. Every man also to whom God hath given riches and wealth, and hath given him power to eat thereof, and to take his portion, and to rejoice in his labour; this is the gift of God. For he shall not much remember the days of his life; because God answereth him in the joy of his heart.

ECCLESIASTES 5:18–20

Make us remember, O God, that every day is your gift, to be used according to your command.
SAMUEL JOHNSON

MY PRAYER STARTER: Lord, may I make the most of every moment, rejoicing as I work for You. Thank You for staying with me today, tomorrow, and always.

What's the greatest thing God gives you? Love. What's the greatest thing He wants you to give Him? Love.

Ask God to free you from everything so that you can love Him with everything.

> *And, behold, a certain lawyer stood up, and tempted him,*
> *saying, Master, what shall I do to inherit eternal life? . . . And*
> *he answering said, Thou shalt love the Lord thy God with all*
> *thy heart, and with all thy soul, and with all thy strength,*
> *and with all thy mind; and thy neighbour as thyself.*
>
> LUKE 10:25, 27

Let my heart be free from every unworthy thing that I may be free to love thee, my Lord God, with all my heart and soul and with all my strength. Free me from such narrow-mindedness as would make me set my affections upon anything apart from thee, O thou, who art the only true Lover and true Lord of all. When I love anything for the reason that it is from thee, then do I truly love thee, in that I love it for thy sake, for thou alone hast every claim over it for our good. Our service of thee, what else is it but a working out of thy loving salvation? Thou didst first show us love to win our love, not needing it, but solely because we cannot become what thou wouldst have us be unless we love thee.

WILLIAM OF SAINT-THIERRY

MY PRAYER STARTER: Savior, Your death on the cross proved Your incomprehensible love for humanity. Purify my cluttered heart so that my own love flows freely back toward You.

Only in God's presence can you find His light, goodness, deliverance, support, wisdom, and mercy. But this place has one gateway: you must seek and love Him with all your heart and mind and soul and might. The word *might* means channeling all your energy into loving God. When you do so diligently and with your whole being, you'll find yourself wanting to obey Him and discover that promised land in Him.

Today, pray to the God whom you seek and love. Do so often, with your entire being, and you'll find His land of promise and power.

> *Hear therefore, O Israel, and observe to do it; that it may be*
> *well with thee, and that ye may increase mightily, as the LORD*
> *God of thy fathers hath promised thee, in the land that floweth*
> *with milk and honey. Hear, O Israel: The LORD our God is*
> *one LORD: and thou shalt love the LORD thy God with all*
> *thine heart, and with all thy soul, and with all thy might.*
> DEUTERONOMY 6:3–5

O eternal Light, shine into our hearts; eternal Goodness, deliver us from evil; eternal Power, be thou our support; eternal Wisdom, scatter our ignorance; eternal Pit, have mercy upon us. Grant that with all our heart and mind and soul and strength we may seek thy face, and finally bring us, by thine infinite mercy, to thy holy presence, through Jesus Christ our Lord. Amen.
ALCUIN

MY PRAYER STARTER: God, I surrender myself to You. If there are any roadblocks deep in my heart, give me the wisdom and courage to find and remove them. I want to be wholly Yours.

Your best answer to prayer isn't the outcome of your pleas but the knowledge that God loves, cares for, and wants the best for you. Glory in God's presence as you pray, and you'll find all the answers you need.

O taste and see that the LORD is good: blessed
is the man that trusteth in him.

PSALM 34:8

We rejoice that in all time men have found a refuge in Thee, and that prayer is the voice of love, the voice of pleading, and the voice of thanksgiving. Our souls overflow toward Thee like a cup when full; nor can we forbear; nor shall we search to see if our prayers have been registered, or whether of the things asked we have received much, or more, or anything. That we have had permission to feel ourselves in Thy presence, to take upon ourselves something of the light of Thy countenance, to have a consciousness that Thy thoughts are upon us, to experience the inspiration of the Holy Spirit in any measure—this is an answer to prayer transcending all things that we can think of. We are glad that we can glorify Thee, that we can rejoice Thee, that it does make a difference to Thee what we do, and that Thou dost enfold us in a consciousness of Thy sympathy with us, of how much Thou art to us, and of what we are to Thee.

HENRY WARD BEECHER

MY PRAYER STARTER: Glorious Father, I praise You for Your never-ending love. As I walk with You, expand my knowledge of this love so that my praise grows ever more sincere.

When you're open to God, when you're willing to receive Him into every moment of your life and readily accept His kingdom no matter what happens in this world, you'll discover the peace found in Jesus alone. He has *overcome* this world.

Knowing that Jesus has gained victory here means you need not fear anything anywhere. The peace you find in Him grants access to all the courage, resilience, and joy you need to thrive. For you know no power in this world can harm you. Jesus is over all!

So on those days when you feel as if the bear has eaten you, go to Jesus. Open yourself up to His ministrations, power, love, and light. Accept all He's willing to give you of His kingdom and Himself. Be as a child in your Father's hands, allowing His arms to protect you, His power to strengthen you, and His love to bind you. Make Jesus your home all the days of your life.

These things I have spoken unto you, that in me ye might
have peace. In the world ye shall have tribulation: but
be of good cheer; I have overcome the world.

JOHN 16:33

Make us receptive and open
and may we accept your kingdom
like children taking bread
from the hands of their father.
Let us live in your peace,
at home with you
all the days of our lives.

·HUUB OOSTERHUIS

MY PRAYER STARTER: All-powerful King, I sometimes feel as if I am losing one battle after another. Remind me of the ultimate victory that I've already won by trusting in You.

The first commandment Jesus gave you was to love God with your entire being. The second was to love others as you love yourself. That means putting others' needs and wants above your own. Doing so may require you to lay aside your work so that you can help with someone else's. To be vulnerable enough to depend on the courage, industry, or honesty of a fellow human being so that that person can shine. To trust in another's wisdom instead of your own.

In order to do this, remember that God is watching. He's taking care of you. And, at times, He'll be counting on you to count on others—to His glory and good end.

> *Be kindly affectioned one to another with brotherly love; in*
> *honour preferring one another; not slothful in business; fervent*
> *in spirit; serving the Lord. . . ; distributing to the necessity*
> *of saints; given to hospitality. . . . Be of the same mind one*
> *toward another. Mind not high things, but condescend to*
> *men of low estate. Be not wise in your own conceits.*
> ROMANS 12:10–11, 13, 16

O God, you have bound us together in this bundle of life; give us grace to understand how our lives depend on the courage, the industry, the honesty and integrity of our fellow men; that we may be mindful of their needs, grateful for their faithfulness, and faithful in our responsibilities to them; through Jesus Christ our Lord.
REINHOLD NIEBUHR

MY PRAYER STARTER: Father, thank You for adopting me as Your son. Help me always treat Your other children with respect, selflessness, and unconditional love.

Today, rise above life's turmoil and into God's love with the power of prayer. Soar up to the Lord, letting your love for Him and His love for you override all.

Let us lift up our heart with our hands unto God in the heavens. . . .
I called upon thy name, O LORD, out of the low dungeon. Thou hast
heard my voice. . . . Thou drewest near. . . : thou saidst, Fear not.
LAMENTATIONS 3:41, 55–57

O God, my God, give me a heart to thank Thee; lift up my heart above myself, to Thee and Thine eternal throne; let it not linger here among the toils and turmoils of this lower world; let it not be oppressed by any earth-born clouds of care or anxiety or fear or suspicion; but bind it wholly to Thee and to Thy love; give me eyes to see Thy love in all things, and Thy grace in all around me; make me to thank Thee for Thy love and Thy grace to all and in all; give me wings of love, that I may soar up to Thee, and cling to Thee, and adore Thee, and praise Thee more and more, until I be fitted to enter into the joys of Thine everlasting love, everlasting to love Thee and Thy grace, whereby Thou didst make me such as Thou couldest love, such as could love Thee, O God, my God. Amen.
EDWARD B. PUSEY

MY PRAYER STARTER: Eternal Refuge, thank You for allowing me to rise to You whenever life becomes unbearable. You are my only oasis in life's desert—may I never forget this truth.

Neither time nor space has dominion over God. He's everywhere, all the time. He's in, around, and over everything. He sees, knows, and understands all things. All things are in His hands—including you. So hold nothing back.

Give God all of you—heart, mind, body, soul, and spirit. Give Him your pen, and the lines you write will dance on the paper. Give Him your instrument, and the notes you play will shimmer in the air. Give Him your brush, and the colors you paint will sing upon the canvas.

God brings out the truest meaning of all things. So pray, surrendering to Him all you have and are. And watch as He uses it to make something amazing.

> *O LORD my God, thou art very great. . . . Who coverest thyself with light as with a garment: who stretchest out the heavens like a curtain: who layeth the beams of his chambers in the waters: who maketh the clouds his chariot: who walketh upon the wings of the wind: who maketh his angels spirits. . . : who laid the foundations of the earth, that it should not be removed for ever.*

PSALM 104:1–5

Thou takest the pen—and the lines dance.
Thou takest the flute—and the notes shimmer.
Thou takest the brush—and the colours sing.
So all things have meaning and beauty in that space beyond time where Thou art. How, then, can I hold back anything from Thee?
DAG HAMMARSKJÖLD

MY PRAYER STARTER: Divine Author, Artist, and Musician, my best efforts are but a dull reflection of Your majesty. I give my instruments of creation to You. Use them as You wish.

Today, use the power of prayer to reaffirm the trust you have in God to give you what you need when you need it.

God. . .is a shield unto them that put their trust in him. . . . Give me neither poverty nor riches; feed me with food convenient for me: lest I be full, and deny thee, and say, Who is the LORD? or lest I be poor, and steal, and take the name of my God in vain.

PROVERBS 30:5, 8–9

O my Lord, in Thine arms I am safe; keep me and I have nothing to fear; give me up, and I have nothing to hope for. I know nothing about the future, but I rely upon Thee. I pray Thee to give me what is good for me; I pray Thee to take from me whatever may imperil my salvation. I leave it all to Thee, because Thou knowest and I do not. If Thou bringest pain or sorrow on me, give me grace to bear it well, keep me from fretfulness and selfishness. If Thou givest me health and strength and success in this world, keep me ever on my guard lest these great gifts carry me away from Thee. Give me to know Thee, to believe on Thee, to love Thee, to serve Thee, to live to and for Thee. Give me to die just at that time and in that way which is most for Thy glory. Amen.

JOHN HENRY NEWMAN

MY PRAYER STARTER: Lord, great Provider, You are the source of all my help. No matter what hunger, pain, or suffering I might endure, I know that You will bring me safely through.

Because you have the Bible, you know Jesus' full story. How He spent His life doing good, helping others, and giving His Father God all the glory. Jesus wants you to do the same, to continue His Father's business. So don't get discouraged or tire of doing good. Continue to follow Jesus' pattern. Do what God has called you to do until He calls you home at last to be with the Holy Three.

> *And his mother said unto him, Son, why hast thou thus dealt*
> *with us? behold, thy father and I have sought thee sorrowing.*
> *And he said unto them, How is it that ye sought me? wist*
> *ye not that I must be about my Father's business?*
>
> LUKE 2:48–49

O Lord Jesus Christ, who when on earth wast ever about thy Father's business: Grant that we may not grow weary in well-doing. Give us grace to do all in thy name. Be thou the beginning and the end of all: the pattern whom we follow, the redeemer in whom we trust, the master whom we serve, the friend to whom we look for sympathy. May we never shrink from our duty from any fear of man. Make us faithful unto death; and bring us at last into thy eternal presence, where with the Father and the Holy Ghost thou livest and reignest for ever.

EDWARD B. PUSEY

MY PRAYER STARTER: God, give me the willpower to follow Jesus' example of hard labor for Your kingdom. Help me work for You on the job, around other people, and at home.

Every day is an opportunity to give your hope a boost. To remember that this life is not the end. To look forward to a better place—the new heaven, where Jesus Christ resides as the Alpha and Omega, the beginning and the end. Because you are a believer—a son who follows his Father's edicts to love Him, yourself, and others—you are blessed. Someday, you will enter the gates of that eternal city, where the bright Morning Star awaits you.

Today, pray for Jesus to awaken you from lethargy and indifference, renewing your hope for that world without end.

I am Alpha and Omega, the beginning and the end, the first and the last. Blessed are they that do his commandments, that they may have right to the tree of life, and may enter in through the gates into the city. . . . I Jesus have sent mine angel to testify unto you these things in the churches. I am the root and the offspring of David, and the bright and morning star. And the Spirit and the bride say, Come.

REVELATION 22:13–14, 16–17

O Christ, our Morning Star,
Splendour of Light Eternal,
shining with the glory of the rainbow,
come and waken us
from the greyness of our apathy
and renew in us your gift of hope. Amen.
SAINT BEDE THE VENERABLE

MY PRAYER STARTER: Lord, my unchanging Hope, energize my spiritual bones. Let me burn with hope for Your heavenly kingdom, spreading that fire to everyone I meet.

For a good night's sleep, remember that God has His angels watching over you. In fact, they have *charge* over you—they are with you, defending and protecting you. They bear you up so that you won't stumble (Psalm 91:11–12). Have faith that God is with you and those you love. That He will reassure those who wake in the night, ease the watchful, comfort the crying, tend the sick, rest the weary, bless the dying, soothe the suffering, and shield the joyful—all because He loves them.

Forget about tomorrow. Know that God will make something good out of all your work and efforts—including your prayers for others. So tonight, before your head hits the pillow, launch your prayers up to God, and then fall asleep in His arms.

> *Except the LORD build the house, they labour in vain that*
> *build it: except the LORD keep the city, the watchman waketh*
> *but in vain. It is vain for you to rise up early, to sit up late,*
> *to eat the bread of sorrows: for so he giveth his beloved sleep.*
>
> PSALM 127:1–2

Watch thou, dear Lord, with those who wake, or watch, or weep tonight, and give thine angels charge over those who sleep. Tend thy sick ones, O Lord Christ; rest thy weary ones; bless thy dying ones. Soothe thy suffering ones; shield thy joyous ones; and all for thy Love's sake. Amen.
SAINT AUGUSTINE

MY PRAYER STARTER: Watchful Father, I am helpless without Your protection. Thank You for sending Your angels to stay with me, even when I am unaware of their presence.

In the Old Testament, Joseph never lost his faith in God. Even after his brothers put him in a pit then sold him to passing strangers. Even when Joseph became a slave in Egypt then a prisoner in a dark dungeon, his faith still held. Eventually, he was lifted up as a great ruler in Egypt, second only to Pharaoh. There, he met up with his brothers again. The men who had once betrayed him cowered in fear. But Joseph told them, "Don't worry. The evil you'd meant has been transformed into something good. And now I'll be able to save you and many others. So don't fear."

No matter what bad things come into your life, no matter how dark your dungeon, don't worry or fear. Instead, believe that God will make something good come out of it all.

> *But as for you, ye thought evil against me; but God*
> *meant it unto good, to bring to pass, as it is this day,*
> *to save much people alive. Now therefore fear ye not.*
> GENESIS 50:20–21

I will not doubt, though all my ships at sea
Come drifting home with broken masts and sails;
I shall believe the Hand which never fails,
From seeming evil worketh good for me;
And though I weep because those sails are battered,
Still will I cry, while my best hopes lie shattered,
"I trust in Thee."

ELLA WHEELER WILCOX

MY PRAYER STARTER: God of all wisdom, let my faith be like Joseph's. When I am met with disappointments and persecution, train my eyes to spot Your hand working behind it all.

God saved you, not because of anything you did but because of His mercy. And God saved you by washing you, renewing you with the Holy Spirit who has come upon you. But this renewal is not just a once-and-done event. It's a power you can access every day as you offer yourself up to God.

So put yourself on God's altar today. Pray for Him to renew all of you—heart, body, mind, and soul—in the power of the Holy Spirit. When you do, your fear will be replaced with courage, your ignorance with knowing, and your discouragement with hope so that in His strength and power, you will carry out whatever work God puts your hand to.

According to his mercy he saved us, by the washing of regeneration, and renewing of the Holy Ghost; which he shed on us abundantly through Jesus Christ our Saviour; that being justified by his grace, we should be made heirs according to the hope of eternal life.

TITUS 3:5–7

O God our Father, who sent your Son to be our Savior: renew in us day by day the power of your Holy Spirit; that with knowledge and zeal, with courage and love, with gratitude and hope, we may strive powerfully in your service: may he keep our vision clear, our aspiration high, our purpose firm and our sympathy wide; that we may live as faithful soldiers and servants of our Lord Jesus Christ.
WILLIAM TEMPLE

MY PRAYER STARTER: Lord, renew my heart again and make me Your effective servant. I surrender my plans, desires, and questions to You.

How wonderful life can be when you truly give yourself up to the Lord, handing your will over to God's. For then you no longer have to worry about anything. When all your being, possessions, and expectations are in His hands—when you let Him do what He thinks best—all the pressure falls away.

So today, tell God that you're His servant and that you're prepared for whatever He has in mind. That you're ready to do and be as He pleases. Experience the reign of freedom such servanthood brings!

> *O LORD, truly I am thy servant; I am thy servant, and*
> *the son of thine handmaid: thou hast loosed my bonds. I*
> *will offer to thee the sacrifice of thanksgiving, and will call*
> *upon the name of the LORD. . . . Praise ye the LORD.*
> PSALM 116:16–17, 19

O Lord, Thou knowest what is best for us, let this or that be done, as Thou shalt please. Give what Thou wilt, and how much Thou wilt, and when Thou wilt. Deal with me as Thou thinkest good, and as best pleaseth Thee. Set me where Thou wilt, and deal with me in all things just as Thou wilt. Behold, I am Thy servant, prepared for all things; for I desire not to live unto myself, but unto Thee; and Oh that I could do it worthily and perfectly! Amen.
THOMAS À KEMPIS

MY PRAYER STARTER: Divine Master, I know that I can only obtain freedom by becoming Your servant. Let me rejoice in this paradox each day as I follow Your lead.

Just as God was with Moses wherever He sent him, whatever He asked him to do, God is also with you. Regardless of how big or small your duty today, God goes before you, preparing your path and removing any obstacles that stand in your way. Because you know He'll give you the tools, strength, and grace to finish the job, there's no need to stress. Simply pray, listening for and following God's voice, and He'll clear your way.

Come now therefore, and I will send thee unto Pharaoh, that thou mayest bring forth my people the children of Israel out of Egypt. And Moses said unto God, Who am I, that I should go unto Pharaoh, and that I should bring forth the children of Israel out of Egypt? And he said, Certainly I will be with thee; . . . I have sent thee.

EXODUS 3:10–12

Give us grace, O Lord, to work while it is day: fulfilling diligently and patiently whatever duty Thou appointest us, doing small things in the day of small things, and great labors if Thou summon us to any: rising and working, sitting still and suffering, according to Thy word. Go with me and I will go, but if Thou go not with me, send me not; go before me if Thou put me forth; let me hear Thy voice when I follow. Amen.

CHRISTINA ROSSETTI

MY PRAYER STARTER: Lord, I know that You are working in my future, clearing out a path. Give me the faith to walk wherever You lead, confident in Your protection.

Children are very precious, especially to God. As recent arrivals, they have a close connection to Him. In fact, they have angels who look upon God's face continually (Matthew 18:10)!

Yet because children are so innocent and vulnerable, they need your support and protection. The best way to provide that is to pray for the young ones in your care. Pray for their health. Pray they would find their way to God, listen to His Spirit, and discover the light of Jesus.

Go to your Father God today as a little child yourself. Ask Him to look out for all the little ones you know. Be secure in the knowledge that although they are on loan to you in this world—a temporary gift for you to love and learn from—they are always safe in God's hands.

Lo, children are an heritage of the LORD: and the fruit of the womb is his reward. As arrows are in the hand of a mighty man; so are children of the youth. Happy is the man that hath his quiver full of them: they shall not be ashamed, but they shall speak with the enemies in the gate.

PSALM 127:3–5

Bless my children with healthful bodies, with good understandings, with the graces and gifts of your Spirit, with sweet dispositions and holy habits, and sanctify them throughout in their bodies and souls and spirits, and keep them unblamable to the coming of the Lord Jesus.

JEREMY TAYLOR

MY PRAYER STARTER: Father, I want Your love for me, Your adopted son, to be reflected in my actions toward children—even if they are not my own. Let me lead them by example.

When Zerubbabel led Jews back to Jerusalem after the exile, he took on the arduous task of governing the land and rebuilding God's temple. Although many forces and numerous delays arose against the Israelites and their leaders, the prophet Haggai—speaking for God—told the high priest Zerubbabel and the people to be strong. To go ahead with the work because God was with them.

When you feel lacking in wisdom and power, go to God. And like Zerubbabel and his people, you'll get even more than you imagined!

> *Yet now be strong, O Zerubbabel, saith the LORD; and be strong, O Joshua, son of Josedech, the high priest; and be strong, all ye people of the land, saith the LORD, and work: for I am with you, saith the LORD of hosts: . . . my spirit remaineth among you: fear ye not.*
>
> HAGGAI 2:4–5

Almighty God, of Thy fulness grant to us who need so much, who lack so much, who have so little, wisdom and strength. Bring our wills unto Thine. Lift our understandings into Thy heavenly light; that we thereby beholding those things which are right, and being drawn by Thy love, may bring our wills and our understanding together to Thy service, until at last, body and soul and spirit may be all Thine, and Thou be our Father and our Eternal Friend. Amen.
GEORGE DAWSON

MY PRAYER STARTER: Unchanging God, just as You empowered Zerubbabel to build Your temple, fill the temple of my body with Your Spirit, empowering me to finish whatever jobs You give.

When you're in the midst of darkness, feeling weak and helpless, pray for Jesus' invigorating light and presence to rest upon you. When you live close to Jesus Christ, abiding in His presence and trusting in Him alone, you'll see His will in everything that comes into your life. You'll also know His purpose—which is for you to have so much confidence in Him that you bring praise and glory to God in every way!

In [Christ] also we have obtained an inheritance, being predestinated according to the purpose of him who worketh all things after the counsel of his own will: that we should be to the praise of his glory, who first trusted in Christ.
EPHESIANS 1:11–12

O Christ Jesus,
when all is darkness
and we feel our weakness and helplessness,
give us the sense of Your presence,
Your love, and Your strength.
Help us to have perfect trust
in Your protecting love
and strengthening power,
so that nothing may frighten or worry us,
for, living close to You,
we shall see Your hand,
Your purpose, Your will through all things.
SAINT IGNATIUS OF LOYOLA

MY PRAYER STARTER: God, Light of my life, I am not afraid of the darkness when You are by my side. Even when I can't make sense of my life, let me see Your plan in action behind the scenes.

When the Israelites begged for a king, God gave them Saul (1 Samuel 9:17–21). At first, Saul saw himself as insignificant, hiding among the baggage when his kingship was announced to the people (1 Samuel 10:22). Yet Saul later became too big for his britches. The prophet Samuel confronted him, saying, "When thou wast little in thine own sight, wast thou not made the head of the tribes of Israel, and the LORD anointed thee king over Israel?" (1 Samuel 15:17). Because Saul had begun following his own wisdom instead of God's, God rejected him as king (1 Samuel 15:23).

It can be easy to lose your perspective when you become "big enough to reach the world." Today, pray for God's love and power to keep you small enough to stay one with Him.

As thou, Father, art in me, and I in thee, that they also may be one in us: that the world may believe that thou hast sent me. And the glory which thou gavest me I have given them; that they may be one, even as we are one: I in them, and thou in me, that they may be made perfect in one; and that the world may know that thou hast sent me, and hast loved them, as thou hast loved me.

JOHN 17:21–23

Grant that with your love, I may be big enough to reach the world, and small enough to be one with you.

MOTHER TERESA

MY PRAYER STARTER: Mighty God, I am infinitely small when compared to You. Whenever I start elevating myself above others, humiliate me so that I stay in tune with Your compassion.

Do you refresh the people you meet?

When the apostle Paul was journeying to Italy as a prisoner, the centurion who was guarding him allowed him to go to his friends to be cared for. If only we all would be as kind as that centurion and as caring as those friends!

Today, pray that God would give you the compassion to refresh and befriend your fellow sojourners.

> *Julius courteously entreated Paul, and gave him*
> *liberty to go unto his friends to refresh himself.*
> ACTS 27:3

Once more a new day lies before us, our Father. As we go out among men to do our work, touching the hands and lives of our fellows, make us, we pray Thee, friends of all the world. Save us from blighting the fresh flower of any heart by the flare of sudden anger or secret hate. May we not bruise the rightful self-respect of any by contempt or malice. Help us to cheer the suffering by our sympathy, to freshen the drooping by our hopefulness, and to strengthen in all the wholesome sense of worth and the joy of life. Save us from the deadly poison of class-pride. Grant that we may look all men in the face with the eyes of a brother. If any one needs us, make us ready to yield our help ungrudgingly, unless higher duties claim us, and may we rejoice that we have it in us to be helpful to our fellow-men.

WALTER RAUSCHENBUSCH

MY PRAYER STARTER: God, thank You for giving me friends who accompany me in my walk with You. Give me the desire and resources to refresh and comfort them when they need support.

Imagine being in a boat upon the sea. At first, it's wonderful. You're awed by all the amazing things the Lord has created. The power of the wind and waves is glorious. The sunrises and sunsets upon the water are magnificent. But then the wind begins to gust, the waves to rage. You and your boat are tossed about. You become terrified. Then you cry out to God, and He rescues you. He calms the storm and stills the waves.

Today's classic prayer helps you rise above the storm. It reminds you that God, your Protector, will bring you to a good place.

They that go down to the sea in ships, that do business in great waters; these see the works of the LORD, and his wonders in the deep. For he commandeth, and raiseth the stormy wind, which lifteth up the waves thereof. They mount up to the heaven, they go down again to the depths: their soul is melted because of trouble. They reel to and fro, and stagger like a drunken man, and are at their wit's end. Then they cry unto the LORD in their trouble, and he bringeth them out of their distresses. He maketh the storm a calm, so that the waves thereof are still.

PSALM 107:23–29

Dear God, be good to me;
The sea is so wide,
and my boat is so small.
PRAYER USED BY BRETON FISHERMEN

MY PRAYER STARTER: Lord, Calmer of storms, I know that You control everything. Whenever I am faced with tumultuous waves of doubt and fear, take my hand and still the winds in my soul.

Have you been tapping your foot recently? Waiting for Jesus to lead you somewhere?

Be patient. You're one of His sheep. He calls you by name and leads you where He wants you to go. All you need to do is follow Him as He clears the way ahead. You'll know His voice.

Today, go to the Good Shepherd. Be still before Him. Listen for His voice. You'll know it when you hear it—it's unlike any other. His powerful and loving words will give you the comfort and patience to either stay where you are or walk forward with Him.

> *But he that entereth in by the door is the shepherd of the sheep. To him the porter openeth; and the sheep hear his voice: and he calleth his own sheep by name, and leadeth them out. And when he putteth forth his own sheep, he goeth before them, and the sheep follow him: for they know his voice. And a stranger will they not follow, but will flee from him: for they know not the voice of strangers.*

JOHN 10:2–5

O Lord, who call your own sheep by name, grant, we beg you, that all whom you call by the voice of conscience may straightway arise to do your most compassionate will, or abide patiently to suffer for it. Amen.
CHRISTINA ROSSETTI

MY PRAYER STARTER: Shepherd of my soul, make me a patient man. Fill me with the willingness to follow Your guidance, even if that means waiting where I am right now.

When you sow peace, you reflect God's character to others. And there's a bonus—God also rewards you for being His son.

Today's prayer asks God to make you a messenger of God's peace. To be the seed of love amid hatred, forgiveness amid hurt, faith amid doubt, hope amid despair, light amid darkness, and joy amid grief—and to go *looking* to help others instead of yourself.

Wear and spread your godly light, and you'll receive so much more in return.

> *Blessed are the peacemakers: for they shall be called the children*
> *of God. . . . Let your light so shine before men, that they may see*
> *your good works, and glorify your Father which is in heaven.*
> MATTHEW 5:9, 16

Lord, make me an instrument of your peace.
Where there is hatred, let me sow love;
Where there is injury, pardon;
Where there is doubt, faith;
Where there is despair, hope;
Where there is darkness, light;
Where there is sadness, joy.
O Divine Master, grant that I may not so much seek
To be consoled as to console;
To be understood as to understand;
To be loved as to love.
For it is in giving that we receive;
It is in pardoning that we are pardoned;
And it is in dying that we are born to eternal life.
SAINT FRANCIS OF ASSISI

MY PRAYER STARTER: Lord, let me not be content with following You solitarily—let me actively seek ways in which I can show Your truth to others.

God is with you through thick and thin, sadness and joy, imprisonment and freedom. Today, defeat your discouragement by prayerfully praising God and affirming His presence, knowing that He won't give you more than you can bear and that Jesus, His Son, seeks you every moment.

> *[The LORD] hath sent me to bind up the brokenhearted, to proclaim*
> *liberty to the captives, and the opening of the prison to them that*
> *are bound. . . , to give unto them. . .the garment of praise for*
> *the spirit of heaviness; that. . .[the LORD] might be glorified.*
> ISAIAH 61:1, 3

O heav'nly Father, I praise and thank Thee for the peace of the night. I praise and thank Thee for this new day. I praise and thank Thee for all Thy goodness and faithfulness throughout my life. Thou hast granted me many blessings: now let me accept tribulation from Thy hand. Thou wilt not lay on me more than I can bear. Thou makest all things work together for good for Thy children. Lord Jesus Christ, Thou wast poor and in misery, a captive and forsaken as I am. . . . Thou dost not forget me but seekest me. Thou willest that I should know Thee and turn to Thee. . . . Lord, whatever this day may bring, Thy name be praised.
DIETRICH BONHOEFFER

MY PRAYER STARTER: Comforting Father, thank You for Your unbreakable love—and for always being near me, giving me strength and courage.

Oh to be like Jesus! Offer your entire self to Him to obtain His light of life. Rejoice that He is in your mind, arranging your thoughts and aligning them with His own. Thank Him for being in your heart, reigning over your emotions, filling you with His love. Invite Jesus into your body, allowing Him to re-create it in the pattern of His perfect health and energy. As you do so, your mental, emotional, and physical power will strengthen, molding you more and more into His image each day. Become the light of His light, the life of His life.

> *Then spake Jesus again unto them, saying, I am the light of the world: he that followeth me shall not walk in darkness, but shall have the light of life.*
>
> JOHN 8:12

Let us praise Him then, for His life in our spirits, increasing in us the consciousness of being His children, light of His light, life of His life. And let us rejoice in His life in our minds, directing and arranging our thoughts, increasing our mental powers, giving us a better grasp of business and more wisdom in every line of work we undertake. Let us thank Him for His life in our hearts, ordering and controlling our emotions and filling us with His own love. And let us give thanks for His life in our bodies, recreating them after the image of His perfect health and strength.

AGNES SANFORD

MY PRAYER STARTER: Perfect Savior, seize control of my thoughts, attitudes, and actions. Use this body as a vehicle for Your divine purposes.

Thank God for His Word, for His good news, for the voice that speaks to you and becomes part of your very being, shoring up your faith in the Father, Son, and Spirit. Pray that God would bless what you read and hear from Him today through that Word. Pray that God would help you, that as you wait upon Him, He would strengthen you so that your faith would mount up with wings like an eagle. That your trust in the Holy Three would stretch its wings and soar higher than the tug of this world.

> *But they that wait upon the LORD shall renew their*
> *strength; they shall mount up with wings as eagles.*
> ISAIAH 40:31

Father, we pray Thy blessings upon the Word given. We pray that Thou wilt help us, that our faith might mount up like an eagle, stretch its broad wings and soar so high that nothing can pull it down, and as the eagle can look upon the son, we pray that we may look upon Thy Holy Son at the right hand of the Majesty, and that we may be grateful to the point of cheers and tenderness, that He who was God and very God, of very God, gave Himself and hung on yonder tree. Bless us. . . . In Christ's name. Amen.

A. W. TOZER

MY PRAYER STARTER: Father, thank You for providing a way to escape this world's discouraging pull. As I read the scriptures, I am comforted by the fact that I am hearing Your voice.

When troubles assail, when temptation comes knocking, run to God. He is your refuge, your strong tower. Know that God is standing with you. Make Him your very present help when you're shaken, in distress, or losing ground. Behind His thick walls, you can ignore the earthquakes, churning waves, and rising waters.

Today, pray that God would engrave His name upon your heart so deeply that nothing will be able to move you from His love when you stand in Him. Know that God will be not only your fortress but your guide, steering you away from all danger—physical and spiritual.

> *God is our refuge and strength, a very present help in trouble.*
> *Therefore will not we fear, though the earth be removed, and*
> *though the mountains be carried into the midst of the sea; though*
> *the waters thereof roar and be troubled, though the mountains*
> *shake with the swelling thereof. . . . The LORD of hosts is with us.*
>
> PSALM 46:1–3, 7

Write thy blessed name, O Lord, upon my heart, there to remain so indelibly engraved, that no prosperity, no adversity, shall ever move me from Thy love. Be Thou to me a strong tower of defence, a comforter in tribulation, a deliverer in distress, a very present help in trouble, and a guide to heaven through the many temptations and dangers of this life.
THOMAS À KEMPIS

MY PRAYER STARTER: Mighty God, I praise You for Your power to protect. When I am rocked by temptation, betrayal, or disaster, You remain sturdy and welcome me into Your fortress.

To a child, few things are scarier than being lost in the dark, uncertain of how to get back to Mom or Dad's loving security. Without light, the child feels lost, afraid of taking the next step in the blackness, terrified of going the wrong way.

The same is true of God's children. At times, you may find yourself shaking in the darkness, afraid of venturing onto the wrong path. That's when you must remember that Father God is not just your defender and rescuer but your light and guide.

Today, pray that God would stretch His hand into your darkness. That He would shine His light upon your path, guiding you back to Him, His love, and His way.

> *Blessed be the LORD my strength. . . : my goodness, and my fortress;*
> *my high tower, and my deliverer; my shield, and he in whom*
> *I trust. . . . Send thine hand from above; rid me, and deliver*
> *me out of great waters, from the hand of strange children.*
>
> PSALM 144:1–2, 7

O God our Father, hear me, who am trembling in this
darkness, and stretch forth thy hand unto me; hold forth thy
light before me; recall me from my wanderings; and, thou
being my guide, may I be restored to myself and to thee.
SAINT AUGUSTINE

MY PRAYER STARTER: Father, as Your son, I am completely dependent on Your guidance. Let Your Word be a flashlight to me in this world's dark, sinful forest. Lead me home to You.

You were born not just to be saved by Jesus, who suffered and died for you, but to live your life as He lived His. He's your example, the pattern for you to follow. He was truthful and right with God. When injured with threats and insults, He bore them without retaliation. He fully committed Himself to God—heart, mind, body, spirit, and soul.

Today's prayer begins with thanking Jesus for all He's done for you. It reminds you of who Jesus is to you—not just your Redeemer but your Friend who loves you unconditionally, your Brother who guides you to a better place. And it ends with asking Jesus to help you know Him better, love Him more, and follow Him more closely—progressively, day by day.

For even hereunto were ye called: because Christ also suffered for us, leaving us an example, that ye should follow his steps: who did no sin, neither was guile found in his mouth: who, when he was reviled, reviled not again; when he suffered, he threatened not; but committed himself to him that judgeth righteously.

1 PETER 2:21–23

Thanks be to thee, my Lord Jesus Christ,
for all the benefits thou hast given me,
for all the pains and insults thou hast borne for me.
O most merciful Redeemer, Friend and Brother,
May I know thee more clearly,
Love thee more dearly,
Follow thee more nearly, day by day.
SAINT RICHARD OF CHICHESTER

MY PRAYER STARTER: Lord, You are the perfect example of humility. Just as You said nothing in the face of extreme pain, may I respond with grace when others voice their hatred against me.

One of the best ways to endure afflictions is to prepare your heart before they arrive. That means reaching out to God, putting aside anything that stands between you and Him. Of course, you'll need God's help to do those things. But that's why He's there—to give you the strength you need, the power to overcome, and the passion to seek His face.

If thou prepare thine heart, and stretch out thine hands toward him; if iniquity be in thine hand, put it far away. . . . For then shalt thou lift up thy face without spot; yea, thou shalt be stedfast, and shalt not fear: because thou shalt forget thy misery, and remember it as waters that pass away: and thine age shall be clearer than the noonday. . . . And thou shalt be secure.

JOB 11:13–18

O God, Who seest all our weaknesses, and the troubles we labour under, have regard unto the prayers of Thy servant, who stands in need of Thy comfort, Thy direction, and Thy help. Thou alone knowest what is best for us; let me never dispute Thy wisdom or Thy goodness. Lord, so prepare my heart, that no affliction may ever so surprise as to overbear me. Dispose me at all times to a readiness to suffer what Thy Providence shall order or permit. Grant that I may never murmur at Thy appointments, nor be exasperated at the ministers of Thy Providence. Amen.

THOMAS WILSON

MY PRAYER STARTER: All-seeing God, only You know my future. Equip my heart with durability and fortitude so that I can stay prepared for any wave of grief or temptation before it hits me.

God is looking for you (Psalm 14:2). He wants you to seek Him (Acts 17:27–28) with all your being (Psalm 63:1). He'll reward you for doing so (Hebrews 11:6), giving you all the guidance you need when you find Him (1 Kings 22:5).

Ask God to teach you how and where to find Him. Perhaps begin by looking for Him in His creation, His Word, and your praises and prayers. Seek Him first with your entire being (Matthew 6:33)—no matter what's happening in your life (2 Chronicles 30:18–20). Be open to God's teaching on how to seek Him. And be assured you'll find Him (Deuteronomy 4:29).

> *Let the heart of them rejoice that seek the LORD. Seek the*
> *LORD and his strength, seek his face continually.*
> 1 CHRONICLES 16:10–11

O Lord my God. Teach my heart this day where and how to find you. You have made me and re-made me, and you have bestowed on me all the good things I possess, and still I do not know you. I have not yet done that for which I was made.

. . . .

Let me seek you in my desire; let me desire you in my seeking. Let me find you by loving you; let me love you when I find you.
SAINT ANSELM

MY PRAYER STARTER: All-important Creator, I know that nothing else apart from You truly matters. Help me direct all my energies toward seeking You—only then will I find contentment.

No matter if you're little or big, young or old, God will support you. When you walk in His strength, you've got His true power. So turn to your Maker today. Know He will forever hold you. Your Deliverer will save you for Himself. Rise to God. Lean on Him for all things in this age, at your age, as you age. When you trust in your Creator, you'll be transported into the loving arms of One who has carried and will continue to carry you—here and beyond.

> *Hearken unto me. . .which are borne by me from the belly,*
> *which are carried from the womb: and even to your old age I*
> *am he; and even to hoar hairs will I carry you: I have made,*
> *and I will bear; even I will carry, and will deliver you.*
> ISAIAH 46:3–4

O Lord, our God, under the shadow of Thy wings let us hope. Thou wilt support us, both when little, and even to gray hairs. When our strength is of Thee, it is strength; but, when our own, it is feebleness. We return unto Thee, O Lord, that from their weariness our souls may rise towards Thee, leaning on the things which Thou hast created, and passing on to Thyself, who hast wonderfully made them; for with Thee is refreshment and true strength. Amen.
SAINT AUGUSTINE

MY PRAYER STARTER: Loving Creator, carry me when I can't walk, and let Your power replace my weakness. Enable me to fight temptations and endure the fear of uncertainty.

Everything you have and are comes from the hand of God, the One who knows your heart. Surrender all of yourself to the Lord of your life today. Give yourself as a willing and living sacrifice, and He'll give you the mind of Jesus Christ and all the joy that follows.

Hear thou in heaven thy dwelling place, and forgive, and do, and give to every man according to his ways, whose heart thou knowest; (for thou, even thou only, knowest the hearts of all the children of men).

1 KINGS 8:39

Searcher of all hearts, Thou knowest my heart, and how it stands with me. Thou has made it, Thou knowest whether I love Thee. All I am or have that has any goodness in it, I am or have alone through Thee, for it is all Thy work in me; but it must be Thine also by the free surrender of my heart. In Thy service, and fulfilling Thy will, I would fain spend every minute of my life. The thought of Thee shall be the sweetest to me of all thoughts; to speak of Thee the dearest and best of all I speak or hear; the joy of Thy love shall be the inmost joy of my soul. Gladly would I devote my whole being to Thee; accept me, then, as a living sacrifice, and give me the mind that was in Christ Jesus, to the glory of God the Father. Amen.

MICHAEL SAILER

MY PRAYER STARTER: Lord, let me not boast in my possessions and talents. Remind me that they are borrowed parts meant to be used for Your glory. Help me fulfill the destiny You've given.

Sometimes, without our even realizing it, our feelings of self-sufficiency may sap our desire for God. That's when it's time to humbly draw near to Him, confident in His goodness and mercy. To come as the blind came to the Giver of sight. As the hungry and thirsty came to the God who satiates. As the afflicted came to the Comforter.

Know that in God you will find ultimate satisfaction. Crave only to be in the presence of your Savior, Source, Provider, Redeemer, Helper, Defender, Protector, Fortress, and Strength. And as you draw near to Him, He will draw nearer to you.

> *God resisteth the proud, but giveth grace unto the humble.*
> *Submit yourselves therefore to God. . . . Draw nigh to*
> *God, and he will draw nigh to you. . . . Humble yourselves*
> *in the sight of the Lord, and he shall lift you up.*
> JAMES 4:6–8, 10

In the confidence of your goodness and great mercy, O Lord,
I draw to you, as a sick person to the healer, as one hungry
and thirsty to the fountain of life, a creature to the creator,
a desolate soul to my own tender comforter. Behold, in
you is everything that I can or ought to desire. You are my
salvation and my redemption, my helper and my strength.
THOMAS À KEMPIS

MY PRAYER STARTER: All-sufficient Lord, You are the eternal Creator, and I am merely a man. Just as the grass needs the sunlight, I need Your Spirit to empower me and fill my life with purpose.

Jesus wants you to abide, to dwell, in Him. To have a personal relationship with Him full of obedience, dependence, and trust. For only then will you experience the full workings of His power and realize your full potential *through* Jesus. Only then will you become the man God created you to be *in* Jesus.

Place yourself before Jesus today. Look up into His face. Ask Him to take you out of yourself and into Him. There, you will find your thankfulness, safety, life, reward, and abundance as He becomes your all in all.

Abide in me, and I in you. As the branch cannot bear fruit of itself, except it abide in the vine; no more can ye, except ye abide in me. I am the vine, ye are the branches: He that abideth in me, and I in him, the same bringeth forth much fruit: for without me ye can do nothing.

JOHN 15:4–5

Sever me from myself that I may be grateful to you;
may I perish to myself that I may be safe in you;
may I die to myself that I may live in you;
may I wither to myself that I may blossom in you;
may I be emptied of myself that I may abound in you;
may I be nothing to myself that I may be all to you.
ERASMUS

MY PRAYER STARTER: Lord, I don't want to just know about You; I want to know You—better than I know anyone else. Lead me closer to You each day, correcting my missteps and accelerating my progress.

Joy in the Lord empowers you spiritually, emotionally, mentally, and physically. Not there yet? No worries. Where there's a will, there's a way.

Your first step is knowing God, loving Him before all others, and rejoicing in Him because He rejoices in you. The second step is praying that you would know, love, and delight in Him. Your progress toward this goal—and the joy that follows—is gradual, but you *will* get there. Begin now with today's prayers.

> *Thou wilt shew me the path of life: in thy presence is fulness of joy; at thy right hand there are pleasures for evermore.*
>
> PSALM 16:11

Grant me, even me, my dearest Lord, to know Thee, and love Thee, and rejoice in Thee. And if I cannot do these perfectly in this life, let me at least advance to higher degrees every day, till I can come to do them in perfection. Let the knowledge of Thee increase in me here, that it may be full hereafter. Let the love of Thee grow every day more and more here, that it may be perfect hereafter; that my joy may be great in itself, and full in Thee. I know, O God, that Thou art a God of truth. O make good Thy gracious promises to me, that my joy may be full. Amen.

SAINT AUGUSTINE

MY PRAYER STARTER: Lord, my Ultimate Goal, steady my steps as I walk toward a deeper knowledge and love of You. When I stumble, take my hand and toughen my resolve.

Luke's Gospel tells of a woman who "could in no wise lift up herself" for eighteen years because of a sickness that kept her bent over (Luke 13:11). But then Jesus saw her. He spoke one sentence: "Woman, thou art loosed from thine infirmity" (Luke 13:12). After He laid His hands on her, "immediately she was made straight, and glorified God" (Luke 13:13).

The Greek adverb for "in no wise" means the woman *could not completely* straighten herself. It is found again only once in the New Testament—in Hebrews 7:25. Here, it has a positive sense, meaning *uttermost*, or "completely, wholly, entirely."

Just as Jesus helped the woman who couldn't completely straighten herself, He helps you, a man equally as feeble, to the uttermost.

Pray for Jesus to help you today. Know that He alone can save you, lift you up, and straighten you out—completely. Know that with one act, one sentence, or one touch, He is saving you. Your job? To glorify God—to the uttermost!

> *But this man [Jesus], because he continueth ever, hath*
> *an unchangeable priesthood. Wherefore he is able also to*
> *save them to the uttermost that come unto God by him,*
> *seeing he ever liveth to make intercession for them.*
>
> HEBREWS 7:24–25

Lord, keep us from sinning, and make us living witnesses
of Thy mighty power to save to the uttermost.
HANNAH WHITALL SMITH

MY PRAYER STARTER: Lord, divine Healer, cure any spiritual sickness that might infect my soul. Help me to stand up straight, refusing to bow to temptations or any force that's opposed to You.

When caught up in the anxiety the world presents, you may begin to lose your footing. Yet that's when the inward light and power of Jesus Christ can shine out to that same world.

When stress threatens to engulf your faith, lean back into God. Pray for the strength, power, and endurance you need to face daily challenges. Commit to knowing God more, increasing your awareness of the Holy Spirit within, and embracing the calmness of Jesus. As you do so in prayer, your faith will decimate anything stress throws at you.

> *But in all things approving ourselves as the ministers of God,*
> *in much patience, in afflictions, in necessities, in distresses. . . ;*
> *by pureness, by knowledge, by longsuffering, by kindness,*
> *by the Holy Ghost, by love unfeigned, by the word of truth,*
> *by the power of God, by the armour of righteousness.*
> 2 CORINTHIANS 6:4, 6–7

O gracious Father, keep me through Thy Holy Spirit; keep my heart soft and tender now in health and amidst the bustle of the world; keep the thought of Thyself present to me as my Father in Jesus Christ; and keep alive in me a spirit of love and meekness to all men, that I may be at once gentle and active and firm. O strengthen me to bear pain, or sickness, or danger, or whatever Thou shalt be pleased to lay upon me, as Christ's soldier and servant; and let my faith overcome the world daily.
THOMAS ARNOLD

MY PRAYER STARTER: God, my secure Fortress, support my often-flailing faith, conquer my worries, and let others see the assistance only You can provide.

You gain so much when you give every bit of yourself to Jesus. When you give Him your hands, He entrusts you with His work. When you give Him your feet, He shows you your path. When you give Him your eyes, He reveals what He sees. And the list goes on.

Today, give Jesus every part of your being. In return, He'll give you all He has and all you need to serve Him.

For this cause I bow my knees unto the Father of our Lord Jesus Christ, of whom the whole family in heaven and earth is named, that he would grant you, according to the riches of his glory, to be strengthened with might by his Spirit in the inner man; that Christ may dwell in your hearts by faith.

EPHESIANS 3:14–17

Lord Jesus,
I give you my hands to do your work.
I give you my feet to go your way.
I give you my eyes to see as you do.
I give you my tongue to speak your words.
I give you my mind that you may think in me.
I give you my spirit that you may pray in me.
Above all, I give you my heart that you may love
in me your Father and all mankind.
I give you my whole self that you may grow in me, so that it
is you, Lord Jesus, who live and work and pray in me.
THE GRAIL PRAYER

MY PRAYER STARTER: Divine Creator of my body, give me the willingness to offer every part of me to You. Let me hold nothing back, even when I'm not sure where You are leading me.

At some point in your life, you may have heard the expression "Mother (or father) knows best." You may have even said, "I know best." But none of these statements are valid. In truth, only Father *God* knows best. He is your true guide to the right path. He knows your needs better than you do. Only He sees what lies before you—the total plan for your life, the road He has laid out for you alone.

Trust that God has the right ideas and guidance for you. He has led servants, prophets, disciples, kings, and His own Son. Let Him lead you.

> *In thee, O LORD, do I put my trust; let me never be ashamed:*
> *deliver me in thy righteousness. Bow down thine ear to me;*
> *deliver me speedily: be thou my strong rock, for an house of*
> *defence to save me. For thou art my rock and my fortress;*
> *therefore for thy name's sake lead me, and guide me.*

PSALM 31:1–3

Lord God Almighty, I charge thee of thy great mercy and by the token of thy holy rood [cross] that thou guide me to thy will and to my soul's need better than I can myself, that above all things I may inwardly love thee with a clean mind and clean body; for thou art my Maker, my help and my hope.

ALFRED THE GREAT

MY PRAYER STARTER: All-wise God, I admit that I don't know best. You, however, know everything, so give me the faith to trust Your decisions over my own.

Tradition says Ireland's Saint Patrick wrote his Breastplate prayer in AD 433. It served as his means of divine protection.

A breastplate is a metal vestlike plate worn to protect the chest. In the Old Testament, part of the high priest Aaron's wardrobe was a breastplate, which he wore when he went into the Holy Place before the Lord (Exodus 28:29–30). In the New Testament, a breastplate is part of the armor of God that we should wear to stand firm before dark spiritual forces.

Part 1 of Saint Patrick's Breastplate prayer appears below. Pray it as you arise, taking up God's strength, might, wisdom, power, and protection.

Wherefore take unto you the whole armour of God, that ye may be able to withstand in the evil day, and having done all, to stand. Stand therefore, having your loins girt about with truth, and having on the breastplate of righteousness.

EPHESIANS 6:13–14

I arise today, through
God's strength to pilot me,
God's might to uphold me,
God's wisdom to guide me,
. . . .
God's host to save me
From snares of devils,
From temptation of vices,
From everyone who shall wish me ill,
afar and near.

SAINT PATRICK'S BREASTPLATE—PART 1

MY PRAYER STARTER: Holy King, I know that Satan tries everything to remind me of my sins and make me fall. May Your divinely imparted righteousness always protect me from such schemes.

God your Father is light. In Him there's no darkness (1 John 1:5). Because God is your Father, you're a child of light. As such, you need to be spiritually alert, putting on the breastplate of faith and love. And your best protection is Jesus and His presence imbuing you—so much that when others see and hear you, they see and hear Him.

Part 2 of Saint Patrick's Breastplate prayer appears below. Pray the power, light, and protection of Jesus Christ to be with you in all ways today.

Ye are all the children of light, and the children of the day. . . . Let us, who are of the day, be sober, putting on the breastplate of faith and love; and for an helmet, the hope of salvation. For God hath not appointed us to wrath, but to obtain salvation by our Lord Jesus Christ, who died for us, that. . .we should live together with him.

1 THESSALONIANS 5:5, 8–10

Christ with me,
Christ before me,
Christ behind me,
Christ in me. . . .
Christ when I lie down,
Christ when I sit down,
Christ when I arise,
Christ in the heart of every man who thinks of me,
Christ in the mouth of everyone who speaks of me,
Christ in every eye that sees me,
Christ in every ear that hears me.

SAINT PATRICK'S BREASTPLATE—PART 2

MY PRAYER STARTER: Righteous Father, just as You have no darkness in You, may I have no darkness in me. Shine through my every action and word, illuminating Your truth for everyone.

When you make it your aim in life to please God rather than yourself or other people, God notices. And so do the people you meet. They begin to smell the sweet fragrance of Jesus all around you. It permeates the air, leaving behind His light, presence, and essence.

After praying today's prayers, make it your quest to be the best *in Jesus Christ*. To preach to others not by what you say but by what you do. To influence them by your Christlikeness—your love, kindness, gentleness, forbearance, grace, mercy, and forgiveness. To be so unlike the world that others see a new door opening to them, one from which Jesus shines through.

Do all this for the love of Jesus Christ.

Now thanks be unto God, which always causeth us to triumph in Christ, and maketh manifest the savour of his knowledge by us in every place. For we are unto God a sweet savour of Christ, in them that are saved, and in them that perish: to the one we are the savour of death unto death; and to the other the savour of life unto life.

2 CORINTHIANS 2:14–16

Help me to spread your fragrance everywhere I go—let me preach you without preaching, not by words but by my example— by the catching force, the sympathetic influence of what I do, the evident fullness of the love my heart bears to you.

JOHN HENRY NEWMAN

MY PRAYER STARTER: God, I want to please You with my life's fragrance. Let others smell it too, and instill in them a desire to find the source, which is Your Spirit.

Think of today's classic prayer as a collective plea from humanity to God.

As you speak these words into God's ears, you'll recall the power of love (translated as "charity" in the verse below) and the grandeur of a Christlike character.

Charity suffereth long, and is kind; charity envieth not; charity vaunteth not itself, is not puffed up, doth not behave itself unseemly, seeketh not her own, is not easily provoked, thinketh no evil; rejoiceth not in iniquity, but rejoiceth in the truth; beareth all things, believeth all things, hopeth all things, endureth all things.

1 CORINTHIANS 13:4–7

Keep us, O God, from pettiness;
let us be large in thought, in word, in deed.
Let us be done with fault-finding
and leave off self-seeking.
May we put away all pretense
and meet each other face to face,
without self-pity and without prejudice.
. . . .

Teach us to put into action our better impulses,
straightforward and unafraid.
. . . .

And may we strive to touch and to know
the great, common [human]-heart of us all.
And, O Lord God,
let us forget not, to be kind!

MARY STEWARD

MY PRAYER STARTER: Lord, to resemble You is my greatest goal. May Your grace, love, and character be found in my interactions with others so that they will want to know You better.

At times, we can make a mess out of our lives. Thank God He can work all things out for His good—and ours. Today, pray for God to take the tangled threads from your hands, and trust that He'll sort them out and weave them into something marvelous.

But I trusted in thee, O LORD: I said, Thou art my God. My times are in thy hand: deliver me. . . . Oh how great is thy goodness, which thou hast laid up for them that fear thee; which thou hast wrought for them that trust in thee before the sons of men!

PSALM 31:14–15, 19

Some things have not gone well today. We have had our troubles. Our hearts have been hurt. You are the healer—will You heal us? Take the tangled threads out of our clumsy hands, disentangle them and weave them into a web of beauty! Take the dark things of the day's providences, the things that seem wrong, and by the power of Your grace, transmute them into blessing. Help us indeed to keep our hands off the strange, complex affairs of our lives— for we would only spoil the pattern which You are fashioning in us, if we attempted to adjust these complicated affairs. May You take entire charge of the myriad things of our lives that are beyond our managing, and bring good and only good out of them.

J. R. MILLER

MY PRAYER STARTER: Omniscient God, I am a shortsighted man. Take each of my confused decisions and weave them into Your perfect tapestry.

Your thoughts can easily lead you astray. But take heart! Since accepting Jesus, you have a new inner being, a new spirit within.

Every day, you must awaken that new inner being. To allow the truth of Jesus to change your thoughts, renewing your mind. Today's classic prayer will help you do that.

Begin by asking God to be all that you love, all that you hope, and all that you strive for. Next, ask for His thoughts to flow into your mind, condensing into His words that pour from your lips. For your daily life to remain in Him. For every breath you take to be for Him.

Speak today's classic prayer slowly, meditatively. Feel God transforming you, His Spirit infusing you, and Jesus' love emanating from you.

If so be that ye have heard him, and have been taught by him, as the truth is in Jesus: that ye put off concerning the former conversation the old man, which is corrupt according to the deceitful lusts; and be renewed in the spirit of your mind; and that ye put on the new man, which after God is created in righteousness and true holiness.

EPHESIANS 4:21–24

O God,
be all my love,
all my hope,
all my striving;
let my thoughts and words flow from You,
my daily life be in You,
and every breath I take be for you.
JOHN CASSIAN

MY PRAYER STARTER: Holy Spirit, take the reins of my soul. Make all my words, thoughts, actions, hopes, and desires point back toward the God who made me.

God directed Abraham, telling him to leave home and go to a place he'd never seen before. In faith, Abraham went, not knowing his destination. By faith, he lived in that land of promise, and God rewarded him for doing so.

Just as God directed Abraham, God's directing you. Today, ask Him to fix your steps and strengthen your determination to abide here as a pilgrim, knowing heaven is your true home.

> *These all died in faith, not having received the promises,*
> *but having seen them afar off, and were persuaded of them,*
> *and embraced them, and confessed that they were strangers*
> *and pilgrims on the earth. . . . But now they desire a better*
> *country, that is, an heavenly: wherefore God is not ashamed*
> *to be called their God: for he hath prepared for them a city.*
>
> HEBREWS 11:13, 16

Fix thou our steps, O Lord, that we stagger not at the uneven motions of the world, but steadily go on to our glorious home; neither censuring our journey by the weather we meet with, nor turning out of the way for anything that befalls us. The winds are often rough, and our own weight presses us downwards. Reach forth, O Lord, thy hand, thy saving hand, and speedily deliver us. Teach us, O Lord, to use this transitory life as pilgrims returning to their beloved home, that we may take what our journey requires, and not think of settling in a foreign country.
JOHN WESLEY

MY PRAYER STARTER: Lord, Guide of my life, Abraham didn't know his destination, but he obeyed You anyway. I, however, know I'm headed toward heaven, so give me the faith to keep walking.

There are some secrets—grudges, habits, tendencies, bitterness, fears, and negative thoughts—that men hide not only from God but from themselves, trying to maintain a facade of toughness or independence. Before long, such hidden sins bring impenetrable darkness into their lives.

Today, pray for God to illuminate your hidden corners. Yield your secrets up to Him and allow His truth to transform you.

> *God is light, and in him is no darkness at all. If we say that*
> *we have fellowship with him, and walk in darkness, we lie,*
> *and do not the truth: but if we walk in the light, as he is*
> *in the light, we have fellowship one with another, and the*
> *blood of Jesus Christ his Son cleanseth us from all sin.*
>
> 1 JOHN 1:5–7

Penetrate those murky corners where we hide memories, and tendencies on which we do not care to look, but which we will not yield freely up to you, that you may purify and transmute them. The persistent buried grudge, the half-acknowledged enmity which is still smouldering; the bitterness of that loss we have not turned into sacrifice, the private comfort we cling to, the secret fear of failure which saps our initiative and is really inverted pride; the pessimism which is an insult to your joy, Lord, we bring all these to you, and we review them with shame and penitence in your steadfast light.
EVELYN UNDERHILL

MY PRAYER STARTER: Eternal Light, You know me better than I know myself. Expose the ugliness and lies in my soul so that I, with Your help, can wash them out with Your love and truth.

God's Word is powerful, God-breathed, alive, and active. It penetrates, judging your heart and mind (see Hebrews 4:12). And your Bible is full of prayers you can pray back to God. Think of the power you can unleash!

Not sure where to start? Begin with the Lord's Prayer. It's bursting with power! Afterward, try the prayer of Jabez (1 Chronicles 4:10). If you're in dire straits, pray Jonah's prayer (Jonah 2:2–9). For comfort, dip into one of David's many prayers (Psalm 23). For praising, try Hannah's (1 Samuel 2:1–10). For direction on finding and abiding in that secret place of God, delve deeply into the prayer of an unknown author (Psalm 91).

Your job: pray. God will answer.

> *The holy scriptures. . .are able to make thee wise unto*
> *salvation through faith which is in Christ Jesus.*
> *All scripture is given by inspiration of God.*
> 2 TIMOTHY 3:15–16

After this manner therefore pray ye: Our Father which art in heaven, Hallowed be thy name. Thy kingdom come, Thy will be done in earth, as it is in heaven. Give us this day our daily bread. And forgive us our debts, as we forgive our debtors. And lead us not into temptation, but deliver us from evil: For thine is the kingdom, and the power, and the glory, for ever. Amen.
MATTHEW 6:9–13

MY PRAYER STARTER: God, thank You for providing so many great examples of prayer in Your Word. May I never forget to access and use them every chance I get.

In *My Utmost for His Highest*, Oswald Chambers wrote, "Keep your life so constant in its contact with God that His surprising power may break out on the right hand and on the left. Always be in a state of expectancy, and see that you leave room for God to come in as He likes."

That's just what King Jehoshaphat did when armies were knocking on the door of his kingdom (2 Chronicles 20). He began by seeking God's face and reminding himself of God's supreme power. Then Jehoshaphat cried to Him for help, admitting his weakness. He didn't know what to do. His eyes were fixed upon God, and so were his expectations. As a result, God moved in a powerful way on behalf of him and his people!

Today, get into constant contact with God. Seek His face. Put your expectations in Him. Watch His power break through on *your* behalf!

For surely there is an end; and thine expectation shall not be cut off.
PROVERBS 23:18

O Lord God of our fathers, art not thou God in heaven? and rulest not thou over all the kingdoms of the heathen? and in thine hand is there not power and might, so that none is able to withstand thee? . . . We have no might against this great company that cometh against us; neither know we what to do: but our eyes are upon thee.
2 CHRONICLES 20:6, 12

MY PRAYER STARTER: Almighty Lord, thank You for fighting on my side. Help me always seek You whenever Satan's battle strategies are too strong for me to resist. Only You can win the war.

When your heart is focused on God's faithfulness to you—on the fact that He does not change and will always love you consistently—you can abide any storm. Because your trust in Him is solid, you'll be able to walk wherever He leads and show love and kindness to everyone you meet.

Today, ask God for that enduring power. Rise with a soul quieted by the knowledge that God will turn all your troubles into something terrific.

> *God is not a man, that he should lie; neither the son of man,*
> *that he should repent: hath he said, and shall he not do it?*
> *or hath he spoken, and shall he not make it good?*
>
> NUMBERS 23:19

Almighty God, Lord of the storm and of the calm, the vexed sea and the quiet haven, of day and of night, of life and of death—grant unto us so to have our hearts stayed upon Thy faithfulness, Thine unchangingness and love, that, whatsoever betide us, however black the cloud or dark the night, with quiet faith trusting in Thee, we may look upon Thee with untroubled eye, and walking in lowliness towards Thee, and in lovingkindness towards one another, abide all storms and troubles of this mortal life, beseeching Thee that they may turn to the soul's true good. We ask it for Thy mercy's sake, shown in Jesus Christ our Lord. Amen.

GEORGE DAWSON

MY PRAYER STARTER: God, thank You for being faithful. Whenever I'm frightened by uncertainties, help me remember that You've never left me—and never will.

Nothing—whether in life or in death—can separate you or your loved ones from Jesus Christ and His love. As a result, you are constantly united with loved ones in this world and the next. Take comfort from this. Embrace this fact, knowing that as you fellowship with Jesus, you also fellowship with those here on earth and in the heavenly realms.

As Jesus lives in you and you in Him, take courage that He is with you on this day and the next, in this world and the one that follows.

According to my earnest expectation and my hope, that in nothing
I shall be ashamed, but that with all boldness, as always, so now
also Christ shall be magnified in my body, whether it be by life,
or by death. For to me to live is Christ, and to die is gain.
PHILIPPIANS 1:20–21

O Lord our God, from whom neither life nor death can separate those who trust in thy love, and whose love holds in its embrace thy children in this world and in the next: So unite us to thyself that in fellowship with thee we may always be united to our loved ones whether here or there: give us courage, constancy and hope; through him who died and was buried and rose again for us, Jesus Christ our Lord.
WILLIAM TEMPLE

MY PRAYER STARTER: Lord, our eternal Hope, it hurts each time a brother or sister in Jesus Christ departs. However, thank You for assuring me that I will see them again someday with You.

Temptations come to men who are weakened by doubts and fears, when they feel as if the forces of evil are more powerful than those of good. Yet Jesus has overcome all evil. Believe He will give you the strength to have victory over things that threaten you.

Today, pray for God to come to your aid, to bless you, to reinforce your resistance through the power of Jesus Christ.

For we have not an high priest which cannot be touched with the feeling of our infirmities; but was in all points tempted like as we are, yet without sin. Let us therefore come boldly unto the throne of grace, that we may obtain mercy, and find grace to help in time of need.

HEBREWS 4:15–16

Strong Son of God, who was tried and tempted to the uttermost, yet without sin; be near me now with Thy strength and give me the victory over this evil desire that threatens to ruin me. I am weak, O Lord, and full of doubts and fears. There are moments when I am afraid of myself, when the world and the flesh and the devil seem more powerful than the forces of good. But now I look to Thee in whom dwelleth all the fulness of grace and might and redemption. Blessed Saviour! I take Thee afresh to be my Refuge, my Covert, my Defence, my strong Tower from the enemy. Hear me and bless me now and ever. Amen.

SAMUEL MCCOMB

MY PRAYER STARTER: Lord God, Strengthener of my spirit, my own power is unable to resist Satan's trickery. Fill me with wisdom and resilience, empowering my will to choose You.

When this day, with all its joys and challenges, is over, God will be watching over you. He is your keeper.

The Hebrew word for "keeper" is *samar*, which *Strong's Concordance* translates as "to *hedge* about (as with thorns), i.e. *guard*; generally to *protect, attend to*, etc."

Tonight, as you lie in bed, imagine the Lord who made heaven and earth guarding you, planting thorns around your bed so that nothing can get through to harm you. He'll be awake all night, watching, protecting, and loving as you drift into your slumber.

> *My help cometh from the LORD, which made heaven and earth. He will not suffer thy foot to be moved: he that keepeth thee will not slumber. Behold, he that keepeth Israel shall neither slumber nor sleep. The LORD is thy keeper.*

PSALM 121:2–5

The day is past and over; all thanks, O Lord, to Thee;
I pray Thee now that sinless the hours of dark may be:
O Jesus, keep me in Thy sight
And guard me through the coming night.
The joys of day are over; I lift my heart to Thee
And ask Thee that offenseless the hours of dark may be.
O Jesus, keep me in Thy sight
And guard me through the coming night.

SAINT ANATOLIUS, *translated by J. M. Neale*

MY PRAYER STARTER: God, my divine Protector, I surrender my safety into Your hands tonight, trusting that You will guard me. Thank You for Your reassuring peace.

When your strength fails, when you're experiencing pain and despair, when you're as low as you can go, it becomes even clearer that without God, you're lost. Without Him, you are nothing.

Today, praise God with your whole heart, banishing whatever darkness and depression that might obscure His light. Know that as you cry out, He's giving you strength. Then rise in His power alone and watch Him work.

> *In the day when I cried thou answeredst me, and strengthenedst*
> *me with strength in my soul. . . . Though the LORD be high,*
> *yet hath he respect unto the lowly: but the proud he knoweth*
> *afar off. Though I walk in the midst of trouble, thou wilt*
> *revive me. . .and thy right hand shall save me. The LORD*
> *will perfect that which concerneth me: thy mercy, O LORD,*
> *endureth for ever: forsake not the works of thine own hands.*
>
> PSALM 138:3, 6–8

My strength fails;
I feel only weakness, irritation, and depression.
I am tempted to complain and to despair. . . .
Lord, destroy my pride;
leave it no resource.
How happy I shall be
if you can teach me by these terrible trials
that I am nothing,
that I can do nothing
and that you are all!
FRANÇOIS FÉNELON

MY PRAYER STARTER: Lord, remind me that I am nothing without You; however, remind me also that with You, I have infinite value. May that knowledge be my power source today.

You may be familiar with the first four lines of today's classic prayer, often called the Serenity Prayer. But the lines that follow are even better! They speak of taking life one day at a time. Of accepting hardships as the path to peace. Of taking the world as it is, not as you would like it to be. Of trusting that as you surrender to Jesus' will, He'll make all things right. Of knowing that you'll be reasonably happy here but extraordinarily happy in your next life with God.

Enjoy this great and powerful prayer—not just today but every day!

Through the tender mercy of our God. . .the dayspring from on high hath visited us, to give light to them that sit in darkness and in the shadow of death, to guide our feet into the way of peace.
LUKE 1:78–79

God grant me the serenity
To accept the things I cannot change;
Courage to change the things I can;
And wisdom to know the difference.
Living one day at a time;
Enjoying one moment at a time;
Accepting hardships as the pathway to peace;
Taking, as Jesus did, this sinful world as it is, not as I would have it;
Trusting that he will make all things right if I surrender to his will;
That I may be reasonably happy in this life
And supremely happy with him forever in the next.
REINHOLD NIEBUHR

MY PRAYER STARTER: Father, Source of my serenity, help me to see everything in my life—even the painful parts—as stepping-stones in my journey home. I look forward to the joy that awaits.

If you're humble and open enough, you can find wisdom all around you. Begin with the Bible, a treasure trove of wisdom. From Genesis to Revelation, it has stories of people who made mistakes you can learn from; in fact, that's one reason their tales were written (Romans 15:4). But you can also learn from your own mistakes—once the dust has settled, of course. And you can learn from the mistakes of others in your life, especially children. For "out of the mouths of babes" God's voice can often be heard.

After praying today's prayers, look for the lessons in your own life.

> *The proverbs of Solomon the son of David, king of Israel; to know wisdom and instruction; to perceive the words of understanding; to receive the instruction of wisdom, justice, and judgment, and equity; to give subtilty to the simple, to the young man knowledge and discretion. A wise man will hear, and will increase learning; and a man of understanding shall attain unto wise counsels.*

PROVERBS 1:1–5

Grant to us, O Father, the wisdom that is necessary in all the conduct of life. And grant that even our mistakes may rise up to guide us and when we behold the mistakes of others, while we seek to rescue them and to sympathize with them, grant that we may read likewise the lessons which they make for us.

HENRY WARD BEECHER

MY PRAYER STARTER: God, thank You for offering wisdom in Your Word and in my daily life. Let me never overlook a lesson You are trying to teach me.

Ah, that God would grant you such grace that you might do what He's calling you to do, take on the work He wants you to perform, and gain the attitude He wants you to have toward Him, yourself, and others. That God would favor you, giving you the grace to speak His words and walk in His footsteps. When you have that grace, you will find a calmness like no other.

Before praying today's prayers, consider the calmness Jesus showed in dire situations. How unruffled He remained when confronted with those who wanted His life. Think about the peace He exuded to the troubled, ill, possessed, and fearfully doubtful.

Then pray, taking on Jesus Christ's persona, making His grace, power, and peace your own. So that you too, no matter what your day brings, remain "calm like waters deep and still"—as did He.

Grace and peace be multiplied unto you through the knowledge of
God, and of Jesus our Lord, according as his divine power hath
given unto us all things that pertain unto life and godliness, through
the knowledge of him that hath called us to glory and virtue.

2 PETER 1:2–3

Grant us such grace that we may work Thy will,
And speak Thy words, and walk before Thy face,
Profound and calm like waters deep and still;
Grant us such grace.
CHRISTINA ROSSETTI

MY PRAYER STARTER: Lord, I am in awe of the grace and peace You bring. I need both every day so that I can speak Your truth fearlessly and with love.

It's easy to have courage when your surroundings are familiar and your task routine. But what about when God calls you to step out of your comfort zone? Do you cower in fear or confidently step out of the boat and walk to Him across the water?

Today, pray for God to give you the courage to go wherever He leads.

And when the disciples saw him walking on the sea, they were troubled, saying, It is a spirit; and they cried out for fear. But straightway Jesus spake unto them, saying, Be of good cheer; it is I; be not afraid. And Peter answered him and said, Lord, if it be thou, bid me come unto thee on the water. And he said, Come. And when Peter was come down out of the ship, he walked on the water, to go to Jesus.

MATTHEW 14:26–29

May he give us all the courage that we need to go the way he shepherds us, that when he calls we may go unfrightened. If he bids us come to him across the waters, that unfrightened we may go. And if he bids us climb the hill, may we not notice that it is a hill, mindful only of the happiness of his company. He made us for himself, that we should travel with him and see him at his last in his unveiled beauty in the abiding city, where he is light and happiness and endless home.

BEDE JARRETT

MY PRAYER STARTER: Sovereign Lord, give me the faith to leap out of my boat when You call me, even when the waters underneath are murky. I know that You will lead me safely across.

When your spirit is quieted by God, your thoughts fixed on His will for you, and your heart steadily trusting Him, there is nothing God cannot do through you. For with such quietness, focus, and determination, you'll be able to *see* what God wants you to do. And you'll perform that task without being self-conscious or overexcited. Without haste, yet without delay. Without fear of what others may say and without worry about results. You'll be working God's will out in His way, with calmness, faith, and love. And in the end, you'll discover that your only true pathway to unsurpassed peace is living and doing God's will.

> *Praise ye the LORD. Blessed is the man that feareth the LORD, that delighteth greatly in his commandments. His seed shall be mighty upon earth: the generation of the upright shall be blessed. . . . His heart is fixed, trusting in the LORD. His heart is established, he shall not be afraid.*
>
> PSALM 112:1–2, 7–8

Dear Lord, quiet my spirit and fix my thoughts on thy will, that I may see what thou wouldst have done, and contemplate its doing without self-consciousness or inner excitement, without haste and without delay, without fear of other people's judgments or anxiety about success, knowing only that it is thy will and therefore must be done quietly, faithfully and lovingly, for in thy will alone is our peace.
GEORGE APPLETON

MY PRAYER STARTER: Heavenly Father, teach me patience and sharpen my spiritual listening skills. Quiet my mind, tuning out the cacophony around me and preparing my ears for Your voice.

It's difficult for a man to feel safe in this tumultuous world. But there's an otherworldly place of protection for you in God. When you commit your will to Him, when you put all of yourself—mind, body, spirit, and soul—into His hands, you're safe forever. No one will ever be able to pluck you from His grip. It's His foolproof protection plan!

> *In thee, O LORD, do I put my trust. . . . For thou art my rock*
> *and my fortress; therefore for thy name's sake lead me, and guide*
> *me. . . . For thou art my strength. Into thine hand I commit*
> *my spirit: thou hast redeemed me, O LORD God of truth. . . .*
> *O love the LORD. . .for the LORD preserveth the faithful.*

PSALM 31:1, 3–5, 23

O my dear Heavenly Father, God and Father of my Lord Jesus Christ, God of all consolation, I give Thee thanks that Thou hast revealed to me Thy dear Son, Jesus Christ, in Whom I have lived and glorified. I pray Thee, my Lord Jesus Christ, to take my poor soul under Thy protection. O my dear Heavenly Father, though I may be obliged to quit this body and quit this life, I am sure I shall dwell forever with Thee, and no one shall pluck me out of Thy hands. Father, into Thy hands I commit my spirit, for Thou hast redeemed me, O Lord God of Truth. Amen.

MARTIN LUTHER

MY PRAYER STARTER: All-powerful God, thank You for saving me from sin and hopelessness. I know I'm safe in Your hands now and forevermore.

When you have a real desire to please God instead of people, you'll never get lost. For the God you trust, the One you live to please above all, will give you continual guidance. In fact, He and His light will be with you, navigating you even through the thickest of shadows.

> *For do I now persuade men, or God? or do I seek to please men?*
> *for if I yet pleased men, I should not be the servant of Christ.*
> GALATIANS 1:10

My Lord God, I have no idea where I am going. I do not see the road ahead of me. I cannot know for certain where it will end. Nor do I really know myself, and the fact that I think that I am following your will does not mean that I am actually doing so. But I believe that the desire to please you does in fact please you. And I hope I have that desire in all that I am doing. I hope that I will never do anything apart from that desire. And I know that if I do this you will lead me by the right road, though I may know nothing about it. Therefore will I trust you always, though I may seem to be lost and in the shadow of death. I will not fear, for you are ever with me, and you will never leave me to face my perils alone.
THOMAS MERTON

MY PRAYER STARTER: Lord, Captain of my ship, align my course with the compass of Your Word. Whenever my mind starts to turn aside, take the wheel and steer it back toward You.

Whatever you want, Jesus has the supply. Whatever your question, Jesus is the answer. You only need to do two things: (1) *trust* in His goodness and mercy, and (2) *go* to Him and ask. If you're sick, go to Jesus, your Great Physician. If you're thirsty, go to Jesus, your Water. If you're hungry, go to Jesus, your Bread. If you're needy, go to Jesus, the King of heaven. It doesn't stop there: Jesus is also your Light, Door, Shepherd, Friend, Way, Truth, Life, and Vine.

Know that Jesus will never fail you. He is all you need no matter what your need. Expect that He will go far beyond your simple requests because He is the God of abundance. He gives till you're overflowing with supply!

Trust Jesus. He's only a prayer away.

But whosoever drinketh of the water that I shall give him shall never thirst; but the water that I shall give him shall be in him a well of water springing up into everlasting life. . . . I am the living bread which came down from heaven: if any man eat of this bread, he shall live for ever.

JOHN 4:14; 6:51

Trusting in your goodness
and great mercy, Lord, I come;
sick—I come to my Saviour;
hungry and thirsty—to the well of Life;
needy—to the King of Heaven.
THOMAS À KEMPIS

MY PRAYER STARTER: Jesus, I stand amazed by the depths of Your provision. You've given me hope for eternal life, and You've filled this life with blessings and contentment. Thank You.

God is love. And you are His child. Therefore, loving Him—from the depths of your heart and with all your being, soul, and mind—is the greatest act you can perform.

Do that today. Give the God of love all your love. Give Him your soul, living only through Him. Give Him your will, loving only for Him. God is your Source of life and breath, your Cause. When you put Him first on your list, when you make loving Him your aim, you'll find the rest you crave and the peace you desire. As He becomes your all in all, you'll find that's all you need.

> *Jesus said unto him, Thou shalt love the Lord thy God*
> *with all thy heart, and with all thy soul, and with all*
> *thy mind. This is the first and great commandment.*
> MATTHEW 22:37–38

My soul is yours,
and must live only through you.
My will is yours,
and must love only for you.
I must love you as my first cause,
since I am from you.
I must love you as my goal and rest,
since I am for you.
I must love you more than my own being,
since my being comes from you.
I must love you more than myself,
since I am all yours and all in you. Amen.
SAINT FRANCIS DE SALES

MY PRAYER STARTER: God, You created me with the capacity to love. Mold my heart so that all that love flows naturally toward You—with no exceptions.

Sometimes, waiting can be hard. Remember Sarah? God promised she'd have a son by Abraham. But it had yet to happen. Time was ticking, and she wasn't getting any younger. So Sarah came up with a plan, one that had disastrous results. Eventually, in accordance with God's timing, Sarah had a son named Isaac—yet the repercussions of her impatience remained.

Years later, Isaac fathered Jacob, who waited seven years to get his wife Rachel. Yet those years "seemed unto him but a few days, for the love he had to her" (Genesis 29:20).

Here's the point: when you hope for what you don't yet see, God will give you the hope and patience you need to wait for it. And the end will be glorious! But when you give up hope, when you lose your patience and take things into your own hands, disaster awaits.

Today, ask God to remove your impatience. To fill you with hope. To help you wait for all the good He's already planned for you!

> *For we are saved by hope: but hope that is seen is not hope: for*
> *what a man seeth, why doth he yet hope for? But if we hope*
> *for that we see not, then do we with patience wait for it.*

ROMANS 8:24–25

Take from us, O God, all tediousness of spirit, all impatience and unquietness. Let us possess ourselves in patience: through Jesus Christ our Lord.
JEREMY TAYLOR

MY PRAYER STARTER: Everlasting Lord, a million years is a second in Your eyes. Help me escape my narrow, impatient attitude and wait expectantly for the fulfillment of Your promises.

Too down to rise up? Pray to God for one word. He'll speak. You'll be comforted.

> *Save me, O God; for the waters are come in unto my soul. . . . I am come into deep waters, where the floods overflow me. I am weary of my crying. . . . I am poor and sorrowful: let thy salvation, O God, set me up on high. I will praise the name of God with a song.*
> PSALM 69:1–3, 29–30

Gracious and most merciful God! thou seest how my heart is filled with sorrow—a stone which I cannot throw off, a load of affliction too heavy to be borne, presses me to the earth—Therefore, I come to thee, almighty God! I pour out my heart into thy bosom, for those art my refuge and my salvation. I cast my troubles from myself upon thee, and beseech thee to save and to assist me. The little bark, driven by fearful winds and waves, is held by the anchor; and so my soul clings to thee, thou living and almighty God. The timid roe [doe] pursued in the chase hastens to the mountains for deliverance, and I lift my eyes to thee, my Rock, my Rescuer, and mighty Defender! I will not despair, for I know that thou art an almighty God—thou canst help me. O send deliverance now, and I am helped; speak but a single word, and my help has come.
JOHANN FRIEDRICH STARCK

MY PRAYER STARTER: God of comfort, Your joy overpowers every sorrow I experience. Thank You for speaking to me, lifting me up from the flood of hopelessness.

The disciple Philip is a great example of obedience—not just to Jesus and God but to the Holy Spirit. After Jesus' resurrection and the Holy Spirit's arrival, an angel of God told Philip to head in a certain direction. He did, then discovered a eunuch there, reading God's Word. When the Spirit told Philip to join the man, he *ran* to obey. Talk about obedience! Later, when Philip was baptizing the eunuch, "the Spirit of the Lord caught away Philip" (Acts 8:39).

Today, realize the power of obedience and pray for God to give you understanding so that you will *run* to obey the Spirit's promptings. You'll find yourself swept away, growing ever closer to God!

> *And the angel of the Lord spake unto Philip, saying, Arise, and go toward the south unto the way that goeth down from Jerusalem unto Gaza, which is desert. And he arose and went: and, behold, a man of Ethiopia, an eunuch. . .[who] had come to Jerusalem for to worship, was returning, and sitting in his chariot read Esaias the prophet. Then the Spirit said unto Philip, Go near, and join thyself to this chariot. And Philip ran thither to him.*

ACTS 8:26–30

Make us of quick understanding and tender conscience, O Lord; that understanding, we may obey every word of thine this day, and discerning, may follow every suggestion of thine indwelling Spirit. Speak, Lord, for thy servant heareth, through Jesus Christ our Lord. Amen.

CHRISTINA ROSSETTI

MY PRAYER STARTER: Lord God, I don't want my obedience to You to feel routine or forced. Give me a sense of urgency that compels me in whatever direction You tell me to go.

The world's problems can seem so huge, so complex. It's difficult to get our minds around them, much less our hands. This is when we need to remember we have a God so much bigger than any troubles this world can present!

Today, ask God to help you love Him and others, even your enemies, and to be with you as you come and go, rise up and lie down, until His new day dawns.

> *The LORD is thy keeper: the LORD is thy shade upon thy right hand. The sun shall not smite thee by day, nor the moon by night. The LORD shall preserve thee from all evil: he shall preserve thy soul. The LORD shall preserve thy going out and thy coming in from this time forth, and even for evermore.*
>
> PSALM 121:5–8

God, we thank you for the inspiration of Jesus. Grant that we will love you with all our hearts, souls, and minds, and love our neighbors as we love ourselves, even our enemy neighbors. And we ask you, God, in these days of emotional tension, when the problems of the world are gigantic in extent and chaotic in detail, to be with us in our going out and our coming in, in our rising up and in our lying down, in our moments of joy and in our moments of sorrow, until the day when there shall be no sunset and no dawn. Amen.
MARTIN LUTHER KING JR.

MY PRAYER STARTER: Powerful Father, I don't know how to deal with tomorrow's uncertainties—but I know that You already have. Thank You for giving me a reason to relax.

You want to spend time in God's presence. But as you begin seeking a blessed communion with Him, thoughts about your missteps and faults begin to creep in. Yet you know God is there, ready to lead, advise, and whisper in your ear.

Today, ask God to renew you as you sense Him. Then sit at His feet, having chosen the better part, with no thought of distraction.

Mary. . .sat at Jesus' feet, and heard his word. . . . And
Jesus. . .said. . .One thing is needful: and Mary hath chosen
that good part, which shall not be taken away from her.
LUKE 10:39, 41–42

Source of all good! Day by day are Your blessings renewed to us, and again we come with thankful hearts to seek the sense of Your presence. O that we could be reborn like the morning. For even as we seek to commune with You, shadows from our past dim the joy of our aspiration. We remember our thoughtless lives, our impatient tempers, our selfish aims; and yet we know that You have neither made us blind nor left us without the guidance of Your still, small voice speaking in our inmost conscience, and Your open word, appealing to us to choose the better part. Take us now to serve You in newness of spirit, and sweep away every dust of care, every trace of unjustified fear, and every trace of an uncharitable mind.
JAMES MARTINEAU

MY PRAYER STARTER: God, Fountain of wisdom, I want to sit at Your feet uninterrupted by pestering doubts and fears. Make my mind a clean slate, ready to receive Your instruction.

Think back to all the blessings you've received from God this week. How events unfolded better than you had imagined. How your fears turned to naught. How you endured what you didn't think you had the strength for. How you had food, shelter, and clothing.

Thank God today for His never-ending, unfailing blessings.

> *Be strong and of good courage, and do it: fear not, nor*
> *be dismayed: for the LORD God, even my God, will be*
> *with thee; he will not fail thee, nor forsake thee.*
>
> 1 CHRONICLES 28:20

Our Father. . .We thank You for all Your mercies. Blessings have come to us in abundant measure. The evils we dreaded when the week began, have not come. The clouds we thought we saw gathering, and which we feared would bring darkness and storm—were either blown away from our sky, or coming, brought only gentle rains which have blessed our fields, leaving them more fertile. The labors we feared would be too great for our strength, have been endured, and we have had strength for them as they came. We thank You, too, for all the blessings of the week, which came to us in so many ways—through Your providences, through our friends, through our work. We have had bread to eat, and clothing to wear. We have had health and life's comforts. You have not once failed us! Amen.

J. R. MILLER

MY PRAYER STARTER: Lord of provision, the future seems daunting until it finally arrives. Thank You for always proving my worries wrong and giving me strength when the trial comes.

You may have issues. . .but with faith, God can make you whole!

The Gospels describe a woman who had an issue of blood (Matthew 9:20–22; Mark 5:25–34; Luke 8:43–48). For twelve years she had been hemorrhaging. She'd seen numerous doctors, but none could cure her. Then she heard Jesus was coming. Although unclean, she crept through a crowd and managed to touch the hem of Jesus' robe. She said to herself, "If I can only touch His robe, I will be made whole." And she was!

The same thing that happened to this woman can happen to a man like you. Take your unresolved issues that have been hounding you for years. Tell yourself that contact with Jesus can make you complete. Reach out to Him. Touch Him. His power will go out from Him and make you whole! Will yourself to believe, and you will believe!

And, behold, a woman, which was diseased with an issue of blood twelve years, came behind him, and touched the hem of his garment. For she said within herself, If I may but touch his garment, I shall be whole. But Jesus turned him about, and when he saw her, he said, Daughter, be of good comfort; thy faith hath made thee whole. And the woman was made whole from that hour.

MATTHEW 9:20–22

Lord, I will believe; I do believe.
HANNAH WHITALL SMITH

MY PRAYER STARTER: Divine Healer, I sometimes feel as if my own soul is bleeding out the joy I need. Cauterize the wound and inject me with the remedy of Your presence.

You're a citizen of God's heavenly kingdom. You need not fear death for yourself or your loved ones. Instead, you can have peace and hope in believing God is good. He has new mercies and compassion for you every morning. He is forever faithful—in life and in death. Strengthen your heart with this belief today.

This I recall to my mind, therefore have I hope. It is of the LORD's mercies that we are not consumed, because his compassions fail not. They are new every morning: great is thy faithfulness. The LORD is my portion, saith my soul; therefore will I hope in him.
LAMENTATIONS 3:21–24

Father in heaven, draw our hearts to you, that our hearts may be where our treasures ought to be, that our minds and thoughts may look to your kingdom, whose citizens we are. Thus, when you shall call us hence, our departure may not be a painful separation from this world, but a joyous meeting with you. Perhaps a long road still lies before us. Yet sometimes our strength is taken from us, a faintness overcomes us, like a mist before our eyes, so that we are in darkness of the night; restless desires stir within us, impatient, wild longings, and the heart groans in anxious anticipation of what is to come: O Lord our God, do teach us then, and strengthen in our hearts the conviction that in life as in death we belong to you.
SØREN KIERKEGAARD

MY PRAYER STARTER: Living God, thank You for taking the sting out of death. Help me to see it not as a separation but as a bridge to Your eternal kingdom.

Because Jesus died for you, you look "right" in God's eyes—you're a member of His kingdom! But it doesn't end there. He's also given you the Holy Spirit and all the peace, joy, and hope found in Him!

So when you feel weak, fearful, and downcast, lift your soul up to God. Ask the Holy Spirit for the strength to face today's work. Ask for the courage to step upon the road God has laid before you. Ask the Spirit for the optimism to bear your load. And ask Him to give you constant inner joy, not just through the pleasant parts of life but through the tough ones as well.

> *For the kingdom of God is not meat and drink; but righteousness,*
> *and peace, and joy in the Holy Ghost. . . . Let us therefore*
> *follow after the things which make for peace, and things*
> *wherewith one may edify another. . . . Now the God of hope*
> *fill you with all joy and peace in believing, that ye may*
> *abound in hope, through the power of the Holy Ghost.*
> ROMANS 14:17, 19; 15:13

These are the gifts I ask
Of Thee, Spirit serene;
Strength for the daily task,
Courage to face the road,
Good cheer to help me bear the traveler's load;
And for the hours that come between,
An inward joy in all things heard and seen.
HENRY VAN DYKE

MY PRAYER STARTER: Father, thank You for giving me Your righteousness, even when I don't deserve it. When my path is rugged, remind me of this truth and grant me grace to persevere.

According to Jewish tradition, entering a Gentile's house would ceremonially defile a Jew. That's why the centurion didn't feel worthy of Jesus coming home with him.

At times, you may feel the same way, as if your soul is unworthy of inviting Jesus in. Yet that's exactly where He wants to be!

Today, pray for Jesus to enter your soul, no matter how unworthy you deem it. Boldly go to Him—and He will lovingly come to you.

> *There came unto him [Jesus] a centurion, beseeching him, and saying, Lord, my servant lieth at home sick. . . . And Jesus saith unto him, I will come and heal him. The centurion answered and said, Lord, I am not worthy that thou shouldest come under my roof: but speak the word only, and my servant shall be healed.*
>
> MATTHEW 8:5–8

I am not worthy, Master and Lord, that You should come beneath the roof of my soul; yet since in Your love towards all, You wish to dwell in me, in boldness I come. Open the gates which You alone have made and enlighten my darkened reasoning. I believe that You will do this; for You did not send away the harlot who came to You with tears. You did not cast out the repenting tax-collector, nor reject the thief who acknowledged Your kingdom. But You counted all of these as members of Your band of friends. You are blessed for evermore.
JOHN CHRYSOSTOM

MY PRAYER STARTER: Righteous Lord, thank You for coming in and cleaning out my soul, even when it is defiled with sin. May I continue allowing You to do so until I meet You face-to-face.

God created everything that surrounds you. And He loves what He's created, calling it not just good but "very good" (Genesis 1:31). The things that God has made and that you are to care for (Genesis 1:28–30) are an extension of Him who "is love" (1 John 4:8).

Look around you. Take in the wonder of God's plants, animals, sand, sky, and air. Praise Him for His gift of things visible *and* invisible. And as you love your Creator, love His creation.

> *The earth is full of the goodness of the LORD. By the word of*
> *the LORD were the heavens made; and all the host of them by*
> *the breath of his mouth. He gathereth the waters of the sea*
> *together as an heap: he layeth up the depth in storehouses.*
> PSALM 33:5–7

Lord, may we love all your creation, all the earth and every grain
of sand in it. May we love every leaf, every ray of your light.
May we love the animals: you have given them the
rudiments of thought and joy untroubled. Let us not
trouble it; let us not harass them, let us not deprive them
of their happiness, let us not work against your intent.
For we acknowledge unto you that all is like an ocean, all is flowing
and bending, and that to withhold any measure of love from anything
in your universe is to withhold that same measure from you.
FYODOR DOSTOEVSKY, *adapted from a passage in The Brothers Karamazov*

MY PRAYER STARTER: Awe-inspiring Creator, whenever I become fixated on my problems, lift my eyes toward the universe You created. Fill me with wonder at the vastness of Your artwork.

No matter where you are—spiritually, physically, mentally, emotionally, or physically—God hears your cry. When you go to Him, He will give you His peace and heal you. He will relieve your stress, calm your fears, and take you out of yourself and into Him.

Today, pray and listen for God's deep voice that assures you Jesus lives and all is well.

Peace, peace to him that is far off, and to him that is near, saith the LORD; and I will heal him.

ISAIAH 57:19

Ever Blessed God, whose word is, "Peace, peace to him that is far off and to him that is near," fulfil Thy promise to this Thy servant for whom we pray. Rescue him from the misery of groundless fears and restless anxieties. Take him more and more out of himself, that duty may be no longer a drudgery but a delight. Lead him into the secret of Thy peace which quiets every misgiving and fills the heart with joy and confidence. Save him from the shame and emptiness of a hurried life. Grant him to possess his soul in patience. Amid the storms and stress of life, let him hear a deeper voice assuring him that Thou livest and that all is well. Strengthen him to do his daily work in quietness and confidence, fearing no tomorrow, nor the evil that it brings, for Thou art with him. And this we ask for Jesus Christ's sake. Amen.

SAMUEL MCCOMB

MY PRAYER STARTER: God, hear me when I'm drowning in fear. Reassure me of my eternal destiny with You.

Although *faith* and *hope* are separate concepts, they're linked. *Faith* is what you believe in now. *Hope* is your confidence in the future, your expectation of something you desire. Hebrews 11:1 says, "Now faith is the substance of things hoped for, the evidence of things not seen." In other words, faith is being certain you'll receive what you hope for, even if you don't see it in the present.

Yet sometimes, we need to shore up our faith, which in turn lifts our hope.

When you need a faith boost, go to Jesus with today's classic prayer. Ask Him to remind you that *all* things are possible for those who believe.

And one of the multitude answered and said, Master, I have brought unto thee my son, which hath a dumb spirit. . . . And ofttimes it hath cast him into the fire, and into the waters, to destroy him: but if thou canst do any thing, have compassion on us, and help us. Jesus said unto him, If thou canst believe, all things are possible to him that believeth. And straightway the father of the child cried out, and said with tears, Lord, I believe; help thou mine unbelief.

MARK 9:17, 22–24

Lord, perfect for me what is lacking in Thy gifts; of faith, help Thou mine unbelief; of hope, establish my trembling hope; of love, kindle its smoking flax.

LANCELOT ANDREWES

MY PRAYER STARTER: Lord, give me the faith to keep Your promises in my mind's eye, even when they seem impossible. May my hope be more than a vain wish—may it be a solid trust in You.

Think back on all the blessings you've received from God. Consider those you're enjoying in this moment. Imagine all the good He has in store for you tomorrow.

Although you can never repay God for all He's done, you can praise Him for all your blessings today—and every day.

> *What shall I render unto the LORD for all his benefits toward me? . . . I will offer to thee the sacrifice of thanksgiving, and will call upon the name of the LORD. . . . Praise ye the LORD.*
>
> PSALM 116:12, 17, 19

O Lord, my God, for life and reason, nurture, preservation,
guidance, education; for Thy gifts of grace and nature, for
Thy calling, recalling, manifold recalling me again and again,
for Thy forbearance, long-suffering, and long long-suffering
toward me, even until now; for all from whom I have received
any good or help; for the use of Thy present good things; for
Thy promise, and my hope, of good things to come.
For all these things and for all other, which I know, which I
know not, manifest or secret, remembered or forgotten by me,
I praise Thee, I bless Thee, I give Thee thanks; and I will praise,
and bless, and give Thee thanks all the days of my life.
What shall I render unto the Lord for all His benefits to me? Thou
art worthy, O Lord, to receive glory, and honor, and power. Amen.
LANCELOT ANDREWES

MY PRAYER STARTER: Gracious Father, I am speechless when I consider Your blessings. Life, salvation, health, family, friends, joy, and peace—all come from You. Thank You.

God is your Wellspring of life, your Fountain of joy. He's the source of your ultimate satisfaction. That's why you can have deep, abiding joy no matter where your path leads. Use God, the Light of your spirit and body, to find your way to Him. Know that at the end of your days, Jesus will be standing at the open gate, ready to usher you in. Oh what joy!

> *O God! . . .the children of men put their trust under the shadow of thy wings. They shall be abundantly satisfied with the fatness of thy house; and thou shalt make them drink of the river of thy pleasures. For with thee is the fountain of life: in thy light shall we see light.*
>
> PSALM 36:7–9

O God, Who has commanded that no man should be idle, give us grace to employ all our talents and faculties in the service appointed for us; that, whatsoever our hand findeth to do, we may do it with all our might. Cheerfully may we go in the road which Thou has marked out, not desiring too earnestly that it should be either more smooth or wise; but daily seeking our way by Thy light, may we trust ourselves and the issue of our journey to Thee, the Fountain of Joy, and sing songs of praise as we go along. Then, O Lord, receive us at the gate of life which Thou has opened for us in Christ Jesus. Amen.
JAMES MARTINEAU

MY PRAYER STARTER: God, Source of all blessings, may every minor joy I feel bring my soul back to You. May I be ever on the move, searching for You in every situation.

Something extraordinary happens when you commune with Father God. He's not just your Lord and Master but your Daddy—your *Abba*. In Him you experience an unfathomable love enveloping you, infusing you with your supernatural Protector's fiery energy and banishing every fear.

Today, use the power of the classic prayer below to experience your Abba like never before.

> *For as many as are led by the Spirit of God, they are the sons*
> *of God. . . . Ye have received the Spirit of adoption, whereby*
> *we cry, Abba, Father. The Spirit itself beareth witness with*
> *our spirit, that we are the children of God: and if children,*
> *then heirs; heirs of God, and joint-heirs with Christ.*
> ROMANS 8:14–17

Eternal God, lead us into the blessedness of the mystery of communion with Thee. Bow our spirits in deepest reverence before Thee, yet uplift us into a sense of kinship. Send the spirit of Thy Son into our hearts, crying "Abba, Father," that all unworthy fear may be banished by the gladness of Thy perfect love. Thy love is like the luminous heaven, receiving only to purify the foulest breath of earth. Thy gentleness is like the sun, seeking to cheer and warm the chilled hearts of men. Touch us, O our Father, with a feeling of Thy great realities, for though our thought about Thee is better than our words, our experience of Thee is better than our thought.
SAMUEL MCCOMB

MY PRAYER STARTER: Abba Father, send the vigorous power of Your love into this man's heart. Without You, I am merely a cold, lifeless shell—I need Your Spirit to constantly awaken me.

Truly believing God is your Protector drastically changes your perspective. At least it did for two of the twelve men sent to spy out the Promised Land.

Ten said that the land of Canaan ate up its inhabitants and that giants lived there: "And we were in our own sight as grasshoppers, and so we were in their sight" (Numbers 13:33). But Joshua and Caleb said the land was good and, because God was with them, ripe for conquering.

Today, pray to God your Protector. He'll change your perspective.

> *And Joshua the son of Nun, and Caleb the son of Jephunneh. . .spake unto. . .Israel, saying, The land, which we passed through to search it, is an exceeding good land. If the LORD delight in us, then he will bring us into this land, and give it us; a land which floweth with milk and honey. Only rebel not ye against the LORD, neither fear ye the people of the land; for they are bread for us: their defence is departed from them, and the LORD is with us: fear them not.*

NUMBERS 14:6–9

O Lord, give us grace, I pray Thee, so to realize Thine Almighty succor pledged to us, Thy protecting Presence surrounding us, Thine all-seeing eye fixed upon us, that we may cease to tremble at man's anger, or shrink from man's ridicule, but may with a good courage perform the work Thou givest us to do.
CHRISTINA ROSSETTI

MY PRAYER STARTER: Lord, reveal Your power to me, just as You did for Joshua and Caleb. May I never stop reaching for Your promised spiritual blessings.

When you truly love someone, you want to do anything for that person, even if it means giving all you have. With that person in your life, nothing's too hard to bear.

Similarly, when you truly love and are loved by God—when you're filled with His love, light, and life—there's no task you cannot perform for Him, no situation unbearable.

Imagine sitting with God, basking in His adoration. He firmly supports you with His left hand and embraces you with His right. He's yours and you're His. Oh such love! There's no greater power than that mutual love between you and your Creator.

Today, pray for that love. Then, "rise up. . .and come away" (Song of Solomon 2:10), able to do all you're asked.

> *I sat down under his shadow with great delight, and his*
> *fruit was sweet to my taste. . . . His banner over me was*
> *love. . . . His left hand is under my head, and his right hand*
> *doth embrace me. . . . My beloved is mine, and I am his.*
> SONG OF SOLOMON 2:3–4, 6, 16

Fill us, we pray, Lord, with your light and life that we may
show forth your wondrous glory. Grant that your love may so
fill our lives that we may count nothing too small to do for you,
nothing too much to give and nothing too hard to bear.
SAINT IGNATIUS OF LOYOLA

MY PRAYER STARTER: God, Your love for me never weakens, despite my imperfections. I love You in return, for You are holy and worthy of all my adoration.

Only by fully trusting God can you give yourself—body, spirit, soul, and heart—completely over to Him. When you abandon yourself to God and His will, He will give you all the strength you need to carry it out.

Today, be as Jesus, the One in whose footsteps you are to follow. Kneel down, pray, and allow the Father to work His will through you, raising you again in strength.

And he was withdrawn from them about a stone's cast, and kneeled down, and prayed, saying, Father, if thou be willing, remove this cup from me: nevertheless not my will, but thine, be done. And there appeared an angel unto him from heaven, strengthening him.

LUKE 22:41–43

Father,
I abandon myself into your hands;
do with me what you will.
Whatever you may do, I thank you:
I am ready for all, I accept all. . . .
Into your hands I commend my soul:
I offer it to you with all the love of my heart,
for I love you, Lord, and so need to give myself,
to surrender myself into your hands without reserve,
and with boundless confidence,
for you are my Father.
CHARLES DE FOUCAULD

MY PRAYER STARTER: Father, just as Jesus surrendered His destiny to You, let me surrender mine. Even if the road ahead is streaked with pain, I know You will bring me through.

Forgiving others can be difficult, especially if they've grievously wounded you. Yet if you don't forgive them, you block God's forgiveness to you (Matthew 6:14–15). Also, by clenching your fists around your bitterness and resentment, you cannot open your hands to the blessings God wants to give!

Today, think about any unforgiveness, bitterness, or resentment you may have amassed in your heart. Turn it over to God and ask Him to help you handle what you cannot.

> *Dearly beloved, avenge not yourselves, but rather give place unto wrath: for it is written, Vengeance is mine; I will repay, saith the Lord. Therefore if thine enemy hunger, feed him; if he thirst, give him drink: for in so doing thou shalt heap coals of fire on his head. Be not overcome of evil, but overcome evil with good.*
>
> ROMANS 12:19–21

Lord, You have plainly told me that all vengeance is thine, not my business at all. You have said that I must forgive. I am willing to, but I've tried over and over, and the resentments keep surging back. Now I will this bitterness over to You. Here—I hold it out to You in my open hand. I promise only that I will not again close my fist and reclaim the resentment. Now I ask You to take it and handle these emotions that I cannot handle.

CATHERINE MARSHALL

MY PRAYER STARTER: God, I sometimes feel angry when others wrong me. Help me to seek reconciliation and not revenge, just like You did when You forgave me.

God grants you so much mercy, grace, and blessings. He's constantly thinking of you, caring for you.

With those thoughts in mind, ask God to broaden your heart so that you can understand His will and walk in the path He's designed for you. All to His glory and praise.

> *I will run the way of thy commandments, when thou*
> *shalt enlarge my heart. . . . Make me to go in the path*
> *of thy commandments; for therein do I delight.*
>
> PSALM 119:32, 35

O most merciful and gracious God, Thou Fountain of all mercy and blessing, Thou hast opened the hand of Thy mercy to fill me with blessings, and the sweet effects of Thy loving-kindness. Thou feedest us like a shepherd. . . . Thou lovest us as a friend, and thinkest on us perpetually, as a careful mother on her helpless babe, and art exceeding merciful to all that fear Thee. . . . As Thou hast spread Thy hand upon me for a covering, so also enlarge my heart with thankfulness. . .and let Thy gracious favors and loving-kindness endure for ever and ever upon Thy servant. . .and let Thy grace so strengthen my purposes that I may sin no more. . .but. . .walk in the paths of Thy commandments; that I, living here to the glory of Thy name, may at last enter into the glory of my Lord, to spend a whole eternity in giving praise to Thy ever glorious name. Amen.

JEREMY TAYLOR

MY PRAYER STARTER: Heavenly Father, I sometimes feel so small compared to the vastness of Your glory. I'm bewildered and amazed by the fact that You still care deeply for me. Thank You.

Three times Balaam's donkey saw God's angry angel standing in her master's way. The first time, she silently turned away into a field. The second time, "she thrust herself unto the wall, and crushed Balaam's foot against the wall" (Numbers 22:25). The third time, "she fell down under Balaam" (Numbers 22:27)!

May you have the patience of a donkey, remaining silent when slandered, unfed, forgotten, and ill-used. As did Jesus.

Then the LORD opened the eyes of Balaam, and he saw the angel of the LORD standing in the way, and his sword drawn in his hand: and he bowed down his head, and fell flat on his face. And the angel of the LORD said unto him, Wherefore hast thou smitten thine ass these three times? behold, I went out to withstand thee, because thy way is perverse before me: and the ass saw me, and turned from me these three times: unless she had turned from me, surely now also I had slain thee, and saved her alive.

NUMBERS 22:31–33

Every time I do not behave like a donkey, it is the worse for me. How does a donkey behave? If it is slandered, it keeps silent; if it is not fed, it keeps silent; if it is forgotten, it keeps silent; it never complains, however much it is beaten or ill-used, because it has a donkey's patience. That is how the servant of God must be. I stand before you, Lord, like a donkey.

SAINT PETER CLAVER

MY PRAYER STARTER: Loving Savior, I've tested Your patience many times, yet You still forgive and bless me. Let me have this attitude as well so that I can show Your grace to others.

Jesus. Oh what love He showered upon you, laying down His life to save yours! Enduring beatings, mocking, rejection so you could be reunited with God.

Today, allow Jesus to fill you with His infinite love. Let it infuse you so that you can see everything through the light of His compassion and extend His undying love to others.

Hereby perceive we the love of God, because he laid down his life for us: and we ought to lay down our lives for the brethren. But whoso hath this world's good, and seeth his brother have need, and shutteth up his bowels of compassion from him, how dwelleth the love of God in him? My little children, let us not love in word, neither in tongue; but in deed and in truth.

1 JOHN 3:16–18

Good Jesus, Fountain of Love,
Fill us with thy love.
Absorb us into thy love;
Compass us with thy love,
That we may see all things in the light of thy love. . . .
Win through thy love others for thy love,
Be kindled day by day with a new glow of thy love,
Until we be fitted to enter into thine everlasting love,
To adore thy love and love to adore thee, our God and all.
Even so come, O Lord Jesus.
EDWARD B. PUSEY

MY PRAYER STARTER: Lord, the love You showed while suffering for me on the cross is unmatched. Let me be a man who lives in constant appreciation, eager to spread Your love to others.

When you began believing in Jesus, you took on a new life. You were transformed within to speak, think, and act like Jesus. Now you need to act in an outward way that matches your new identity within! That means speaking God's words, thinking God's thoughts, and doing whatever God would have you do!

There's only one way to do all that: you must have God always with you, giving you the strength, energy, love, thoughts, and words to behave like Jesus.

Before praying today's prayers, reflect upon Jesus' life. Take note of His character—giving, loving, forgiving, blessing, healing, watching, waiting, and serving. Then ask God to stick with you so that you can find the willpower to put on the wardrobe tailored by Jesus.

Put off all these; anger, wrath, malice, blasphemy, filthy communication out of your mouth. Lie not one to another, seeing that ye have put off the old man with his deeds; and have put on the new man, which is renewed in knowledge after the image of him that created him.

COLOSSIANS 3:8–10

O God, stay with me; let no word cross my lips that is not your word, no thoughts enter my mind that are not your thoughts, no deed ever be done or entertained by me that is not your deed.
MALCOLM MUGGERIDGE

MY PRAYER STARTER: Perfect Creator, my soul is still under construction—and You have the blueprints. Let me be receptive to every change You want to make.

Every man has hidden faults or sins, ones he either doesn't remember or has committed unknowingly. Yet just as nothing can hide from the sun's heat, so nothing can hide from God's illuminating light (Psalm 19:6). God calls you to walk in that light (1 John 1:7). But to do so, you must admit you've erred, knowingly and unknowingly.

Today, confess your errors to God and ask for His light to illuminate them, knowing Jesus will forgive and cleanse you (1 John 1:9) and make you right with God again.

> *Who can understand his errors? cleanse thou me from secret*
> *faults. Keep back thy servant also from presumptuous sins; let*
> *them not have dominion over me: then shall I be upright, and*
> *I shall be innocent from the great transgression. Let the words*
> *of my mouth, and the meditation of my heart, be acceptable*
> *in thy sight, O LORD, my strength, and my redeemer.*
>
> PSALM 19:12–14

Forgive me my sins, O Lord—the sins of my present and the sins of my past, the sins of my soul and the sins of my body, the sins which I have done to please myself and the sins which I have done to please others. Forgive me my casual sins and my deliberate sins and those which I have laboured so to hide that I have hidden them even from myself. Forgive me them, O Lord, forgive them all; for Jesus Christ's sake.

THOMAS WILSON

MY PRAYER STARTER: God, I'm sorry for all the times I've ignored or unintentionally broken Your laws. Please forgive me and give me the strength to improve.

Sometimes, you may feel as if you're walking in the dark. But with God, you have light because "in him is no darkness at all" (1 John 1:5). Even when you feel lonely, your God will never leave or forsake you (Hebrews 13:5). If you're feeling restless, Jesus will give you peace (John 16:33). When you're bitter, God will teach you the joy of patience (James 5:11). And although you may not understand God's ways, He knows yours (Proverbs 3:5–7).

Today, reaffirm God as the light, companion, peace, patience, and guide upon your life path. And walk in the power of that knowledge.

O the depth of the riches both of the wisdom and knowledge of God!
how unsearchable are his judgments, and his ways past finding
out! For who hath known the mind of the Lord? or who hath
been his counsellor? Or who hath first given to him, and it shall
be recompensed unto him again? For of him, and through him,
and to him, are all things: to whom be glory for ever. Amen.

ROMANS 11:33–36

In me there is darkness.
But with Thee there is light.
I am lonely, but Thou leavest me not.
I am restless, but with Thee there is peace.
In me there is bitterness, but with Thee there is patience.
Thy ways are past understanding, but Thou knowest the way for me.

DIETRICH BONHOEFFER

MY PRAYER STARTER: God, I am an imperfect man. Erase the smudges of darkness and bitterness in my soul and replace them with Your holiness and love.

The first four of the Ten Commandments concern your relationship to God: you shall have no other gods, not make a graven image, not curse using God's name, and keep the Sabbath (Exodus 20:3–11). The last five concern your relationships with others: you shall not murder, commit adultery, steal, lie, or covet (Exodus 20:13–17). Between those two categories is the commandment about honoring your parents (Exodus 20:12). And it's the only one with a promise: honor your folks that you may live long and prosper!

Both Jesus and Paul stress the importance of this command (Mark 7:1–13; Ephesians 6:1–3; 1 Timothy 5:4). May today's classic prayer empower you to obey this directive from God.

Honour thy father and thy mother, as the Lord thy God hath commanded thee; that thy days may be prolonged, and that it may go well with thee, in the land which the Lord thy God giveth thee.
DEUTERONOMY 5:16

O Lord God, whose will it is that, next to yourself, we should hold our parents in highest honour; it is not the least of our duties to beseech your goodness towards them. Preserve, I pray, my parents and home, in the love of your religion and in health of body and mind. Grant, that through me no sorrow may befall them; and finally, as they are kind to me, so may you be to them, O supreme Father of all.
ERASMUS

MY PRAYER STARTER: God, I know that family relations are vitally important in Your eyes. Help me be a loyal son, honoring and caring for my parents while I still have the chance.

Jesus wants you to come to Him as a little child. To be simple and helpless in His presence, trustingly depending upon Him alone. This means admitting that you have no resources of your own—nothing to recommend yourself to Him and no accomplishments to offer. Only then, as humble as a little one, can you truly see Jesus Christ and enter His kingdom.

Today, ask Jesus to give you the humbleness of a child as you come to Him in prayer. Ask Him to give you a childlike love for Him—the perfect love that will cast out any fear (1 John 4:18) that troubles you. Embrace the tranquility and love He gives you in return.

> *At the same time came the disciples unto Jesus, saying, Who is the greatest in the kingdom of heaven? And Jesus called a little child unto him, and set him in the midst of them, and said, Verily I say unto you, Except ye be converted, and become as little children, ye shall not enter into the kingdom of heaven. Whosoever therefore shall humble himself as this little child, the same is greatest in the kingdom of heaven. And whoso shall receive one such little child in my name receiveth me.*

MATTHEW 18:1–5

Most loving Lord, give me a childlike love of
Thee, which may cast out all fear. Amen.
EDWARD B. PUSEY

MY PRAYER STARTER: Father, as Your son, I want to completely rely on Your provision. Give me the faith to trust You for every need, and fill me with a wonder-struck admiration for You.

God's Word gives you comfort, strength, guidance, and wisdom (see verses below). It also gives light for your path (Psalm 119:105), joy (Psalm 119:111), refuge and protection (Psalm 119:114), delight (Psalm 119:143), and so much more!

Be sure to pray today's classic prayer before launching into God's Word. May its power help transform your mind into that of Jesus Christ's.

Strengthen thou me according unto thy word. . . . Give me understanding, and I shall keep thy law. . . . Make me to go in the path of thy commandments; for therein do I delight. . . . This is my comfort in my affliction: for thy word hath quickened me. . . . I thought on my ways, and turned my feet unto thy testimonies. . . . The entrance of thy words giveth light; it giveth understanding unto the simple.

PSALM 119:28, 34–35, 50, 59, 130

As we read Your word, may its lessons be made plain to us. Help us to receive its instruction into our hearts, so that our lives shall be controlled by it. As we pray, may Heaven's blessings be given to us:

comfort for our sorrow,
strength for our weakness,
guidance for our feet, and
wisdom for our ignorance.

As we seek to be a blessing to others—may we receive the mind that was in Christ Jesus. We ask all in Jesus' precious name. Amen.

J. R. MILLER

MY PRAYER STARTER: Eternal God, I praise You for giving us Your Word to study. As I read it, lead me with Your Spirit into the truth and comfort You want me to receive.

Sometimes, it's good to talk to yourself—especially to your heart through prayer.

In the verses below, the Hebrew word for "heart" is *lēb*. Figuratively, says *Strong's Concordance*, it's used "very widely for the feelings, the will and even the intellect; likewise for the *centre* of anything."

Speak to your heart with today's classic prayer, encouraging it to turn aside from all things and rest in God. Pray it from your core and find true rest in God's presence.

One thing have I desired of the LORD, that will I seek after; that I may dwell in the house of the LORD all the days of my life, to behold the beauty of the LORD, and to enquire in his temple. . . . When thou saidst, Seek ye my face; my heart said unto thee, Thy face, LORD, will I seek.

PSALM 27:4, 8

Come now, little one, turn aside for a while from your daily employment, escape for a moment from the tumult of your thoughts. Put aside your weighty cares, let your burdensome distractions wait, free yourself awhile for God and rest awhile in him. Enter the inner chamber of your soul, shut out everything except God and that which can help you in seeking him. And when you have shut the door, seek God. Now, my whole heart, say to God, "I seek your face, Lord, it is your face I seek."

SAINT ANSELM

MY PRAYER STARTER: God of peace, quiet my restless heart. Amid my doubts, insecurities, and fearful thoughts, let me find solace in Your promises.

God is looking for you to look to Him as you serve Him. That means following "the least indications" of His will, allowing Him to rule your inner being and pervade all your thoughts.

Today, pray for God to help you serve Him. Then go and do so—in His power.

If any man serve me, let him follow me; and where I am, there shall also my servant be: if any man serve me, him will my Father honour.

JOHN 12:26

O Lord, we acknowledge Thy dominion over us; our life, our death, our soul and body, all belong to Thee. Oh, grant that we may willingly consecrate them all to Thee. . . . Let us walk before Thee in childlike simplicity, steadfast in prayer; looking ever unto Thee, that whatsoever we do or abstain from we may in all things follow the least indications of Thy will. Become Lord of our hearts and spirits. . .that Thy life of love and righteousness may pervade all our thoughts and energies and the very ground of our souls; that we may be wholly filled with it. Come, O Lord and King, enter into our hearts, and live and reign there for ever and ever. O faithful Lord, teach us to trust Thee for life and death, and to take Thee for our All in All. Amen.

GERHARD TERSTEEGEN

MY PRAYER STARTER: Lord, make me into a man of action. Let me jump at every opportunity—no matter how small—to glorify You and spread the news about Your love.

Life can be scary. Sometimes, you don't know your next step or even which direction you should go. Other times, you begin on the right track but eventually lose your way. And then there are the distractions, attention grabbers, and time consumers that stall you in your tracks.

Thank God you have Jesus! He has already given you the two most important commandments (Matthew 22:37–40) to abide by. And He's lived His life as an example for you to follow. Thus, you need not ever feel as if you've lost your way. You haven't! Jesus has got your pathway covered!

Today, pray that nothing would distract you from following Jesus and the course He's laid out for you. Doing so will keep your feet on the right path.

> *For I have given you an example, that ye should do as I have done to you. Verily, verily, I say unto you, The servant is not greater than his lord; neither he that is sent greater than he that sent him. If ye know these things, happy are ye if ye do them.*
> JOHN 13:15–17

O Lord, let nothing divert our advance towards you, but in this dangerous labyrinth of the world and the whole course of our pilgrimage here, your heavenly dictates be our map and your holy life be our guide.
JOHN WESLEY

MY PRAYER STARTER: God, Anchor of my soul, a million voices in this world are all vying for my attention. Stop up my ears to all of them except Your own. Tie my devotion to the mast of Your truth.

David was in a tough spot. When he and his men came back from war, they found their homes burned and families taken captive. First, they wept. Then "David encouraged himself in the LORD his God" (1 Samuel 30:6) and "enquired at the LORD" (1 Samuel 30:8).

It's fine to grieve over discouragements. But don't linger there, reacting negatively to God's will for you or seeking comfort elsewhere. Instead, run to God. Use today's prayers to ask Him what to do. Know He will encourage you, bring good out of your disappointment, and prepare you for your next step.

> *David and the people that were with him lifted up their voice*
> *and wept, until they had no more power to weep. . . . And*
> *David was greatly distressed. . .but David encouraged himself*
> *in the LORD his God. . . . And David enquired at the LORD.*
>
> 1 SAMUEL 30:4, 6, 8

O God, the Father of Consolation, let me neither desire anything against Thy will, nor in disappointment seek comfort away from Thee; but, knowing Thy will to comprehend what is best, in both my own life and my neighbor's, and in that of all creatures, let me ever resign myself to Thy disposal, who out of evil bringest good, and to whom our prayer should be in perfect peace. Give us what Thou seest fit, only fit us for what Thou givest. Amen.
ROWLAND WILLIAMS

MY PRAYER STARTER: Lord God, let me be a man of forward-moving faith, just like David. When tragedy knocks me down, may I always land on my knees, asking You for the strength to get up.

The disciple Peter admired Jesus. In fact, he proclaimed He was "the Christ, the Son of the living God" (Matthew 16:16) and vowed to lay down his life for Jesus (John 13:37–38). Yet Peter was also the one who sunk in the water due to his lack of faith in Jesus (Matthew 14:28–31) and who denied knowing Jesus three times (John 18:15–17, 25–27), just as Jesus predicted.

Yet Jesus didn't want Peter to just respect and appreciate Him. He wanted him to follow and resemble Him. And in spite of all Peter's shortcomings, Jesus gave him a second chance, and Peter leaped at it (John 21:7, 15–17).

Today's classic prayer invites you to tap into the power found in willingly following and resembling Jesus. Leap at this chance.

> *Whither I go, ye cannot come; so now I say to you. A new commandment I give unto you, That ye love one another; as I have loved you, that ye also love one another. By this shall all men know that ye are my disciples, if ye have love one to another. Simon Peter said unto him, Lord, whither goest thou? Jesus answered him, Whither I go, thou canst not follow me now; but thou shalt follow me afterwards.*
>
> JOHN 13:33–36

O Lord Jesus Christ. . .save us from the error of wishing to admire Thee instead of being willing to follow Thee and to resemble Thee.
SØREN KIERKEGAARD

MY PRAYER STARTER: Lord Jesus, I'm just like Peter sometimes—eager to follow You but riddled with imperfections. Thank You for giving me a second chance. May I never pass it up.

People prayed for Peter while he was imprisoned. As a result, God's angel came, shined a light into the prison, woke Peter, and raised him up. After Peter's chains fell off, the angel led him through the city gates and then departed. When Peter realized what had happened, he made his way to the house where people had been praying for him.

Today, experience the power of praying for others.

> *Peter therefore was kept in prison: but prayer was made without ceasing of the church unto God for him. . . . When Peter was come to himself, he said, Now I know of a surety, that the LORD hath. . .delivered me. . . . When he had considered the thing, he came to the house of Mary the mother of John, whose surname was Mark; where many were gathered together praying.*
>
> ACTS 12:5, 11–12

O Lord of love, who art not far from any of thy children, watch with thy care those who are far away from us; be thou about their path; be thou within their hearts; give them unfailing trust in thee; grant them power against temptation; qualify them for whatever task thou givest them to do; make it their joy to do thy will. Let not distance break the bonds of love which bind them to us and to thee, but unite us closer in thy love; for the sake of Jesus Christ our Lord.
WILLIAM BOYD CARPENTER

MY PRAYER STARTER: God, many of my brothers and sisters around the world are suffering and afraid. Guide them with Your light and comfort them with assurance of Your presence.

Every opportunity to do good and walk right, every inward and outward success, you owe to God. Thank Him for all that and more, knowing that the best thanks you can offer to Him is to grow in the knowledge of His will for you and live accordingly.

I pray, that your love may abound yet more and more in knowledge and in all judgment; that ye may approve things that are excellent; that ye may be sincere and without offence till the day of Christ; being filled with the fruits of righteousness.

PHILIPPIANS 1:9–11

Father, with thankful and humble hearts we appear before Thee. We would thank Thee for all the benefits that we have received from Thy goodness: It is to Thy blessing we owe what success we have found. Every opportunity for doing good; every impulse in the right way; each victory we have gained over ourselves; every thought of Thy presence, O Father; every silent but loving glance on the example of our Pattern, Thy Son our Lord—all are alike. Thy gifts to us. Give us strength and wisdom to walk faithfully and joyfully in the way of willing obedience to Thy laws, and cheerful trust in Thy love. The best thanksgiving we can offer to Thee is to live according to Thy holy will; grant us every day to offer it more perfectly, and to grow in the knowledge of Thy will and the love thereof for evermore. Amen.

MICHAEL SAILER

MY PRAYER STARTER: Righteous God, I take no credit for any good thing I'll ever do. I know that it is Your Spirit working through me, and I praise You for using me to fulfill Your plans.

Elisha was a man of God. When his servant saw that "an host compassed the city both with horses and chariots" (2 Kings 6:15), he panicked. But Elisha told him not to fear because "they that be with us are more than they that be with them" (v. 16). Then Elisha said, "LORD, I pray thee, open his eyes, that he may see" (v. 17). The servant then saw that "the mountain was full of horses and chariots of fire round about Elisha" (v. 17).

Child of God, use today's prayers to ask the Lord to open your spiritual eyes so that you can see not the visible threats charging toward you but His unseen chariots coming to save you.

The chariots of God are twenty thousand, even thousands of angels: the Lord is among them. . . . Blessed be the Lord, who daily loadeth us with benefits, even the God of our salvation. . . . To him that rideth upon the heavens of heavens, which were of old; lo, he doth send out his voice, and that a mighty voice. Ascribe ye strength unto God: his excellency is over Israel, and his strength is in the clouds. . . . The God of Israel is he that giveth strength and power unto his people. Blessed be God.

PSALM 68:17, 19, 33–35

Lord, open my eyes that I may see, not the visible enemy, but Thy unseen chariots of deliverance.
HANNAH WHITALL SMITH

MY PRAYER STARTER: Invisible God, I need spiritual eyesight. When the world around me looks bleak and hopeless, give me a glimpse of Your master plan.

Elijah was on his way to being swept up in a whirlwind, taken up by horses and chariots to God. He told Elisha, his friend and pupil, to wait in Gilgal. Elisha said, "As God and my soul lives, I will not leave you." So they went to Bethel. There, Elijah again told Elisha to stay behind. He again refused, and they went to Jericho together. At Jericho, Elijah repeated his request and Elisha again refused. Three times Elisha declared he wouldn't leave his friend.

Today, thank God for the joy your worthy friends bring you—and pray that you might be such a worthy, joy-bringing friend to them at every turn.

And it came to pass, when the LORD would take up Elijah into heaven by a whirlwind, that Elijah went with Elisha from Gilgal. And Elijah said unto Elisha, Tarry here, I pray thee; for the LORD hath sent me to Bethel. And Elisha said unto him, As the LORD liveth, and as thy soul liveth, I will not leave thee. So they went down to Bethel.

2 KINGS 2:1–2

It is my joy in life to find
At every turning of the road,
The strong arm of a comrade kind
To help me onward with my load.
And since I have no gold to give,
And love alone must make amends,
My only prayer is, while I live,—
God make me worthy of my friends!

FRANK DEMPSTER SHERMAN

MY PRAYER STARTER: Lord, thank You for the loyal friends that encourage me on my journey home. Help me be loyal to them as well, assisting them on their walk with You.

When you feel as if your life is parched like a desert, it's time to change up your thoughts. To get a new perspective. To get a *God* perspective.

Today, ask God to fill you with thoughts of Him, making your desert bloom as His magnificence rests upon and surrounds you.

> *Remember ye not the former things, neither consider the*
> *things of old. Behold, I will do a new thing; now it shall*
> *spring forth; shall ye not know it? I will even make a way*
> *in the wilderness, and rivers in the desert. . . . This people*
> *have I formed for myself; they shall shew forth my praise.*
> ISAIAH 43:18–19, 21

O Lord of life, and Lord of love! Love us into life, and give us life to love Thee. Grant us life enough to put life into all things, that when we travel through this part of our life, and it seems but dust and barrenness, we may be full of hope in Thee. Touch this barrenness, till all things bloom. Lord, forgive us that our life is so poor, and grant us thoughts of God that we may be enabled for the time to come to make this very desert blossom. Grant that the Spirit of God may so come and so dwell, that the beauty of the Lord may be upon us: through Jesus Christ our Lord. Amen.
GEORGE DAWSON

MY PRAYER STARTER: God, Refresher of my soul, life occasionally feels like a thirsty wasteland. During these moments, lift my eyes and help me see the oasis of Your love.

When God called Jonah, telling him to take His message to Nineveh, Jonah ran in another direction. He boarded a ship he thought would take him away from God. So the Lord created a storm that threatened to break up the ship. Jonah, realizing he was the cause of all this tumult, told the sailors to throw him into the sea. Reluctantly, they did. And the sea calmed. Yet Jonah's troubles weren't over—God then sent a great fish to swallow him.

After three days and three nights in the fish's belly, Jonah finally prayed to God. He began by recognizing God as his supreme ruler and ended with giving his life to God. Hearing Jonah's prayer, God had the fish vomit Jonah onto dry land.

Although you may not be running from God's will physically, you may be emotionally, mentally, or spiritually. Today's prayers will help you come out of yourself so that you can give yourself fully to God. No great fish necessary.

> *Submit yourselves therefore to God. . . . Draw nigh to*
> *God, and he will draw nigh to you. . . . Humble yourselves*
> *in the sight of the Lord, and he shall lift you up.*
> JAMES 4:7–8, 10

O Lord, help us to go out of ourselves, so that we
may give ourselves over to Thee, with all our powers,
with all that we are and all that we have.
JAKOB BÖHME

MY PRAYER STARTER: Father, Ruler of my life, Jonah's story proves that running from You is futile. Give me the strength to submit to You at every moment, even when I feel like walking away.

It's good for a child to have an adult in its life who provides food, clothing, shelter, love, compassion, help, teaching, security, protection, and joy so that it can grow up to adulthood. But it's infinitely better for that child to have God, who provides supernatural versions of all these things—including salvation and fulfilled potential!

Kids surround us, whether they are our children, grandchildren, nieces, nephews, siblings, fosters, or church kids. They all deserve the opportunity to grow up in God. But how will they know of Him unless you tell them?

Today, thank God for the children in your life. Ask Him for the grace to lovingly train them up in the way He wants them to go so that they will find a firm foundation in Jesus Christ.

> *Train up a child in the way he should go: and*
> *when he is old, he will not depart from it.*
> PROVERBS 22:6

Almighty God and heavenly Father, we thank you for the children which you have given us; give us also grace to train them in your faith, fear, and love; that as they advance in years they may grow in grace, and may hereafter be found in the number of your children; through Jesus Christ our Lord. Amen.
JOHN COSIN

MY PRAYER STARTER: Father, the children in my life are blessings. They represent the next generation, so help me teach them at an early age about You.

The Bible is full of paradoxes, statements that seem to be contradictory but are in fact true (see Mark 8:35; John 12:24; Acts 20:35; Romans 6:18; 2 Corinthians 12:10; Philippians 3:7–8; James 4:10).

Today, pray God would help you learn to see the world through His eyes.

> *He that findeth his life shall lose it: and he that*
> *loseth his life for my sake shall find it.*
> MATTHEW 10:39

Lord, high and holy, meek and lowly, Thou hast brought me to the valley of vision, where I live in the depths but see thee in the heights; hemmed in by mountains of sin I behold thy glory. Let me learn by paradox that the way down is the way up, that to be low is to be high, that the broken heart is the healed heart, that the contrite spirit is the rejoicing spirit, that the repenting soul is the victorious soul, that to have nothing is to possess all, that to bear the cross is to wear the crown, that to give is to receive, that the valley is the place of vision.

. . . .

Let me find thy light in my darkness, thy life in my death, thy joy in my sorrow, thy grace in my sin, thy riches in my poverty, thy glory in my valley.

PURITAN PRAYER

MY PRAYER STARTER: Divine Creator, Your perfect ways often seem baffling to us. Help me to see that the more I weaken and suffer physically for You, the stronger I become in Your eyes.

Following rules in your own power takes you nowhere in your relationship with Jesus or your right standing with God. In fact, you'd only be cutting yourself off from God's grace. But if you rely on the Spirit for help and wait in faith for a good connection with Him, then you'll find true faith activated, generated by, and expressed through love.

Today, pray that God would increase your trust in Him so that you can rise up and glorify Him in true faith.

For we through the Spirit wait for the hope of righteousness
by faith. For in Jesus Christ neither circumcision availeth any
thing, nor uncircumcision; but faith which worketh by love.

GALATIANS 5:5–6

We desire, O Lord, that You will, to all Your other mercies, add that gift by which we shall trust in You—faith that works by love; faith that abides with us; faith that transforms material things, and gives them to us in spiritual meanings; faith that illumines the world by a light that never sets, that shines brighter than the day, and that clears the night quite out of our experience. . . . We beg You to grant us this faith, that shall give us victory over the world and over ourselves; that shall make us valiant in all temptation and bring us off conquerors and more than conquerors through Him that loved us. Amen.

HENRY WARD BEECHER

MY PRAYER STARTER: Almighty God, I have no power to make myself righteous, nor should I try. I need Your Spirit every second to help me follow Your commands and glorify Your name.

Today's classic prayer is wrapped up in love. It acknowledges that "love is of God" (1 John 4:7) and "God *is* love" (1 John 4:8, emphasis added). The deeper you plunge into God, the more you'll realize these truths.

Jesus felt, lived, and personified God's love. He admitted God loved Him before the world was ever created, before the Spirit of God hovered over the waters. He prayed that God's love for Him would be in His followers, and He Himself in them.

What's with all the love that keeps circling back? It's God Himself. For when you have the grace of love and God who is love, all your days will empty into the fullness of His eternal love.

> *Father, I will that they also, whom thou hast given me, be with*
> *me where I am; that they may behold my glory, which thou hast*
> *given me: for thou lovedst me before the foundation of the world.*
> *O righteous Father, the world hath not known thee: but I have*
> *known thee, and these have known that thou hast sent me. And I*
> *have declared unto them thy name, and will declare it: that the love*
> *wherewith thou hast loved me may be in them, and I in them.*
> JOHN 17:24–26

You who are love itself,
give me the grace of love,
give me yourself,
so that all my days may finally empty
into the one day of your eternal life.
KARL RAHNER

MY PRAYER STARTER: Lord God, there's nothing shallow about Your love for us. Just as You gave Your life for me, help me love You—and others— enough to offer myself as well.

Esther was a Jewish orphan who, through providence, ended up as Persia's queen. When her cousin Mordecai refused to bow to Haman—one of the king's officials—Haman had the king sign an edict to destroy the Jews.

When Mordecai heard of the plot, he urged Esther to take action, saying, "Perhaps this is why you have become queen during such a time." After instituting a fast for her people, Esther thwarted the plot, and Haman was destroyed instead of the Jews.

Why are you here? Could it be for such a time as this? Today, be a man of faith and action, asking God to help you work out your part in His plan and make a creative contribution to this world.

> *Who knoweth whether thou art come to the*
> *kingdom for such a time as this?*
> ESTHER 4:14

O God, we thank you for the lives of great saints and prophets in the past, who have revealed to us that we can stand up amid the problems and difficulties and trials of life and not give in. We thank you for our foreparents, who've given us something in the midst of the darkness of exploitation and oppression to keep going. Grant that we will go on with the proper faith and the proper determination of will, so that we will be able to make a creative contribution to this world. In the name and spirit of Jesus we pray.
MARTIN LUTHER KING JR.

MY PRAYER STARTER: Lord, Author of history, I know You have an eternally significant part for me to play in Your divine plan. Give me the wisdom to hear Your voice and the courage to act.

Jesus was an untiring worker for the kingdom. Even as a twelve-year-old boy, He stayed behind instead of accompanying His parents home from Jerusalem. After three days of searching, they finally found Him "in the temple, sitting in the midst of the doctors, both hearing them, and asking them questions. And all that heard him were astonished" (Luke 2:46–47). He was about His Father's business.

When you find yourself weary of doing good for God, ask Jesus for the encouragement and grace to continue in your Father's business. He'll exceed your expectations!

Son, why hast thou thus dealt with us? behold, thy father and I have sought thee sorrowing. And he said unto them, How is it that ye sought me? wist ye not that I must be about my Father's business?

LUKE 2:48–49

O Lord Jesus Christ, who when on earth wast ever about thy Father's business: Grant that we may not grow weary in well-doing. Give us grace to do all in thy name. Be thou the beginning and the end of all: the pattern whom we follow, the redeemer in whom we trust, the master whom we serve, the friend to whom we look for sympathy. May we never shrink from our duty from any fear of man. Make us faithful unto death; and bring us at last into thy eternal presence, where with the Father and the Holy Ghost thou livest and reignest for ever.

EDWARD B. PUSEY

MY PRAYER STARTER: Father, I want to be Your loyal son. Don't let me forget that I'm in this world to follow Your plan, not my own. Let me always be about Your business.

At times, you might not feel very generous toward others, or even toward God. You might be tired of continually serving and giving, wondering how much more energy or resources you can expend. Or maybe you're weary of fighting and only want rest. Perhaps you've worked and worked without a single thank-you or reward.

Yet when you go to God realizing that the mere *knowledge* that you're doing the Lord's will *is* your reward, you *can* find a generous heart, energy to serve, strength to fight, and determination to work. For in doing His will, you'll find your joy in the Lord!

Whatever you do, do it as if you are working for God alone, not your fellow humans. Seek the reward of joy in the Lord and nowhere else. Today's prayers will help you begin.

> *And whatsoever ye do, do it heartily, as to the Lord, and not unto men; knowing that of the Lord ye shall receive the reward of the inheritance: for ye serve the Lord Christ.*
> COLOSSIANS 3:23–24

Dearest Lord, teach me to be generous;
Teach me to serve thee as thou deserves;
To give and not to count the cost,
To fight and not to seek for rest,
To labour and not to seek reward,
Save that of knowing that I do thy will.
SAINT IGNATIUS OF LOYOLA

MY PRAYER STARTER: God, show me the importance of every seemingly mundane task I perform for You. Even in the most thankless of jobs, let me be thankful to You for the chance to do them.

How often do you wake up, read the Bible, pray, and then go about your day, trying to live and work in your own power instead of tapping into God's? Doing so can become exhausting to your body, mind, and spirit! As a result, you might find yourself laid up (or laid down) because you've been trying to plow through on your own.

Today's classic prayer reminds you that God's power is the strongest when you're at your weakest. That whether you're sick or well, it's wiser to live in God's power than to struggle in your own.

There was given to me a thorn in the flesh, the messenger of Satan to buffet me, lest I should be exalted above measure. For this thing I besought the Lord thrice, that it might depart from me. And he said unto me, My grace is sufficient for thee: for my strength is made perfect in weakness. Most gladly therefore will I rather glory in my infirmities, that the power of Christ may rest upon me.

2 CORINTHIANS 12:7–9

Lord, teach me the art of patience whilst I am well, and give me the use of it when I am sick. In that day either lighten my burden or strengthen my back. Make me, who so often in my health have discovered my weakness presuming on my own strength, to be strong in my sickness when I solely rely on Thy assistance.

THOMAS FULLER

MY PRAYER STARTER: Mighty God, I might sometimes think I'm tough enough to handle anything, but in reality, I can't do a thing without Your help. Give me the strength to lean on You.

Whatever you're requesting of God, know that what He has in mind for you is better than you can imagine.

> *Now unto him that is able to do exceeding abundantly*
> *above all that we ask or think, according to the*
> *power that worketh in us, unto him be glory.*
> EPHESIANS 3:20–21

Thou hast called us to Thyself, most merciful Father, with love and with promises abundant; and we are witnesses that it is not in vain that we draw near to Thee. We bear witness to Thy faithfulness. . . . Thy blessings are exceeding and abundant more than we know or think. We thank Thee for the privilege of prayer, and for Thine answers to prayer; and we rejoice that Thou dost not answer according to our petitions. We are blind, and are constantly seeking things which are not best for us. If Thou didst grant all our desires according to our requests, we should be ruined. . . . We are, day by day, saved from peril and from ruin by Thy better knowledge and Thy careful love. Amen.

HENRY WARD BEECHER

MY PRAYER STARTER: All-knowing Lord, You know what I need much better than I do. Help me to trust You, even when it seems like my prayers are going unanswered.

You may think that you control your destiny, that you own yourself. But that's not true. As a believer, you are joined to God. You are one with Him. As such, your body belongs to the Lord. It's a part of Jesus Christ and a temple of the Holy Spirit.

You are God's property, having been bought with the precious blood of Jesus. Today's classic prayer invites you into that reality. It asks you to acknowledge that God owns all of you—spirit, heart, body, soul, gifts, and personality. And it's up to Him to send you where He wants, to use you as He wills. Be willing.

> *But he that is joined unto the Lord is one spirit. . . . What?*
> *know ye not that your body is the temple of the Holy Ghost*
> *which is in you, which ye have of God, and ye are not your*
> *own? For ye are bought with a price: therefore glorify God*
> *in your body, and in your spirit, which are God's.*
> 1 CORINTHIANS 6:17, 19–20

Heavenly Father, here I am. I am Thy property. Thou hast bought me with a price. I acknowledge Thine ownership, and surrender myself and all that I am absolutely to Thee. Send me where Thou wilt; do with me what Thou wilt; use me as Thou wilt.
R. A. TORREY

MY PRAYER STARTER: Master, I surrender all illusions of control. Take my reins and steer me wherever You want. I am willing.

It can be hard, if not downright impossible, for a man to find peace in this world. Thank God for Jesus! He leaves you with true peace—peace that guarantees calm in the face of trouble, removes your fear, and reigns over your heart. He's promised this peace to those who believe, and it can never be taken away!

Today's classic prayer leads you into Jesus' peace. It asks you to invite His peace into your heart, mind, spirit, and soul so that God can act within you.

Stop looking elsewhere for peace. Look to God alone, and you'll find His calm. That's a promise!

> *Peace I leave with you, my peace I give unto you: not*
> *as the world giveth, give I unto you. Let not your*
> *heart be troubled, neither let it be afraid.*
>
> JOHN 14:27

O Lord, calm the waves of this heart; calm its tempest! Calm thyself, O my soul, so that the divine can act in thee! Calm thyself, O my soul, so that God is able to repose in thee, so that his peace may cover thee! Yes, Father in heaven, often have we found that the world cannot give us peace. O but make us feel that thou art able to give peace; let us know the truth of thy promise: that the whole world may not be able to take away thy peace.

SØREN KIERKEGAARD

MY PRAYER STARTER: Lord, thank You for being the source of my unbreakable peace. Calm my turbulent storms of doubt and replace them with the assuring stillness of Your Spirit.

Have you ever tried counting the times you've done wrong, grieved someone else, or offended God? Keeping track of these stats would be impossible, not to mention depressing. Yet God has forgiven you for all these sins—*if* you've forgiven those who have sinned against you. Thus, God's forgiveness is conditional. You only gain it *after* you've forgiven everyone else.

God requires us to forgive "from [our] hearts" (Matthew 18:35), which means not mentioning or dwelling on the ways others have offended us. It also means loving those who have wronged us, just as God unconditionally loves us. That may sound like a tall order, but with God's help, it *can* be done.

So today, ask God to help you forgive.

And when ye stand praying, forgive, if ye have ought against any: that your Father also which is in heaven may forgive you your trespasses. But if ye do not forgive, neither will your Father which is in heaven forgive your trespasses.

MARK 11:25–26

O Lord, because we often sin and have to ask for pardon, help us to forgive as we would be forgiven; neither mentioning old offences committed against us, nor dwelling upon them in thought, but loving our brother freely as you freely love us; for your name's sake.
CHRISTINA ROSSETTI

MY PRAYER STARTER: Father, thank You for erasing my sins from Your record. Help me to display the same level of unconditional patience and love toward others as well.

Many heroes have gone before you (see Hebrews 11). Consider Moses, born to brave parents who, in defiance of the king's edict that all newborn Jewish males were to be killed, kept him hidden. Later, even though Moses could have lived a privileged life as the pharaoh's grandson, he chose instead to take on the challenge of leading his people to freedom.

God, through Jesus, will give you the courage to tackle the adventures He's planned for you. You only need to ask.

> *By faith Moses, when he was born, was hid three months of his parents, because they saw he was a proper child; and they were not afraid of the king's commandment. By faith Moses, when he was come to years, refused to be called the son of Pharaoh's daughter. . . . By faith he forsook Egypt, not fearing the wrath of the king: for he endured, as seeing him who is invisible. . . . By faith they passed through the Red sea as by dry land.*
>
> HEBREWS 11:23–24, 27, 29

O thou who art heroic love, keep alive in our hearts that adventurous spirit which makes men scorn the way of safety, so that thy will be done. For so only, O Lord, shall we be worthy of those courageous souls who in every age have ventured all in obedience to thy call, and for whom the trumpets have sounded on the other side; through Jesus Christ our Lord.

JOHN OLDHAM

MY PRAYER STARTER: Eternal God, You've guided countless men of faith into victory throughout the millennia, and I know You can do the same for me. Grant me the courage to follow.

When God told Moses to confront Pharaoh and free the Israelites from Egypt, Moses had lots of questions. "Who am I," he asked, "to lead the Israelites?" "Why will they believe my message is from God?" "How will I know what to say?" But God told Moses not to worry. The One who had made his mouth, eyes, and mind would be in him, helping him at every step.

What God said to Moses pertains to you as well. There is "one God and Father of all, who is above all, and through all, and in you all" (Ephesians 4:6). Today, ask God to be in every part of you as you journey toward freedom.

And Moses said unto the LORD, O my LORD, I am not eloquent. . .but I am slow of speech, and of a slow tongue. And the LORD said unto him, Who hath made man's mouth? or who maketh the dumb, or deaf, or the seeing, or the blind? have not I the LORD? Now therefore go, and I will be with thy mouth, and teach thee what thou shalt say.

EXODUS 4:10–12

God be in [my] head and in my understanding;
God be in my eyes and in my looking;
God be in my mouth and in my speaking;
God be in my heart and in my thinking;
God be at my end and at my departing.

OLD SARUM PRAYER

MY PRAYER STARTER: God, Creator of my body and mind, empower me to use all of my faculties for Your glory.

When you're looking for love, look no further than God—He *is* love! He loves you more than you could ever imagine. And when you consider that He loved you enough to sacrifice His one and only Son—and that Jesus loved you enough to willingly go along with the plan—you'll start overflowing with love too. Then, you'll have the love you need to love *everyone*!

Today, pray for the ability to love others from the depths of your heart.

*Beloved, let us love one another: for love is of God; and every
one that loveth is born of God, and knoweth God. He that
loveth not knoweth not God; for God is love. . . . Beloved,
if God so loved us, we ought also to love one another.*

1 JOHN 4:7–8, 11

Grant unto us, O Lord God, that we may love one another unfeignedly; for where love is, there art Thou; and he that loveth his brother is born of Thee, and dwelleth in Thee, and Thou in him. And where brethren do glorify Thee with one accord, there dost Thou pour out Thy blessing upon them. Love us, therefore, O Lord, and shed Thy love into our hearts, that we may love Thee, and our brethren in Thee and for Thee, as all children to Thee, through Jesus Christ our Lord. Amen.

ANONYMOUS

MY PRAYER STARTER: Father, You are love personified. As I think on Your love, may I burn with the desire to reflect it toward others so that they too can know Your goodness.

As one of arid Israel's main sources of water was dew, your key source of refreshment is the Holy Spirit.

Today, awaken the sense of the Holy Spirit within you, asking Him to renew you and restore your energy and vitality. He will refill you with the light, joy, strength, direction, power, and protection that accompany His presence.

I will be as the dew unto Israel: he shall grow as the lily, and cast forth his roots as Lebanon. His branches shall spread, and his beauty shall be as the olive tree, and his smell as Lebanon. They that dwell under his shadow shall return; they shall revive as the corn, and grow as the vine.

HOSEA 14:5–7

O Holy Spirit, Love of God, infuse Thy grace, and descend plentifully into my heart; enlighten the dark corners of this neglected dwelling, and scatter there Thy cheerful beams; dwell in that soul that longs to be Thy temple; water that barren soil, over-run with weeds and briars, and lost for want of cultivating, and make it fruitful with Thy dew from heaven. O come, Thou refreshment of them that languish and faint. Come, Thou Star and Guide of them that sail in the tempestuous sea of the world; Thou only Haven of the tossed and shipwrecked. Come, Thou Glory and Crown of the living, and only Safeguard of the dying. Come, Holy Spirit, in much mercy, and make me fit to receive Thee. Amen.

SAINT AUGUSTINE

MY PRAYER STARTER: Holy Spirit, my soul feels like a spiritual desert sometimes. Send Your rain, refreshing my soul and enabling Your fruits to grow therein.

It's easy for us to pray only for ourselves. However, we are called to intercede "for all men" as well. But how can we do that if we're not exactly sure how to pray for others?

First, pray today's prayers, asking God to make you so bound up in your love for others that you feel their needs as much as you do your own.

Second, try dreaming up some creative ideas for how to pray for someone else. For example, you might find a psalm and personalize it for another person. Perhaps Psalm 23 will look something like, "Lord, You are Jane's good shepherd. Help her not to feel lack. . ."

Ask God for more ideas to revitalize your intercessions!

I exhort therefore, that, first of all, supplications, prayers, intercessions, and giving of thanks, be made for all men. . . . For this is good and acceptable in the sight of God our Saviour.

1 TIMOTHY 2:1, 3

Lord, save us from being self-centered in our prayers and teach us to remember to pray for others. May we be so bound up in love with those for whom we pray, that we may feel their needs as acutely as our own, and intercede for them with sensitivity, with understanding and with imagination.
JOHN CALVIN

MY PRAYER STARTER: Compassionate Savior, the world is broken and filled with suffering. Help me to feel the pain of others so that I can sincerely lift them up to You in prayer.

True contentment is found not in what you possess but in surrendering it all to Jesus and freely receiving His love and grace.

Today's classic prayer asks you to give the Lord all your freedom, memory, understanding, and will. To restore to Him all He has given you, surrendering it to His direction. And ultimately, to ask that you love Him alone. For if you have His love and grace, what more do you need?

> *Again, the kingdom of heaven is like unto treasure hid in a field; the which when a man hath found, he hideth, and for joy thereof goeth and selleth all that he hath, and buyeth that field. Again, the kingdom of heaven is like unto a merchant man, seeking goodly pearls: who, when he had found one pearl of great price, went and sold all that he had, and bought it.*

MATTHEW 13:44–46

Take, Lord, all my liberty. Receive my memory,
my understanding, and my whole will.
Whatever I have and possess, you have given to me;
to you I restore it wholly, and to your will
I utterly surrender it for your direction. Give me the love of you only,
with your grace, and I am rich enough; nor ask I anything beside.
SAINT IGNATIUS OF LOYOLA

MY PRAYER STARTER: Lord, help me be grateful for the material blessings You've given me. But most importantly, help me to cling to Your grace, even when all else fades away.

Not many things can top a good night's sleep. And you can attain it when you lift yourself to God just before you close your eyes.

Know that fear is unnecessary, for God is your Guide and Protector who's strong enough to keep you from all danger. When you're sleeping in His light, you need not fear the dark. Pray today for that good night's sleep. Sweet dreams!

> *When thou liest down, thou shalt not be afraid: yea, thou shalt*
> *lie down, and thy sleep shall be sweet. . . . For the LORD shall*
> *be thy confidence, and shall keep thy foot from being taken.*
> PROVERBS 3:24, 26

O Lord my God, I thank thee that thou hast brought this day to a close; I thank thee for giving me rest in body and soul. Thy hand has been over me and has guarded and preserved me. Forgive my lack of faith and any wrong that I have done today, and help me to forgive all who have wronged us. Let me sleep in peace under thy protection, and keep me from all the temptations of darkness. Into thy hands I commend my loved ones and all who dwell in this house; I commend to thee my body and soul. O God, thy holy name be praised.
DIETRICH BONHOEFFER

MY PRAYER STARTER: Almighty God, I'm placing myself in Your full protection tonight. Keep me safe and help me to wake with Your praises on my lips.

Jesus. The more you learn about Him, the more you will trust Him. The closer you live by His Word, the nearer you will get to Him. And He will show Himself to you if you keep on knocking. He will answer your questions if you keep on asking. You will find Him if you keep on seeking.

As you pursue this cycle of asking, seeking, and knocking, you will awaken a boundless love within and your thoughts will return to Him alone.

Today, pray with the intention of seeking Jesus in all His wonder—and you will find Him.

> *Ask, and it shall be given you; seek, and ye shall find; knock, and it shall be opened unto you: for every one that asketh receiveth; and he that seeketh findeth; and to him that knocketh it shall be opened.*

MATTHEW 7:7–8

O beloved Saviour, show yourself to us who knock, that knowing you, we may love you alone, desire only you, think always of you alone, meditating day and night on your words. Awaken in us such a love as may be rightly and fittingly rendered to you. O God, may your love take possession of our whole being and make it totally yours.

SAINT COLUMBANUS

MY PRAYER STARTER: Savior, I want to seek Your splendor in everything I do. Give me spiritual eyes so that I can see the mysteries of Your grace and love.

God is love. And Jesus taught us the way of that love through His words and actions.

Even when the mob came to arrest Jesus, He did not strike back. But someone in the surrounding crowd did. After this man cut off the right ear of the high priest's servant, Jesus said, "Let them take Me." Then Jesus "touched his ear, and healed him" (Luke 22:51).

Pray that God would make you willing to follow His lead and to walk peacefully in Jesus' love, just as He taught through word and deed.

> *Ye have heard that it hath been said, An eye for an eye, and a tooth for a tooth: but I say unto you, That ye resist not evil: but whosoever shall smite thee on thy right cheek, turn to him the other also. . . . Love your enemies, bless them that curse you, do good to them that hate you, and pray for them which despitefully use you, and persecute you; that ye may be the children of your Father which is in heaven.*
>
> MATTHEW 5:38–39, 44–45

O God, make us willing to do your will, come what may. Increase the number of persons of good will and moral sensitivity. Give us renewed confidence in nonviolence and the way of love as taught by Christ. Amen.
MARTIN LUTHER KING JR.

MY PRAYER STARTER: Lord, You responded with peace when others treated You violently. Help me follow in Your footsteps and love my enemies, even if they hate me in return.

After David had cut off part of King Saul's robe—and later, after he had taken a census—his heart "smote him" (1 Samuel 24:5; 2 Samuel 24:10). Weighed down with guilt, David was "not able to look up" (Psalm 40:12). Yet he knew if he confessed to God, he'd be forgiven.

Because God has put His laws into our hearts and written them in our minds (Hebrews 10:16), we know when we've done wrong. There's nothing like a guilty conscience to drag us into depression, but God has provided a remedy to lift us out.

If you want to clear things up between you and God, confess your wrongdoings to Him and take refuge in His forgiveness. As you look up afterward, He'll lift you up.

> *Let us draw near with a true heart in full assurance*
> *of faith, having our hearts sprinkled from an evil*
> *conscience, and our bodies washed with pure water.*
> HEBREWS 10:22

O God, animate us to cheerfulness. May we have a joyful sense of our blessings, learn to look on the bright circumstances of our lot, and maintain a perpetual contentedness under thy allotments. Fortify our minds against disappointment and calamity. Preserve us from despondency, from yielding to dejection. Teach us that no evil is intolerable but a guilty conscience, and that nothing can hurt us, if, with true loyalty of affection, we keep thy commandments and take refuge in thee; through Jesus Christ our Lord. Amen.
WILLIAM ELLERY CHANNING

MY PRAYER STARTER: God of forgiveness, thank You for offering me so many second chances. Help me to keep confessing to You whenever I slip up.

Jesus says if you love Him, you'll obey His words. And as you obey, He and God will make Their home with you.

Are you obeying Jesus' words? Are you loving God with all your being and loving others as yourself? Are you forgiving others as God forgives you? Are you listening to the Spirit's promptings, God's directions, and Jesus' calls?

When you fully love and trust the Holy Three, obedience will become easier. To nurture that love and trust, dig into the Word and ask God for it to permeate your whole being.

You owe God all your love and obedience, just as a son owes them to his father and a servant to his lord. Be assured that when you walk in obedience to God and follow Jesus' Word, the Spirit will lead you to level ground (Psalm 143:10).

Jesus answered and said unto him, If a man love me,
he will keep my words: and my Father will love him,
and we will come unto him, and make our abode with him.

JOHN 14:23

Most gracious God and Father. . .inasmuch as it hath pleased Thee to remember us with Thy servants and children, grant that we may render unto Thee the love and obedience which we owe Thee, as children to their father and servants to their lord. We ask all for the sake of Jesus Christ our only Saviour. Amen.

JOHN CALVIN

MY PRAYER STARTER: Father, You are worthy of my utmost respect and obedience. I surrender any notions of control—fill me with Your Spirit and cause Your love to dwell within my heart.

When trouble arrives, a man's first reaction may not be to smile. Yet Jesus wants you to face all trials with joy! And you *can* have that joy when you know that He's with you and sustaining you with His presence.

Use today's prayers as a reminder of the peace and patience that Jesus' presence brings, no matter what comes your way.

Count it all joy when ye fall into divers temptations; knowing this, that the trying of your faith worketh patience. But let patience have her perfect work, that ye may be perfect and entire, wanting nothing.

JAMES 1:2–4

Holy Father. . .we rejoice that we can turn to Thee in the midst of great anxiety, and commit all our troubles to Thy sure help. As Thou art with us in the sunlight, oh, be Thou with us in the cloud. In the path by which Thou guidest us, though it be through desert and stormy sea, suffer not our faith to fail, but sustain us by Thy near presence, and let the comforts which are in Jesus Christ fill our hearts with peace. And, O God, grant that the fiery trial which trieth us may not be in vain, but may lead us to a cheerful courage, and a holy patience; and let patience have her perfect work, that we may be perfect and entire, wanting nothing, wholly consecrate to Thee, through Jesus Christ our Lord. Amen.

HENRY W. FOOTE

MY PRAYER STARTER: God of hope, grant me the optimism to view every trial as an opportunity for growth. Remind me of the ultimate peace I have in You.

Other than the fact that they rhyme, the words *meek* and *weak* have nothing in common. Meekness, as Jesus taught, is strength under control. And that's just what He exhibited when He was arrested, beaten, questioned, and crucified. As the Son of God, He could have annihilated all who came against Him. But that was neither His message nor His mission. So He stayed meek, keeping His extreme power under control—for you.

Jesus wants each Christian man to display that same meekness. When we do, we will be blessed and inherit the earth (Matthew 5:5). So today, ask Jesus to pour not just His spirit of meekness but His spirit of love upon you. To wipe out your ego, replacing it with His gentleness. To guide your hand as it rests upon the Rock of ages, trusting in "the LORD JEHOVAH [who] is everlasting strength" (Isaiah 26:4).

> *Put on therefore, as the elect of God, holy and beloved,*
> *bowels of mercies, kindness, humbleness of mind, meekness,*
> *longsuffering; forbearing one another, and forgiving one*
> *another. . . . And above all these things put on charity.*
> COLOSSIANS 3:12–14

O Savior, pour upon me thy spirit of meekness and love, annihilate the selfhood in me, be thou all my life. Guide thou my hand which trembles exceedingly upon the rock of ages.
WILLIAM BLAKE

MY PRAYER STARTER: Lord, thank You for holding back Your infinite power at the cross in order to save us. Help me follow in Your footsteps and use my own strength for love and not retaliation.

Although you may get so enmeshed in the busyness of your day that you forget about God, rest assured that He won't forget about you.

God isn't a parent who can't keep track of His kids. He's always aware of your actions, thoughts, and words. He knows where you are and when. He knows your every movement, understands your every thought, and sees all your habits—good and bad.

Today's classic prayer helps you rest easy in the assurance that God will not forget about you, even though you may forget about Him.

O Lord, thou hast searched me, and known me. Thou knowest my downsitting and mine uprising, thou understandest my thought afar off. Thou compassest my path and my lying down, and art acquainted with all my ways. For there is not a word in my tongue, but, lo, O LORD, thou knowest it altogether. Thou hast beset me behind and before, and laid thine hand upon me. . . . Thine eyes did see my substance, yet being unperfect; and in thy book all my members were written, which in continuance were fashioned, when as yet there was none of them. How precious also are thy thoughts unto me, O God! How great is the sum of them!

PSALM 139:1–5, 16–17

O Lord, Thou knowest how busy
I must be this day.
If I forget Thee,
do not forget me.
JACOB ASTLEY

MY PRAYER STARTER: All-seeing Father, I am only a man, so I sometimes forget about You. Thank You for always watching over and protecting me. Thank You for never forgetting.

When you get to the heart of the matter, "God is love" (1 John 4:8). He loved you before you loved Him (1 John 4:19). He chose you and picked you out in Jesus Christ before He made the world (Ephesians 1:4). And because you are His child—a child of Love—He wants you to walk in love, just as Jesus loved you and gave Himself up for you (Ephesians 5:1–2). What love for you to build your faith on!

Today, get down on your knees. Pray God would strengthen you with His Spirit so that the Son of Love would live in your heart by faith. And pray that once you find security in that love, you will grasp the enormity of His magnificent love and be filled with God's presence.

I bow my knees unto the Father of our Lord Jesus. . .that he would grant you, according to the riches of his glory, to be strengthened with might by his Spirit in the inner man; that Christ may dwell in your hearts by faith; that ye, being rooted and grounded in love, may be able to comprehend with all saints what is the breadth, and length, and depth, and height; and to know the love of Christ, which passeth knowledge, that ye might be filled with all the fulness of God.

EPHESIANS 3:14, 16–19

God, thou art Love. I build my faith on that!
ROBERT BROWNING

MY PRAYER STARTER: God, Your love is so powerful that I am unable to comprehend its magnitude. Help me grasp it enough to show it to others so that they will find security in You as well.

Take yourself—and all that's weighing you down—to Jesus. Only in Him will you find true rest, release, relief, and refreshment for your soul.

Come unto me, all ye that labour and are heavy laden, and I will give you rest. Take my yoke upon you, and learn of me; for I am meek and lowly in heart: and ye shall find rest unto your souls. For my yoke is easy, and my burden is light.

MATTHEW 11:28–31

O Lord, Thy hands have formed us, and Thou hast sent us into this world, that we may walk in the way that leads to heaven and Thyself, and may find a lasting rest in Thee, Who art the Source and Centre of our souls. Look in pity on us poor pilgrims in the narrow way; let us not go astray, but reach at last our true home where our Father dwells. . . . Forgive us for having hitherto so often wavered or looked back, and let us hence-forward march straight on in the way of Thy laws, and may our last step be a safe and peaceful passage to the arms of Thy love, and the blessed fellowship of the saints in light. Hear us, O Lord, and glorify Thy name in us, that we may glorify Thee for ever and ever. Amen.

GERHARD TERSTEEGEN

MY PRAYER STARTER: Divine Master, I can do nothing to earn my way to heaven, and I'll never deserve Your love. That's why I surrender my life to You and praise You for making a way.

In the verses below, the word *charity* means "love." Love endures, shows kindness, doesn't envy, and doesn't seek itself. Today, pray that you'll become that love to others and thereby bless them. When you do, you become like Jesus, who is love personified.

> *Charity suffereth long, and is kind; charity envieth not;*
> *charity vaunteth not itself, is not puffed up, doth not behave*
> *itself unseemly, seeketh not her own. . .beareth all things,*
> *believeth all things, hopeth all things, endureth all things.*
>
> 1 CORINTHIANS 13:4–5, 7

O Thou, Whose name is Love, Who never turnest away from the cry of Thy needy children, give ear to my prayer this morning. Make this a day of blessings to me, and make me a blessing to others. . . . Preserve me from outward transgression and from secret sin. Help me to control my temper. . . . If I meet with unkindness or ill-treatment, give me that charity which suffereth long and beareth all things. Make me kind and gentle towards all, loving even those who love me not. Let me live this day as if it were to be my last. . . . May I take no step that is not ordered by Thee, and go nowhere except Thou, Lord, go with me. Amen.
ASHTON OXENDEN

MY PRAYER STARTER: Lord, Your love is multifaceted, displaying all admirable traits toward everyone it encounters. Help me show these traits toward others, shining Your light everywhere I go.

When you give cheerfully, God multiplies your rewards! In Malachi 3:10, God asks you to prove Him in this, seeing if He "will not open you the windows of heaven, and pour you out a blessing, that there shall not be room enough to receive it." God's blessings prompt you to do even more to bless others.

Today's classic prayer asks God for more grace and gratitude for what you have. Just as God has willingly and joyfully given to you, you should do the same for others. Bless and be blessed.

And God is able to make all grace abound toward you; that ye, always having all sufficiency in all things, may abound to every good work: (as it is written, He hath dispersed abroad; he hath given to the poor: his righteousness remaineth for ever. Now he that ministereth seed to the sower both minister bread for your food, and multiply your seed sown, and increase the fruits of your righteousness;) being enriched in every thing to all bountifulness, which causeth through us thanksgiving to God. For the administration of this service not only supplieth the want of the saints, but is abundant also by many thanksgivings unto God.

2 CORINTHIANS 9:8–12

Lord, give me more grace and more gratitude,
now that You multiply Your favors.
CHARLES SPURGEON

MY PRAYER STARTER: Generous Giver of life, I don't deserve Your many blessings. Help me to handle them wisely, sharing them with others and using them to glorify You.

God's love has created you, moved you, and rested upon you. Seek His face with today's prayers. Know Him, reach out to Him, and feel Him rising up within you, energizing your soul with His light, life, healing, and peace—all for His glory and grace.

> *For God, who commanded the light to shine out of darkness,*
> *hath shined in our hearts, to give the light of the knowledge*
> *of the glory of God in the face of Jesus Christ.*
> 2 CORINTHIANS 4:6

O God, Thou hast found us, and not we Thee. At times we but dimly discern Thee; the dismal mists of earth obscure Thy glory. Yet in other and more blessed moments, Thou dost rise upon our souls, and we know Thee as the Light of all our seeing, the Life of all that is not dead within us, the Bringer of health and cure, the Revealer of peace and truth. We will not doubt our better moments, for in them Thou dost speak to us. We rejoice that Thou hast created us in Thine image. Thy love has stirred us into being, has endowed us with spiritual substance. In the intellect, whose thoughts wander through eternity; in the conscience that bears witness to Thy eternal righteousness; in the affects that make life sweet, and reach forth to Thee, O Lover of Mankind—in these, we are made heirs to the riches of Thy grace.
SAMUEL MCCOMB

MY PRAYER STARTER: Holy Creator, I praise You for moving within my soul, giving me glimpses of Your eternal majesty. Let me never lose sight of Your glory.

In the verses below, Paul tells how God figuratively delivered him "out of the mouth of the lion." Hopefully, you've never literally been in a lion's mouth. Yet during times of trial, you may have *felt* as if you were.

But here's the good news: no matter what you're going through, God will stand with you and give you all the strength and comfort you need to reach the end. Use today's prayers to embed that knowledge deep within so that you'll always be able to stand with Him.

Notwithstanding the Lord stood with me, and strengthened me; that by me the preaching might be fully known, and that all the Gentiles might hear: and I was delivered out of the mouth of the lion. And the Lord shall deliver me from every evil work, and will preserve me unto his heavenly kingdom: to whom be glory for ever and ever. Amen.

2 TIMOTHY 4:17–18

Lord, do not permit my trials to be above my strength; and do thou vouchsafe to be my strength and comfort in the time of trial. Give me grace to take in good part whatever shall befall me; and let my heart acknowledge it to be the Lord's doing, and to come from thy providence, and not by chance. . . . May I receive everything from thy hand with patience and joy.

THOMAS WILSON

MY PRAYER STARTER: Lord, life sometimes feels like a den of anxiety, depression, and fear. Close these lions' mouths and remind me that You will deliver me in the end.

It's great to have close friends who share your interests. But it's even more special to have brothers and sisters in Jesus Christ. With these people, you have a *spiritual* connection. You're actually siblings, related through your Brother Jesus and Father God!

Today, pray for your friends who may not be part of your spiritual family tree. Ask for the Holy Spirit to sow Jesus in their hearts.

> *But he answered and said unto him that told him, Who is my*
> *mother? and who are my brethren? And he stretched forth his*
> *hand toward his disciples, and said, Behold my mother and my*
> *brethren! For whosoever shall do the will of my Father which*
> *is in heaven, the same is my brother, and sister, and mother.*
>
> MATTHEW 12:48–50

I shook hands with my friend, Lord,
And suddenly when I saw his sad and anxious face,
I feared that you were not in his heart.
I am troubled as I am before a closed tabernacle
when there is no light to show that you are there.
If you were not there, Lord, my friend and I would be separated.
For his hand in mine would be only flesh in flesh
And his love for me that of man for man.
I want your life for him as well as for me.
For it is only in you that he can be my brother.
MICHEL QUOIST

MY PRAYER STARTER: Father, thank You for uniting me with the millions of people who trust in You. Please reveal Yourself to my friends who don't know You so that they can share in this unity as well.

When you're feeling restless, try applauding God. You won't find true peace until you do so.

Know that God has called you by name. He created you for Himself and for His glory, choosing you before the foundation of the world to be a part of Him and His family. He delights in you, especially when you delight in Him.

So today, lift your voice in praise to the One who raised you into His heavenly arms. Remember all He has done, is doing, and will continue to do for you. When you wake up, thank Him with all your heart, mind, and soul.

> *Even every one that is called by my name: for I have created him*
> *for my glory, I have formed him; yea, I have made him. . . . Ye are*
> *my witnesses, saith the LORD, and my servant whom I have chosen:*
> *that ye may know and believe me, and understand that I am he:*
> *before me there was no God formed, neither shall there be after me.*
> *I, even I, am the LORD; and beside me there is no saviour. . . . This*
> *people have I formed for myself; they shall shew forth my praise.*
>
> ISAIAH 43:7, 10–11, 21

You awaken us to delight in your praises; for you made us for yourself, and our heart is restless until it reposes in you.
SAINT AUGUSTINE

MY PRAYER STARTER: Lord, Giver of meaning, You created me to serve You, so I will never find satisfaction in anything else. Help me fulfill my destiny by honoring You with my life.

Today, confess your shortcomings to God and receive the power to become the man He created you to be.

This is my commandment, That ye love one another, as I have loved you. Greater love hath no man than this, that a man lay down his life for his friends. Ye are my friends, if ye do whatsoever I command you.
JOHN 15:12–14

Thou Eternal God, out of whose absolute power and infinite intelligence the whole universe has come into being, we humbly confess that we have not loved thee with our hearts, souls and minds, and we have not loved our neighbors as Christ loved us. We have all too often lived by our own selfish impulses rather than by the life of sacrificial love as revealed by Christ. We often give in order to receive. We love our friends and hate our enemies. . . . And so. . .we are confronted with the appalling fact that the history of our lives is the history of an eternal revolt against you. But thou, O God, have mercy upon us. . . . Give us the intelligence to know your will. Give us the courage to do your will. Give us the devotion to love your will. In the name and spirit of Jesus, we pray. Amen.
MARTIN LUTHER KING JR.

MY PRAYER STARTER: Almighty Father, forgive me for the times I failed to live up to Your standards. Help me to keep journeying upward toward You as I try to live out Your will.

God knows that we are frail creatures who need His strength to stand firm—that to turn *from* Him is to fall but to turn *to* Him is to rise.

It's okay to tell God your laundry list of what you need to stand strong. So today, pray to God with the intention of being renewed in every way. Ask for His help to carry out His will for upcoming duties. Ask for His guidance to clear up any confusion you may have. Ask for His protection from any dangers you may be facing. Ask for His peace to help you overcome any sorrow you may be feeling.

Ask for these things, knowing that He's already answering and granting you all you need—and more.

Therefore, my brethren dearly beloved and longed for, my joy and crown, so stand fast in the Lord, my dearly beloved. . . . My God shall supply all your need according to his riches in glory by Christ Jesus.
PHILIPPIANS 4:1, 19

O Lord, to be turned from you is to fall, to be turned to you is to rise, and to stand in you is to abide for ever; grant us in all our duties your help, in all our perplexities your guidance, in all our dangers your protection, and in all our sorrows your peace; through Jesus Christ our Lord.
SAINT AUGUSTINE

MY PRAYER STARTER: God, my Source of strength and comfort, thank You for allowing me to come to You for anything. Grant me the humility to take every need to You, no matter how small.

Someone once said, "Worry is a thin stream of fear that trickles through the mind, which, if encouraged, will cut a channel so wide that all other thoughts will be drained out." Today's prayer aims to discourage that fear and encourage your awe of God. When a man's eyes are set on God and his trusting heart is quiet, God and His angels rush in to defend him! So pray away your worries and rest in God. He's got this.

> *I sought the LORD, and he heard me, and delivered me from all my fears. . . . This poor man cried, and the LORD heard him, and saved him out of all his troubles. The angel of the LORD encampeth round about them that fear him, and delivereth them.*

PSALM 34:4, 6–7

Grant unto us, Almighty God, of Thy good Spirit, that quiet heart, and that patient lowliness to which Thy comforting Spirit comes; that we, being humble toward Thee, and loving toward one another, may have our hearts prepared for that peace of Thine which passeth understanding; which, if we have, the storms of life can hurt us but little, and the cares of life vex us not at all; in the presence of which death shall lose its sting, and the grave its terror; and we, in calm joy, walk all the days of our appointed time, until our great change shall come. Amen.
GEORGE DAWSON

MY PRAYER STARTER: Unshakable God, all my worries are but grains of sand compared to Your power. Thank You for erasing my reason to fear and enabling me to rest in Your security.

Some occasions call for short and sweet SOS prayers to God. You need His direction so badly that you just start crying out for help. That's the prayer you have today—plea for God to teach you what to ask for, how to ask for it, and what to do next.

As you pray this prayer, do so knowing that God is your most important guide in this life and the next. That if you ask, He will lead you. And when you follow, your peace will flow like a river and you'll have all the living water you need in these desert places.

Pray. God's help is already on its way.

> Thus saith the LORD, thy Redeemer, the Holy One of Israel; I am
> the LORD thy God which teacheth thee to profit, which leadeth thee
> by the way that thou shouldest go. O that thou hadst hearkened to
> my commandments! then had thy peace been as a river, and thy
> righteousness as the waves of the sea. . . . And they thirsted not when
> he led them through the deserts: he caused the waters to flow out of
> the rock for them: he clave the rock also, and the waters gushed out.
> ISAIAH 48:17–18, 21

Lord, help me! Lord, help me! Teach me what to
ask for! Teach me how to ask for it! Teach me what
to think of next! Teach me what to do next.
CHARLES SPURGEON

MY PRAYER STARTER: Lord, deliver me from life's tumult and heartbreak. But if it's Your will that I face them, give me the courage, wisdom, and endurance to power through.

When you trust in God's results as you labor in His name, your work no longer seems arduous. You become refreshed, no longer worrying about outcomes. You suddenly have new strength, new goals, and new joy. For you know you're working not for yourself, your family, or your boss, but for God alone.

Today's prayer allows you to change your work attitude—to gain the courage to face your daily tasks and complete them with joy in your heart and a smile on your face. At the end of the day, you can go to bed tired but content, knowing you've done a good day's job for the Lord and expecting a peaceful sleep in Jesus' arms.

But thanks be to God, which giveth us the victory through our Lord Jesus Christ. Therefore, my beloved brethren, be ye stedfast, unmoveable, always abounding in the work of the Lord, forasmuch as ye know that your labour is not in vain in the Lord.

1 CORINTHIANS 15:57–58

The day returns and brings us the petty round of irritating concerns and duties. Help us to play the man, help us to perform them with laughter and kind faces, let cheerfulness abound with industry. Give us to go blithely on our business all this day, bring us to our resting beds weary and content and undishonoured, and grant us in the end the gift of sleep. Amen.
ROBERT LOUIS STEVENSON

MY PRAYER STARTER: Father, let my work be motivated by devotion to You, not by a sense of dull obligation. Let me find satisfaction and peace as I strive to fulfill Your will.

All men experience stress. But God can lift us out. He reminds us that in Him we live, move, and have our being. He opens our eyes to His presence all around us. He draws our hearts to Him through His love. He soothes us with His Word, telling us to be anxious for nothing and to leave in His hands the work He's given us to do. He removes our doubts, erases our mistrust.

Today, lift your thoughts to God, allowing Him to relieve the burden of stress as you pray.

They should seek the LORD, if haply they might feel after him, and find him, though he be not far from every one of us: for in him we live, and move, and have our being.
ACTS 17:27–28

O Lord God, in whom we live, and move, and have our being, open our eyes that we may behold Thy Fatherly presence ever about us. Draw our hearts to Thee with the power of Thy love. Teach us to be anxious for nothing, and when we have done what Thou hast given us to do, help us, O God, our Saviour, to leave the issue to Thy wisdom. Take for us all doubt and mistrust. Lift our thoughts up to Thee in heaven, and make us to know that all things are possible to us through Thy Son our Redeemer. Amen.
BROOKE FOSS WESTCOTT

MY PRAYER STARTER: Lord of peace, I know that stress is unavoidable in this life. But I thank You for making a way for me to overcome it by dwelling on the promises in Your Word.

Even our most insignificant decisions or desires can turn into a wrestling match between God's will and our own. That's when we must remind ourselves that God can defeat any foe—that Jesus is the ultimate conqueror.

The "victory verses" below can shore up your confidence in God's overwhelming power. And when you're about to get pinned on the mat, add in today's prayers to strengthen you. Then you'll be sure to win the day—God willing.

For the LORD your God is he that goeth with you, to fight for
you against your enemies, to save you. . . . And the LORD said
unto Joshua, Fear them not: for I have delivered them into
thine hand; there shall not a man of them stand before thee. . . .
If God be for us, who can be against us? . . . Thanks be to God,
which giveth us the victory through our Lord Jesus Christ. . . .
My brethren, be strong in the Lord, and in the power of his
might. . . . For whatsoever is born of God overcometh the world.
DEUTERONOMY 20:4; JOSHUA 10:8; ROMANS 8:31;
1 CORINTHIANS 15:57; EPHESIANS 6:10; 1 JOHN 5:4

Victory in Jesus' name: victory in Jesus' name; to-day: to-day: Thy will be being done: the other will undone: victory in Jesus' name.
S. D. GORDON

MY PRAYER STARTER: Lord God, I'm a fallen man living in a fallen world, and as a result, Your voice can easily get lost in the noise around me. Tune my spiritual ears to hear only Your will.

Reduced levels of sunlight can mess up your circadian rhythm (your biological clock) and drop your serotonin levels (a brain chemical that affects your mood), causing a type of depression called Seasonal Affective Disorder (SAD). Just as less sunlight can cause physical and emotional distress, a shortage of the Son's light can affect you spiritually.

Rise up today—the light of Jesus is here! Pray for God's illuminating presence to stick close to you. Then you'll find your joy. . .and power.

> *Arise, shine; for thy light is come, and the glory of the LORD is risen upon thee. . . . The sun shall be no more thy light by day; neither for brightness shall the moon give light unto thee: but the LORD shall be unto thee an everlasting light, and thy God thy glory. Thy sun shall no more go down; neither shall thy moon withdraw itself: for the LORD shall be thine everlasting light.*
> ISAIAH 60:1, 19–20

Grant me, O Lord, the royalty of inward happiness and the serenity which comes from living close to thee. Daily renew the sense of joy, and let the eternal spirit of the Father dwell in my soul and body, filling every corner of my heart with light and grace, so that bearing about with me the infection of a good courage, I may be a diffuser of life and may meet all ills and crosses with gallant and high-hearted happiness, giving thee thanks always for all things.
ROBERT LOUIS STEVENSON

MY PRAYER STARTER: Savior, my soul has the tendency to darken sometimes, sinking me into a spiritual depression. When this happens, fill me with Your light and restore my health within.

Someone once wrote, "Pray as though everything depended on God. Work as though everything depended on you." Just sitting back, waiting for God to provide but putting forth no effort, is productive neither for Him nor for you. And working as if God won't help will burn you out and leave no room for Him to work. However, if you leave it all up to God in prayer but work as if it all depends on you, you'll most likely find rewards at both ends! For then you'll please God *and* be pleased with God. It's a win-win!

> *For even when we were with you, this we commanded you, that if*
> *any would not work, neither should he eat. For we hear that there*
> *are some which walk among you disorderly, working not at all, but*
> *are busybodies. Now them that are such we command and exhort*
> *by our Lord Jesus Christ, that with quietness they work, and eat*
> *their own bread. But ye, brethren, be not weary in well doing. . . .*
> *The grace of our Lord Jesus Christ be with you all. Amen.*
> 2 THESSALONIANS 3:10–13, 18

The things that we pray for, good Lord, give us your grace to work for.
SIR THOMAS MORE

MY PRAYER STARTER: Almighty God, I know You can handle everything. But I also know You want me to work while trusting You for the results. Help me strike the balance between faith and action.

Both life and love are eternal. So when faced with the deaths of saved loved ones, remember that you will see them again. And when you're in heaven with the Lord, you'll share even more time together. For now, take comfort knowing that the closer you are to the Lord, the closer you are to them.

For whether we live, we live unto the Lord; and whether we die, we die unto the Lord: whether we live therefore, or die, we are the Lord's. For to this end Christ both died, and rose, and revived, that he might be Lord both of the dead and living.

ROMANS 14:8–9

We give back to you, O God, those whom you gave to us. You did not lose them when you gave them to us, and we do not lose them by their return to you. Your dear Son has taught us that life is eternal and love cannot die. So death is only a horizon, and a horizon is only the limit of our sight. Open our eyes to see more clearly, and draw us closer to you that we may know that we are nearer to our loved ones, who are with you. You have told us that you are preparing a place for us: prepare for us also that happy place, that where you are we may also be always, O dear Lord of life and death.

WILLIAM PENN

MY PRAYER STARTER: Everlasting God, losing a brother or sister in Jesus Christ hurts deeply. However, I praise You through the sadness, knowing that death is only a segue into eternal joy.

When a man focuses on things other than God and His Word, his vision can become clouded, causing him to stumble. Today's classic prayer invites you to clear up your eyesight. To look away from pride and false idols and turn to God.

As you pray, let all distractions fall away. Imagine yourself in God's presence, your eyes firmly fixed on Him as His light, power, majesty, strength, love, and compassion reach out to envelop you. Then, you'll begin to understand what God is. . .and what you are not.

> *Make me to go in the path of thy commandments; for therein*
> *do I delight. Incline my heart unto thy testimonies, and*
> *not to covetousness. Turn away mine eyes from beholding*
> *vanity; and quicken thou me in thy way. . . . I thought on*
> *my ways, and turned my feet unto thy testimonies.*
>
> PSALM 119:35–37, 59

Nothingness strives to be something, and the Omnipotent becomes nothing! I will be nothing with Thee, my Lord! I offer Thee the pride and vanity which have possessed me hitherto. Help Thou my will; remove from me occasions of my stumbling; turn away mine eyes from beholding vanity (Psalm 119:37); let me behold nothing but Thee and myself in Thy presence, that I may understand what I am and what Thou art.

FRANÇOIS FÉNELON

MY PRAYER STARTER: All-enveloping Creator, whenever I see some object that I desire, let me always contrast it with Your splendor, keeping my priorities and perception constantly in check.

Many times, afflicted people are cranky, demanding, and irrational, making it hard for caregivers to see Jesus in them. Yet Jesus says you'll be blessed when you nourish the hungry and thirsty, take in strangers, clothe the unclothed, care for the sick, and visit the imprisoned. For when you do those things for others, you're really doing them for Jesus.

Today's prayers help you start recognizing Jesus within those you minister to. Believe it, and you'll start to see it.

> *Come, ye blessed of my Father, inherit the kingdom prepared for you from the foundation of the world: for I was an hungred, and ye gave me meat: I was thirsty, and ye gave me drink: I was a stranger, and ye took me in: naked, and ye clothed me: I was sick, and ye visited me: I was in prison, and ye came unto me. . . . Inasmuch as ye have done it unto one of the least of these my brethren, ye have done it unto me.*
>
> MATTHEW 25:34–36, 40

Dearest Lord, may I see you today and every day in the person of your sick, and, whilst nursing them, minister unto you. Though you hid yourself behind the unattractive disguise of the irritable, the exacting, the unreasonable, may I still recognize you, and say: "Jesus, my patient, how sweet it is to serve you." Lord, give me this seeing faith.

MOTHER TERESA

MY PRAYER STARTER: Father, thank You for taking care of me, even when I don't deserve Your grace and protection. Help me display the same sort of patience and compassion toward others.

You have access to the greatest teacher, the One to whom God the Father has given all knowledge. That teacher is the Holy Spirit. He has been sent in Jesus' name, and He will instruct you in all things, including the power of prayer.

Invite the Holy Spirit in with prayer today. Ask Him to teach you what to pray and how. He will search your heart and speak to God for you, translating your groans, sighs, tears, laughter, and smiles. He will tell God what you are feeling, thinking, hoping, and desiring. What a gift of comfort! What an inspiring partner to have as you close your eyes and seek the face of God.

But the Comforter, which is the Holy Ghost, whom the Father will send in my name, he shall teach you all things, and bring all things to your remembrance, whatsoever I have said unto you. . . . Likewise the Spirit also helpeth our infirmities: for we know not what we should pray for as we ought: but the Spirit itself maketh intercession for us with groanings which cannot be uttered. And he that searcheth the hearts knoweth what is the mind of the Spirit, because he maketh intercession for the saints according to the will of God.

JOHN 14:26; ROMANS 8:26–27

Blessed Prayer-Spirit, Master-Spirit, teach me how to pray.
S. D. GORDON

MY PRAYER STARTER: All-knowing God, I am a man with flawed understanding. Thank You for sending Your Holy Spirit, who teaches me and makes sense of my confused cries for help.

Wars, threats of wars, terrorist attacks, and bombings seem to be on the rise. But Jesus tells us not to panic (Matthew 24:6; Mark 13:7). Such things are part of fallen humanity. Yet we can pray for world peace, for God to draw us together and help us realize that we're all the same under our skin—that we all share a common blood and destiny.

Today, pray for God to step into the fray, waking people up to our commonality so that peace and brotherhood would reign on earth at last.

> *The people that walked in darkness have seen a great light:*
> *they that dwell in the land of the shadow of death, upon them*
> *hath the light shined. . . . For unto us a child is born, unto us*
> *a son is given: and the government shall be upon his shoulder:*
> *and his name shall be called Wonderful, Counsellor, The mighty*
> *God, The everlasting Father, The Prince of Peace. Of the*
> *increase of his government and peace there shall be no end.*
>
> ISAIAH 9:2, 6–7

O Thou strong Father of all nations, draw all Thy great family together with an increasing sense of our common blood and destiny, that peace may come on earth at last, and Thy sun may shed its light rejoicing on a holy brotherhood of peoples.

WALTER RAUSCHENBUSCH

MY PRAYER STARTER: God of peace, I am appalled by the darkness and division that reigns in our culture. Only You can unite us with Your Spirit and love. We need Your help today.

Overcoming evil with good can be difficult when you focus on the negatives. So instead of getting dragged down by falsehood, cheating, injustice, immorality, ugliness, and bad news, fix your attention on truth, honesty, justice, purity, beauty, and good news. Then, as you overcome the baseness of the world through willing obedience to God, you'll be reenergized.

Today, ask God to move within you, opening your eyes to the worthy things in life and thereby making you an overcomer.

> *Whatsoever things are true, whatsoever things are honest,*
> *whatsoever things are just, whatsoever things are pure,*
> *whatsoever things are lovely, whatsoever things are of good*
> *report; if there be any virtue, and if there be any praise, think*
> *on these things. . . . And the God of peace shall be with you.*
> PHILIPPIANS 4:8–9

Almighty God, Who art over all things, Life of all life—stir in our souls, that we, being moved by Thy Spirit, may see those things which are fairest and truest in life, and clinging thereunto, be enabled to get the victory over that which is mean and base; that so at last, all evil passion and unholy desire, all self-will and contrariness to Thee, may be overcome, and we come at last to that sublime state of willing obedience, when Thy will shall be in us supreme. Of Thy mercy hear us, through Jesus Christ our Lord. Amen.
GEORGE DAWSON

MY PRAYER STARTER: Lord, thank You for providing a host of pure things to dwell upon as I walk through this world. Help me fix my eyes on Your kingdom and not on fading distractions.

The travelers on the road to Emmaus didn't realize they'd been talking with Jesus until He blessed their dinner and then vanished. After this, "they said one to another, Did not our heart burn within us, while he talked with us by the way, and while he opened to us the scriptures?" (Luke 24:32).

Jesus, the living Flame of love, is available to you. Ask that He would burn within you, setting you on fire to become more and more like Him.

> *[I saw] one like unto the Son of man. . . . And his eyes were as a*
> *flame of fire. . . . I saw heaven opened, and behold a white horse;*
> *and he that sat upon him was called Faithful and True. . . .*
> *His eyes were as a flame of fire, and on his head were many*
> *crowns; and he had a name written, that no man knew, but*
> *he himself. . . . And his name is called The Word of God.*
> REVELATION 1:13–14; 19:11–13

Enter my heart substantially and personally, and fill it with fervour by filling it with Thee. Thou alone canst fill the soul of man, and Thou hast promised to do so. Thou art the living Flame, and ever burnest with love of man: enter into me and set me on fire after Thy pattern and likeness.

JOHN HENRY NEWMAN

MY PRAYER STARTER: Everlasting Savior, make Yourself known to me in a way that will affect every aspect of my being. Kindle my passion to spread Your love and the message of salvation.

As long as you stick with Jesus, you're never lost. Why? Because He's the Way, the Truth, and the Life! He's your way to being reconciled with God. He's got God's truth that you need to hear and follow. He's able to give you eternal life.

With today's prayers, ask Jesus to keep you on track with His way. To trust in His truth. To rest only in His life. To teach you, via the Holy Spirit, what to believe, what to do, and where to rest. In so doing, you'll find all the guidance you need.

> *And if I go and prepare a place for you, I will come again, and receive you unto myself; that where I am, there ye may be also. And whither I go ye know, and the way ye know. . . . I am the way, the truth, and the life: no man cometh unto the Father, but by me.*
>
> JOHN 14:3–4, 6

O Lord Jesus Christ, who art the Way, the Truth, and the Life, we pray thee suffer us not to stray from thee, who art the Way, nor to distrust thee, who art the Truth, nor to rest in any other thing than thee, who art the Life. Teach us, by thy Holy Spirit what to believe, what to do, and wherein to take our rest. Amen.
ERASMUS

MY PRAYER STARTER: Jesus, I want to walk in Your path and learn from Your teaching as I prepare to live eternally with You. Be my Guide, today and always.

When trouble arises, your first reaction may be fear, grief, doubt, panic, or worry. That's when you need to go to Jesus in prayer.

Ask Jesus to be with your spirit, and He will. Ask Him to live in your heart by faith, and He'll enter immediately, giving you the strength to face any challenge. But He won't stop there. With Jesus in your life, He'll make whatever befalls you work out for good.

Know that you've got a Savior by your side who will stick to you like glue!

> *For this cause I bow my knees unto the Father of our Lord Jesus*
> *Christn. . .that he would grant you, according to the riches of*
> *his glory, to be strengthened with might by his Spirit in the*
> *inner man; that Christ may dwell in your hearts by faith.*
> EPHESIANS 3:14, 16–17

Lord Jesus. . .be with my spirit, and dwell in my heart by faith. Be with me, O my Saviour, everywhere, and at all times. . .in all events and circumstances of my life; let thy presence sanctify and sweeten to me whatever befalls me. Never leave nor forsake me in my present pilgrimage, but abide with me till thou hast brought me safe, through all trials and dangers, to thy heavenly kingdom; that I may there dwell in thy sight, and enjoy thy love, and inherit thy glory for evermore. Amen.

BENJAMIN JENKS

MY PRAYER STARTER: Lord, train my mind so that it responds to life's difficulties by crying out to You. Stay by my side and keep me aware of Your presence.

Only God can break the spell of the things that blind your mind. Ask Him to do so today, and He'll show you what He wants you to see.

One thing I know, that, whereas I was blind, now I see.
JOHN 9:25

Most gracious and all wise God, before whose face the generations rise and fall; Thou in whom we live, and move, and have our being. We thank thee [for] all of thy good and gracious gifts. . . . We come before thee painfully aware of our inadequacies and shortcomings. We realize that we stand surrounded with the mountains of love and we deliberately dwell in the valley of hate. We stand amid the forces of truth and deliberately lie. We are forever offered the high road and yet we choose to travel the low road. For these sins O God forgive. Break the spell of that which blinds our minds. Purify our hearts that we may see thee. O God in these turbulent days when fear and doubt are mounting high give us broad visions, penetrating eyes, and power of endurance. Help us to work with renewed vigor for a warless world, for a better distribution of wealth and for a brother/sisterhood that transcends race or color. In the name and spirit of Jesus we pray. Amen.
MARTIN LUTHER KING JR.

MY PRAYER STARTER: Lord God, help me see past this world's veil of temporal, futile pleasures and open my eyes to Your eternal plan for my life.

God's words hold power. That's why Moses told the people to put them in their hearts, teaching them and talking about them while staying at home, walking, lying down, and rising (Deuteronomy 6:6–7). After Moses died, God told Joshua to meditate on His words day and night. By doing so, Joshua would then be able to follow those words, making him prosperous and successful (Joshua 1:8).

Today, ask God to help you keep His words close as you meditate on them day and night—to help you understand and implement them, growing closer to God and prospering for Him along the way.

> *[The blessed man's] delight is in the law of the LORD; and in his law doth he meditate day and night. And he shall be like a tree planted by the rivers of water, that bringeth forth his fruit in his season; his leaf also shall not wither; and whatsoever he doeth shall prosper.*

PSALM 1:2–3

Lord God, let us keep your Scriptures in mind and meditate on them day and night, persevering in prayer; always on the watch. We beg you, Lord, to give us real knowledge of what we read and to show us not only how to understand it, but how to put it into practice, so that we may deserve to obtain spiritual grace, enlightened by the law of the Holy Spirit, through Jesus Christ our Lord, whose power and glory will endure throughout all ages.

ORIGEN

MY PRAYER STARTER: Father, thank You for giving me instructions on how to live for You. Solidify them in my consciousness and help me to never neglect them or take them for granted.

The Holy Three is a mystery that we can hardly wrap our minds around. Although three, They are one. And They and Their power reside within you. Prayerfully meditate upon this today.

For there are three that bear record in heaven, the Father,
the Word, and the Holy Ghost: and these three are one.

1 JOHN 5:7

Our God, God of all men,
God of heaven and earth, seas and rivers,
God of sun and moon, of all the stars,
. . . .

He has a dwelling
In heaven and earth and sea
And in all things that are in them.
He gives a being to all things,
He gives life to all things,
He is lord over all things,
He nurtures all things.
He makes the light of the sun to shine.
He surrounds the moon and stars.
. . . .

He has a son co-eternal with himself
Like Himself. . .
And the Holy Spirit breathes in them.
They are not separate beings,
Father and Son and Holy Spirit.
SAINT PATRICK

MY PRAYER STARTER: Mysterious and divine Creator, I can't begin to understand Your secrets. Thank You for filling my chasms in knowledge with the comfort of Your presence.

It's true. Every man is imperfect—some days more than others. Yet Jesus still died for us so that our mistakes would not stand between us and God. And although we can neither erase what we've done nor carry the weight of our worries, Jesus can. He and God are strong enough to roll away both our sins and our burdens.

Leave all you are, all you've done, and all you're carrying at the foot of the cross today. Then, in Jesus' name, take on the strength and power of the Spirit so that you can live as God would have you live.

> *[Mary Magdalene, Mary the mother of James, and Salome]*
> *came unto the sepulchre at the rising of the sun. And they said*
> *among themselves, Who shall roll us away the stone from*
> *the door of the sepulchre? And when they looked, they saw*
> *that the stone was rolled away: for it was very great.*

MARK 16:2–4

When we think of ourselves and of the meanness and ugliness and weakness of our lives, we thank Thee for Jesus Christ our Saviour. Grant unto us a true penitence for our sins. Grant that at the foot of the Cross, we may find our burdens rolled away. And so strengthen us by Thy Spirit that in the days to come, we may live more nearly as we ought. Through Jesus Christ our Lord.

WILLIAM BARCLAY

MY PRAYER STARTER: Lord God, just as You rolled the stone away from Jesus' empty tomb, roll my guilt away and help me see that all my past sins have vanished.

There's a lot about Jesus that attracts us: His love, His compassion, His pure life. Today, give in to His attraction, allowing Him to draw you deeply into Himself. For in Him you live, move, and have your being (Acts 17:28). And once your spirit is joined to His, you'll find a secret power—the energy of your existence—and a love that is better than wine.

Today, let all the world's distractions fall away. Follow the path of your spirit when it senses Jesus' presence. Allow His purity to wash over you. And while you're in this sacred chamber with Him, revel and rejoice in His love.

> *Thy love is better than wine. Because of the savour of thy good ointments thy name is as ointment poured forth, therefore do the virgins love thee. Draw me, we will run after thee: the king hath brought me into his chambers: we will be glad and rejoice in thee, we will remember thy love more than wine: the upright love thee.*
>
> SONG OF SOLOMON 1:2–4

Lord, You attract us by the fragrance of Your very being, and You draw us so deeply within to Yourself! Draw me to Yourself, Oh my Divine Center, by the secret springs of my existence, and all my powers and senses will follow You!

JEANNE GUYON

MY PRAYER STARTER: Father, tune my soul to be one with Yours. Let me hear the music of Your love as I lose myself in devotion to You.

God's grace is a free gift that's much more powerful than your mistakes, your urges, and the world's wiles.

Today, put your fears aside. Reach out with all your heart to receive the grace that draws you into Jesus' presence. Humbly allow God's gift to supply all your daily needs—physical, emotional, mental, and spiritual. Then, God will do all those things you cannot do by yourself.

But he giveth more grace. Wherefore he saith, God resisteth the
proud, but giveth grace unto the humble. Submit yourselves therefore
to God. . . . Draw nigh to God, and he will draw nigh to you.
JAMES 4:6–8

I come to thee, O Lord, not only because I am unhappy without thee; not only because I feel I need thee, but because thy grace draws me on to seek thee for thy own sake, because thou art so glorious and beautiful. I come in great fear, but in greater love. Oh may I never lose, as years pass away, and the heart shuts up, and all things are a burden, let me never lose this youthful, eager, elastic love of thee. Make thy grace supply the failure of nature. Do the more for me, the less I can do for myself.
JOHN HENRY NEWMAN

MY PRAYER STARTER: Generous Father, I am a man who needs Your grace for every aspect of my life. Thank You for not only offering Your grace but making it free of charge.

The Bible has a lot to say about words. In fact, Proverbs 18:21 says, "Death and life are in the power of the tongue." A pretty strong statement, but oh how true it is!

You'll never have enough power to tame your tongue. But God does.

Today, reflect on some things you've said but now regret. Then ask God for the wisdom to speak as He wants you to, bearing good fruit in all you say. Pray for His power to tame your tongue.

> *But the tongue can no man tame. . . . Out of the same mouth proceedeth blessing and cursing. My brethren, these things ought not so to be. . . . Who is a wise man and endued with knowledge among you? let him shew out of a good conversation his works with meekness of wisdom. . . . The wisdom that is from above is first pure, then peaceable, gentle, and easy to be intreated, full of mercy and good fruits, without partiality, and without hypocrisy.*
>
> JAMES 3:8, 10, 13, 17

We must praise your goodness that you have left nothing undone to draw us to yourself. But one thing we ask of you, our God, not to cease to work in our improvement. Let us tend towards you, no matter by what means, and be fruitful in good words, for the sake of Jesus Christ our Lord.

LUDWIG VAN BEETHOVEN

MY PRAYER STARTER: Almighty Lord, I sometimes say things I shouldn't. Let Your Spirit catch every improper word before it leaves my mouth, and give me kind words to speak instead.

Pride and attitudes of self-sufficiency have no place in your relationship with God, for all you are and all you own have been given to you *by* God.

Today, ask God to teach you respect for the earth. To help you remember you're fed and clothed by the efforts of others. To make you compassionate toward the hungry and willing to teach them how to harvest God's plenty. As you trust God to help you do this, you'll receive a full reward (Ruth 2:12).

Then said Boaz unto Ruth, Hearest thou not, my daughter? Go not to glean in another field, neither go from hence, but abide here fast by my maidens: let thine eyes be on the field that they do reap, and go thou after them. . .and when thou art athirst, go unto the vessels, and drink of that which the young men have drawn.

RUTH 2:8–9

O God, from whose unfailing bounty we draw our life and all that we possess, forgive our pride and self-sufficiency. Teach us to reverence the earth, which thou hast made fruitful. Help us to remember our unity with those by whose work we are fed and clothed. Touch us with compassion for all who have not enough to eat. As thou hast given us the knowledge which can produce plenty, so give us also the wisdom to bring it within the reach of all: through Jesus Christ our Lord.

JOHN OLDHAM

MY PRAYER STARTER: Compassionate Creator, You never cease to provide for humanity. Help me reflect Your kindness by leading others to Your eternal joy.

All men suffer sometimes. But Jesus took it upon Himself to carry away our weakness, sickness, disease, and even death so that we can be wholly healed someday.

In the meantime, although we're often faced with trouble, we have Jesus to shine within us. In fact, the weaker we are, the more His presence is revealed through us. And we can be encouraged knowing that although we may be fading outwardly, we're being renewed day by day within (2 Corinthians 4:16).

Today, pray for those who are burdened with worry, sorrow, and illness. Ask Jesus to reveal to them who He is—the God who loves them more than they can imagine.

> *But we have this treasure in earthen vessels, that the excellency*
> *of the power may be of God, and not of us. We are troubled on*
> *every side, yet not distressed; we are perplexed, but not in despair;*
> *persecuted, but not forsaken; cast down, but not destroyed; always*
> *bearing about in the body the dying of the Lord Jesus, that the life*
> *also of Jesus might be made manifest in our body. For we which*
> *live are always delivered unto death for Jesus' sake, that the life*
> *also of Jesus might be made manifest in our mortal flesh.*
>
> 2 CORINTHIANS 4:7–11

Lord, we pray for all those who are weighed down with the mystery of suffering. Reveal yourself to them as the God of love, who yourself bear all our suffering.
GEORGE APPLETON

MY PRAYER STARTER: Mighty God, let me not look down on the weak. Without Your presence, I am just as weak as they are. Help me love them by showing them the way to Your power.

You're never lost if you're walking in Jesus' footsteps. He has left you an example, a pattern for you to follow so that you can know how God wants you to live.

Look upon Jesus today. May His pierced heart win your love for Him. May His torn hands inspire you to do good work, His wounded feet urge you toward errands of mercy, and His crown of thorns banish your idle thoughts. Most of all, may His life be your pattern as you live for Him.

> *Be ye followers of me, even as I also am of Christ. . . . For even hereunto were ye called: because Christ also suffered for us, leaving us an example, that ye should follow his steps. . . . For ye were as sheep going astray; but are now returned unto the Shepherd and Bishop of your souls.*
> 1 CORINTHIANS 11:1; 1 PETER 2:21, 25

By virtue of Thy victory, give us also, I entreat Thee, victory. Let Thy pierced heart win us to love Thee, Thy torn hands incite us to every good work, Thy wounded feet urge us on errands of mercy, Thy crown of thorns prick us out of sloth, Thy thirst draw us to thirst after the Living Water Thou givest; let Thy life be our pattern while we live and Thy death our triumph over death when we come to die.
CHRISTINA ROSSETTI

MY PRAYER STARTER: Sacrificial Savior, let the picture of You on the cross be the catalyst that stirs my love toward You and humanity. Give me the opportunity to joyfully follow Your example.

No one really knows what heaven will be like. But the Bible gives a few hints, such as the fact that it will be a city. God will be there, and so will angels and lots of other people. Best of all, believers will be able to meet Jesus face-to-face. What's not to like?

This vision of heaven comforts us when we think of our loved ones who have passed on. We know we will meet them again one day in the company of God, angels, and all the saints.

Today, ask God to welcome these loved ones, knowing they have passed into a better life filled with rest, calm, and eternal peace.

But ye are come unto mount Sion, and unto the city of the living God, the heavenly Jerusalem, and to an innumerable company of angels, to the general assembly and church of the firstborn, which are written in heaven, and to God the Judge of all, and to the spirits of just men made perfect, and to Jesus the mediator of the new covenant.
HEBREWS 12:22–24

Lord, welcome into your calm and peaceful kingdom those who have departed out of this present life to be with you. Grant them rest and a place with the spirits of the just. Give them the life that knows no age, the reward that passes not away, through Christ our Lord. Amen.
SAINT IGNATIUS OF LOYOLA

MY PRAYER STARTER: God of mysteries, please welcome all my saved loved ones when they pass. I look forward to reuniting with them again someday as we behold Your eternal glory.

Without love, a man is nothing. In fact, love is more powerful than faith and hope. So put aside all else and focus solely on loving today. Pray that God would fill you with love, making you completely His.

And though I have the gift of prophecy, and understand all mysteries,
and all knowledge; and though I have all faith, so that I could remove
mountains, and have not charity, I am nothing. . . . And now abideth
faith, hope, charity, these three; but the greatest of these is charity.
1 CORINTHIANS 13:2, 13

Lord, because you have made me, I owe you the whole of my love;
because you have redeemed me, I owe you the whole of myself; because
you have promised so much, I owe you my whole being. Moreover, I
owe you as much more love than myself as you are greater than I, for
whom you gave yourself and to whom you promised yourself. I pray
you, Lord, make me taste by love what I taste by knowledge; let me
know by love what I know by understanding. I owe you more than
my whole self, but I have no more, and by myself I cannot render
the whole of it to you. Draw me to you, Lord, in the fullness of your
love. I am wholly yours by creation; make me all yours, too, in love.
SAINT ANSELM

MY PRAYER STARTER: God of love, I sometimes find myself chasing possessions and temporary emotion. But all I need is to experience and reflect
Your love. Only then will I find fulfillment.

Jesus wants you to be "clear as crystal" (Revelation 21:11) so that His light can shine through you (Matthew 5:16), making you a child of light (John 12:36).

But before you can spread Jesus' light, your eye (or conscience) needs to be healthy, cleansed of guilt, distrust, greed, and anything else that would cloud your transparency.

Today's classic prayer is short and sweet. It asks God to make you clear as crystal so that His light can shine through. So that others will see Him alone. So that His love will spread, drawing others to Him.

It's good to repeat this simple prayer every day. As you do, you'll help tremendously in lighting up this dark world.

> *The light of the body is the eye: therefore when thine eye is single, thy whole body also is full of light; but when thine eye is evil, thy body also is full of darkness. Take heed therefore that the light which is in thee be not darkness. If thy whole body therefore be full of light, having no part dark, the whole shall be full of light, as when the bright shining of a candle doth give thee light.*
>
> LUKE 11:34–36

Lord, make me like crystal that your light may shine through me.
KATHERINE MANSFIELD

MY PRAYER STARTER: Father of lights, make my soul a prism that purely reflects the intricacies of Your love. Use my hands to do Your work and my mouth to speak Your words.

To have true companionship with Jesus, you need to bring to Him all your dirt—your misdeeds, missteps, and mistakes. Only when you come to Him just as you are can He begin to clean you up, forgive you, and fellowship with you heart to heart and spirit to spirit.

Today, ask Jesus to wash your feet. Then bask in His presence and love.

> *[Jesus] riseth from supper, and laid aside his garments; and took a towel, and girded himself. After that he poureth water into a bason, and began to wash the disciples' feet, and to wipe them with the towel wherewith he was girded. . . . Peter saith unto him, Thou shalt never wash my feet. Jesus answered him, If I wash thee not, thou hast no part with me. . . . Ye also ought to wash one another's feet. For I have given you an example, that ye should do as I have done to you.*
>
> JOHN 13:4–5, 8, 14–15

Jesus, my feet are dirty. Come even as a slave to me, pour water into your bowl, come and wash my feet. In asking such a thing I know I am overbold, but I dread what was threatened when you said to me, "If I do not wash your feet I have no fellowship with you." Wash my feet then, because I long for your companionship.
ORIGEN

MY PRAYER STARTER: Savior, I bring all my sins and ugly thoughts and lay them at Your feet. Wash me clean with Your forgiveness and flood me with adoration toward You.

Some days, the people you thought would help you may leave you feeling naked, wounded, bleeding, left for dead, and ignored. That's when you must go to Jesus, your Good Samaritan. He comes to you and shows compassion, binding you, healing you, and carrying you to comfort. There, He takes care of you—to His praise and your joy.

> *But a certain Samaritan, as he journeyed, came where he was: and when he saw him, he had compassion on him, and went to him, and bound up his wounds, pouring in oil and wine, and set him on his own beast, and brought him to an inn, and took care of him. And on the morrow when he departed, he took out two pence, and gave them to the host, and said unto him, Take care of him; and whatsoever thou spendest more, when I come again, I will repay thee.*
>
> LUKE 10:33–35

O Lord, show Your mercy to me and gladden my heart. I am like the man on the way to Jericho who was overtaken by robbers, wounded and left for dead. O Good Samaritan, come to my aid. I am like the sheep that went astray. O Good Shepherd, seek me out and bring me home in accord with Your will. Let me dwell in Your house all the days of my life and praise You for ever and ever with those who are there. Amen.

SAINT JEROME

MY PRAYER STARTER: Faithful Lord, friends sometimes betray me and the world turns its back during my darkest day. But not You. Thank You for sticking close, even when everyone else has fled.

God has a plan for your life. He's steering your boat. He's with you through the raging waters and narrow currents. Nothing can stop His purposes for you.

Your job is to grow closer to God, trusting Him so much that you remain unshakable, certain He'll eventually bring you to a safe, wonderful haven. Pray that you'll reach that goal today.

> *But he is in one mind, and who can turn him? and what his soul desireth, even that he doeth. For he performeth the thing that is appointed for me: and many such things are with him.*
> JOB 23:13–14

Preserve my soul, O Lord, because it belongs to Thee, and preserve my body because it belongs to my soul. Thou alone dost steer my boat through all its voyage, but hast a more especial care of it, when it comes to a narrow current, or to a dangerous fall of waters. Thou hast a care of the preservation of my body in all the ways of my life; but, in the straits of death, open Thine eyes wider, and enlarge Thy Providence towards me so far that no illness or agony may shake and benumb the soul. Do Thou so make my bed in all my sickness that, being used to Thy hand, I may be content with any bed of Thy making. Amen.
JOHN DONNE

MY PRAYER STARTER: Divine Captain, thank You for steering my ship through life's crashing waters and into the harbor of Your mercy. Fix my eyes on the lighthouse of Your truth.

Speak to God and God will speak to you.

And the LORD. . .will not fail thee.
DEUTERONOMY 31:8

I do need thee, Lord. I need thee now.
I needed thee when sorrow came, when shadows were thrown
across the threshold of my life, and thou didst not fail me
then. I needed thee when sickness laid a clammy hand upon
my family, and I cried to thee, and thou didst hear. I needed
thee when perplexity brought me to a parting of the ways, and
I knew not how to turn. Thou didst not fail me then, but in
many ways, big and little, didst indicate the better way. . . .
I give thee my gratitude for that constant sense of need
that keeps me close to thy side. Help me to keep my hand
in thine and my ears open to the wisdom of thy voice.
Speak to me, that I may hear thee giving me courage
for hard times and strength for difficult places; giving
me determination for challenging tasks.
PETER MARSHALL

MY PRAYER STARTER: God, thank You for whispering in my ear when this
world's cacophony of fear threatens to take away my sanity. Help me to
keep our conversation alive at each moment.

We men often take on projects without considering their ramifications. Consequently, we may find ourselves stretching our resources or doing things God doesn't want us to do. But if we ask God to bless all our thoughts and advise us what to do and when, He'll open our eyes to His wisdom, plan, and intentions. Then, we'll do our work in His strength. What peace of mind that will bring!

> *Know thou the God of thy father, and serve him with a*
> *perfect heart and with a willing mind: for the LORD searcheth*
> *all hearts, and understandeth all the imaginations of the*
> *thoughts: if thou seek him, he will be found of thee.*
>
> 1 CHRONICLES 28:9

Almighty God, Who alone gavest us the breath of life, and alone canst keep alive in us the breathing of our holy desires, we beseech Thee for Thy compassion's sake to sanctify all our thoughts and endeavors, that we may neither begin any action without a pure intention, nor continue it without Thy blessing; and grant that, having the eyes of our understanding purged to behold things invisible and unseen, we may in heart be inspired with Thy wisdom, and in work be upheld by Thy strength, and in the end be accepted of Thee, as Thy faithful servants, having done all things to Thy glory, and thereby to our endless peace. Grant this prayer, O Lord. Amen.

ROWLAND WILLIAMS

MY PRAYER STARTER: All-wise God, without Your help, all my plans will fail. Help me seek Your wisdom each time I make a decision.

The Bible's stories cover roughly 1,500 years, from about 1450 BC to AD 100. The complete volume we have today was canonized before AD 375. That means the Bible you now read has been around for over 1,500 years. Yet God's story and all its participants are still relevant to you today! They still speak to your heart, mind, and soul.

God's promises still have the power to bear fruit and give hope. May that knowledge give you patience as you wait on the promises of the God who inspired the Word, His Son who became the Word, and the Spirit who translates the Word that lives in you.

> *For whatsoever things were written aforetime were written*
> *for our learning, that we through patience and comfort of*
> *the scriptures might have hope. Now the God of patience and*
> *consolation grant you to be likeminded one toward another*
> *according to Christ Jesus: that ye may with one mind and one*
> *mouth glorify God, even the Father of our Lord Jesus Christ.*
>
> ROMANS 15:4–6

O God, by whose command the order of time runs its course: Forgive, we pray thee, the impatience of our hearts; make perfect that which is lacking in our faith; and, while we tarry the fulfilment of thy promises, grant us to have a good hope because of thy word; through Jesus Christ our Lord.

SAINT GREGORY OF NAZIANZUS

MY PRAYER STARTER: Unchanging God, the Bible was written to give us examples of how—and how not—to live. May I never overlook these lessons as I study Your holy Word.

Jesus knew He would be rejected, despised, misunderstood, reviled, mocked, beaten, and killed by those He came to save. But none of those things deterred Him from His mission.

Just before His arrest, Jesus went into a garden, putting some distance between Himself and His disciples so He could get down on His knees and pray—not for His will but for God's will to be done. As He prayed, an angel from heaven came and gave Him the spiritual strength and courage He would need to face His duty, to overcome all that would come against Him, and to rise again.

Each day you have the same opportunity to ask God for His will to be done. . .and for the courage and strength for you to live out His will. As you do, know God will bless and empower you.

And he was withdrawn from them about a stone's cast, and kneeled down, and prayed, saying, Father, if thou be willing, remove this cup from me: nevertheless not my will, but thine, be done. And there appeared an angel unto him from heaven, strengthening him.

LUKE 22:41–43

Make us, O blessed Master, strong in heart, full of courage, fearless of danger, holding pain and danger cheap when they lie in the path of duty. May we be strengthened with all might by thy Spirit in our hearts.

F. B. MEYER

MY PRAYER STARTER: Lord God, let Your will take precedence in my mind. If my plans ever clash with Yours, give me the wisdom to see the conflict and the courage to surrender.

Disagreements can be uncomfortable, and you probably won't rest easy until you settle the matter with another conversation. It's the same way with God. When you're not walking in His way, you won't rest until you have a heart-to-heart, spirit-to-spirit conversation with Him.

Do that today. Bring before Him whatever's standing between your delight in Him and His delight in you. Then enjoy the peace that follows.

Trust in the LORD, and do good. . . . Delight thyself also in the LORD: and he shall give thee the desires of thine heart. Commit thy way unto the LORD; trust also in him; and he shall bring it to pass. . . . The steps of a good man are ordered by the LORD: and he delighteth in his way.

PSALM 37:3–5, 23

O God, Who puttest into our hearts such deep desire, that we cannot be at peace until we enjoy the feeling of Thy love; mercifully grant that the unspeakable sighing of our souls' need may not go unsatisfied because of any unrighteousness of heart, which must divide us from the All-holy One; but strengthen us to do right by whomsoever we have wronged in thought, word, or deed; to renounce all plans of wrong-doing for the future; to purify our thoughts and govern our appetites, so that we may have no bar between us and Thy glory, but enjoy Thy peace which passeth understanding. Amen.
ROWLAND WILLIAMS

MY PRAYER STARTER: Father, whenever I mess up, don't let these sins grow in my conscience. Give me the humility to spill out my heart to You, confessing my wrongs and praising Your holiness.

Sometimes, when we run ahead of God's plan, God begins working on us. Then we come to our senses and begin slowly making our way back to Him. But God isn't slow. He sees us coming and runs to meet us. He then hugs and kisses us, and when we begin to explain, He interrupts us by clothing us, feeding us, and supping with us merrily.

Come to your senses today. Use today's prayers to run to God before He can run to you. Allow Him to draw you into His loving arms. Make merry in His presence.

He arose, and came to his father. But when he was yet a great way off, his father saw him, and had compassion, and ran, and fell on his neck, and kissed him. And the son said unto him, Father, I have sinned against heaven, and in thy sight, and am no more worthy to be called thy son. But the father said to his servants, Bring forth the best robe. . .and let us eat, and be merry: for this my son was dead, and is alive again; he was lost, and is found. And they began to be merry.

LUKE 15:20–24

Come, Lord, work upon us, set us on fire and clasp us close, be fragrant to us, draw us to your loveliness, let us love, let us run to you.
SAINT AUGUSTINE

MY PRAYER STARTER: Gracious Lord, I am overwhelmed by the depth of Your forgiveness. When I start drifting away, You bring me to my senses and lead me back to You. Thank You.

Jesus had been killed, and Mary Magdalene was devastated. But when she went to His tomb, His body was gone! She told the disciples, two of whom came to look for themselves. Then they went away. But she remained, weeping.

When angels asked her why she was crying, she told them she didn't know where Jesus was. Then she turned and saw a man standing there. She didn't know He was Jesus. . .until He called her name.

God is with you. Ask Him to reveal Himself, to startle you, to remind you He is always everywhere in your life.

> *[The angels] say unto [Mary], Woman, why weepest thou? She saith unto them, Because they have taken away my LORD, and I know not where they have laid him. And when she had thus said, she turned herself back, and saw Jesus standing, and knew not that it was Jesus. Jesus saith unto her, Woman, why weepest thou? whom seekest thou? She, supposing him to be the gardener, saith unto him, Sir, if thou have borne him hence, tell me where thou hast laid him, and I will take him away. Jesus saith unto her, Mary.*
>
> JOHN 20:13–16

Lord, catch me off guard today. Surprise me with some moment of beauty or pain so that for at least a moment I may be startled into seeing that you are with me here in all your splendor, always and everywhere, barely hidden, beneath, beyond, within this life I breathe.
FREDERICK BUECHNER

MY PRAYER STARTER: Lord God, don't let my life become a tiresome string of mundane events. When I start getting complacent, show me glimpses of Your glory.

It's one thing to say, "In You, O Lord, I put my trust." But it's another thing to actually do it.

Today, admit you trust in God. Say it, pray it, and believe it. Then walk in the power, strength, and grace that God readily grants to those who trust in Him alone.

In thee, O LORD, do I put my trust. . . . I trusted in thee, O LORD: I said, Thou art my God. . . . The LORD preserveth the faithful, and plentifully rewardeth the proud doer. Be of good courage, and he shall strengthen your heart, all ye that hope in the LORD.

PSALM 31:1, 14, 23–24

O Lord God Almighty, Who givest power to the faint, and increasest strength to them that have no might! Without Thee I can do nothing, but by Thy gracious assistance I am enabled for the performance of every duty laid upon me. Lord of power and love, I come, trusting in Thine Almighty strength, and Thine infinite goodness, to beg from Thee what is wanting in myself, even that grace which shall help me such to be, and such to do, as Thou wouldest have me. O my God! let Thy grace be sufficient for me, and ever present with me, that I may do all things as I ought. I will trust in Thee, in Whom is everlasting strength.

BENJAMIN JENKS

MY PRAYER STARTER: Father, when I say I trust in You, I want my actions to prove it. Fill me with Your Spirit and grant me the faith and courage to face today, knowing You have my back.

DAY 353

When God looks upon you, His light vanquishes all the darkness within you. He fills you with His love and reveals the treasures of wisdom in His Word.

Today, seek God's face. Allow Him to open you up to all He has to offer. Ask Him to water the seeds of desire He's sown in you. Permit His Spirit to awaken you to what you should pray for.

As you do these things, know God will satisfy all your longings and fill your hungry soul with His goodness (Psalm 107:9), leading you to perfect peace.

One thing have I desired of the LORD, that will I seek after; that I may dwell in the house of the LORD all the days of my life, to behold the beauty of the LORD, and to enquire in his temple. . . . When thou saidst, Seek ye my face; my heart said unto thee, Thy face, LORD, will I seek.

PSALM 27:4, 8

Look upon us, O Lord,
and let all the darkness of our souls
vanish before the beams of thy brightness.
Fill us with holy love,
and open to us the treasures of thy wisdom.
All our desire is known unto thee,
therefore perfect what thou hast begun,
and what thy Spirit has awakened us to ask in prayer.
We seek thy face,
turn thy face unto us and show us thy glory.
Then shall our longing be satisfied,
and our peace shall be perfect.
SAINT AUGUSTINE

MY PRAYER STARTER: Almighty God, I need to know that You're looking upon me now. I need the joy that only Your Spirit provides and the wisdom found only in Your Word.

Hoarders hate to have visitors. Although their home may look orderly on the outside, on the inside it's a nightmare. The last thing they want is to open their door to someone else's surprise, disgust, or pity.

Although you may not be a physical hoarder, you might have some spiritual clutter you need to deal with. Today is your day!

Go to God with all the mess in your heart. Clear it of bitterness, hatred, fear, doubt, wrong desires, past missteps, and whatever else that's blocking the door. Have a heart that Jesus is glad to enter when you open it from within.

Behold, I stand at the door, and knock: if any man hear my voice, and open the door, I will come in to him, and will sup with him, and he with me. To him that overcometh will I grant to sit with me in my throne, even as I also overcame, and am set down with my Father in his throne. He that hath an ear, let him hear what the Spirit saith.

REVELATION 3:20–22

Let us have clean hearts ready inside us for the Lord Jesus, so that he will be glad to come in, gratefully accepting the hospitality of those worlds, our hearts: he whose glory and power will endure throughout the ages. Amen.

ORIGEN

MY PRAYER STARTER: Holy God, I want my soul to be filled with Your Spirit and nothing else. Come in today and clear out any junk that might be strewn in the shadows of my heart.

Parents don't like it when kids whine. And Father God is no exception.

Trapped between the Egyptian army and the Red Sea, the Israelites cried out to God and then complained to Moses. He told them not to fear—to be quiet and stand firm as God fought for them.

That's good advice for all men of God. Know that amid the direst circumstances, God is with you. He'll give you courage to stand firm and accept your situation, knowing He has secured your victory.

> *The children of Israel. . .were sore afraid. . . . And they said unto Moses, Because there were no graves in Egypt, hast thou taken us away to die in the wilderness? wherefore hast thou dealt thus with us, to carry us forth out of Egypt? . . . And Moses said unto the people, Fear ye not, stand still, and see the salvation of the LORD. . . . The LORD shall fight for you, and ye shall hold your peace.*
> EXODUS 14:10–11, 13–14

O Father, who hast ordained that we be set within a scheme of circumstance, and that in stern conflict we should find our strength and triumph over all; withhold not from us the courage by which we alone can conquer. Still our tongues of their weak complainings, steel our hearts against all fear, and in joyfully accepting the conditions of our earthly pilgrimage may we come to possess our souls and achieve our purposed destiny.
WILLIAM EDWIN ORCHARD

MY PRAYER STARTER: Almighty Protector, let me not fear life's uncertainties. Give me the quiet confidence that comes with knowing You are fighting my battles.

The verse below equates your conscience with your "spirit"—the candle given to you by God. This candle searches every secret place, bringing to light whatever needs to be seen. But *God's* Spirit is even brighter, going even deeper within your being.

Today's prayers invite the Spirit's candle to illuminate the hidden things within you—the things your conscience may be breezing by. It shines upon your dreams, your forgotten memories, the past hurts you've suffered. Then it goes even deeper, telling you who you truly are and revealing the seed that God, before the foundation of the world, planned to plant within you.

Go deep with God. Allow Him to lighten you within so that you can see the road ahead.

> *The spirit of man is the candle of the LORD,*
> *searching all the inward parts of the belly.*
> PROVERBS 20:27

Give me a candle of the Spirit, O God, as I go down into the deeps of my being. Show me the hidden things, the creatures of my dreams, the storehouse of forgotten memories and hurts. Take me down to the spring of my life, and tell me my nature and my name. Give me freedom to grow, so that I may become that self, the seed of which You planted in me at my making. Out of the depths I cry to You.

GEORGE APPLETON

MY PRAYER STARTER: Divine Light, if there be any ugliness inside my soul, please reveal it to me. The temporary shock will be worth the long-term benefits as You purify me and prepare me for eternity.

Think about your blessings—past and present, and future. Then use today's classic prayer to thank God for all of them. Finally, ask for one last thing: a grateful heart. Ask that you'll be grateful not just for the big things but for *all* things.

To begin, thank God for Jesus and His love for you. For His mercy and compassion that never fail. For His Word that explores His wisdom, tells stories about prior men of faith, and reveals His plan for you.

Renew your passion for thanking God by daily writing down something new for which you can praise Him. By doing so, you'll begin developing a heart with a pulse of praise.

> *Rejoice the soul of thy servant: for unto thee, O Lord, do I lift up my*
> *soul. For thou, Lord, art good, and ready to forgive; and plenteous*
> *in mercy unto all them that call upon thee. . . . Among the gods*
> *there is none like unto thee, O Lord; neither are there any works*
> *like unto thy works. . . . For thou art great, and doest wondrous*
> *things. . . . I will praise thee, O Lord my God, with all my heart.*
> PSALM 86:4–5, 8, 10, 12

Thou has given much to me;
Give one thing more—a grateful heart.
Not thankful when it pleaseth me,
As if thy blessings had spare days,
But such a heart whose pulse may be
Thy praise.
GEORGE HERBERT

MY PRAYER STARTER: Generous Lord, let my thanksgiving be more than rote, obligatory prayers. Let it flow from my heart as You open my eyes to all You've done for me.

Many paths lie before you. But God wants you to take the road He's paved for you.

Today, ask God for the desire, wisdom, and resources to take the path He's already surveyed and prepared for you. Ask Him to open your ears to His voice so that you'll know the right route for certain, not being swayed toward a path that's less pleasing to Him. Ask Him to give you the knowledge, passion, and ability to do all He's required you to do so that your pathway to Him will be safe and smooth to the end.

> *But the path of the just is as the shining light, that shineth*
> *more and more unto the perfect day. . . . Let thine eyes look*
> *right on, and let thine eyelids look straight before thee. Ponder*
> *the path of thy feet, and let all thy ways be established.*
>
> PROVERBS 4:18, 25–26

Grant me, I beseech Thee, Almighty and most merciful God, fervently to desire, wisely to search out, and perfectly to fulfil, all that is well-pleasing unto Thee. Order Thou my worldly condition to the glory of Thy name; and, of all that Thou requirest me to do, grant me the knowledge, the desire, and the ability, that I may so fulfil it as I ought, and may my path to Thee, I pray, be safe, straightforward, and perfect to the end.
SAINT THOMAS AQUINAS

MY PRAYER STARTER: All-wise God, I don't know which route to choose—each one looks equally frightening. Please guide me to the right path and give me peace as I decide.

Focusing on the world's darkness is a quick way for a man to reach the depths of despair. But there's a solution—God's Word and His Spirit.

To stay above the fray and find the saving light, remember the words of Jesus. Build yourself up in faith by delving into the Word, pray in the Spirit, and keep yourself in God's love. He, the Giver and Sustainer of life, will lift you from the dark valley of despair and set you upon the mountain of hope.

> *Beloved, remember ye the words which were spoken before of the apostles of our Lord Jesus Christ. . . . Ye, beloved, building up yourselves on your most holy faith, praying in the Holy Ghost, keep yourselves in the love of God, looking for the mercy of our Lord Jesus Christ unto eternal life. And of some have compassion, making a difference. . . . Now unto him that is able to keep you from falling, and to present you faultless before the presence of his glory with exceeding joy, to the only wise God our Saviour. . .*
>
> JUDE 17, 20–22, 24–25

And now unto him who is able to keep us from falling and lift us from the dark valley of despair to the mountains of hope, from the midnight of desperation to the daybreak of joy; to him be power and authority for ever and ever. Amen.
MARTIN LUTHER KING JR.

MY PRAYER STARTER: God, this world is an ocean that's trying to drown me in misery. Take my hand and lift me from the waters, reminding me that You have given me hope.

David was the smallest and youngest of his brothers—yet he was a man after God's heart (1 Samuel 13:14), and God chose him to be Israel's king. Gideon was the least of his clan—yet God called him to live as a "mighty man of valour" (Judges 6:12). Mary was a teenager—yet God made her the mother of His Son (Luke 1:35).

Even if you feel unworthy, God can use you. No matter who you are, rise up to God like an eagle, daring to fly toward the Son.

> *Lift up your eyes on high, and behold who hath created these things. . . . The everlasting God, the LORD, the Creator of the ends of the earth, fainteth not, neither is weary[.] . . . He giveth power to the faint; and to them that have no might he increaseth strength. Even the youths shall faint and be weary, and the young men shall utterly fall: but they that wait upon the LORD shall renew their strength; they shall mount up with wings as eagles; they shall run, and not be weary; and they shall walk, and not faint.*
>
> ISAIAH 40:26, 28–31

Lord Jesus, I am not an eagle. All I have are the eyes and the heart of one. In spite of my littleness, I dare to gaze at the sun of love, and long to fly toward it.
SAINT THÉRÈSE OF LISIEUX

MY PRAYER STARTER: All-powerful God, when I ponder Your glory and consider Your love toward me, I start to see my worth. Thank You for lending purpose to my existence.

Too often, we find ourselves looking for peace in all the wrong places. We look to other people or possessions for solace. All will be well, we tell ourselves, if we can get clothes, houses, jobs, and cars. But once we reach those goals, we immediately look for something else.

Yet the only perfect peace is found by focusing on, trusting in, and desiring God alone—all day and all night. Use the prayers below to seek that peace today and every day.

> *Thou wilt keep him in perfect peace, whose mind is*
> *stayed on thee: because he trusteth in thee.*
> *Trust ye in the LORD for ever: for in the LORD JEHOVAH*
> *is everlasting strength. . . . With my soul have I desired*
> *thee in the night; yea, with my spirit within me will I seek*
> *thee early. . . . LORD, thou wilt ordain peace for us.*
> ISAIAH 26:3–4, 9, 12

Grant us, O Lord, the blessing of those whose minds are stayed on you, so that we may be kept in perfect peace: a peace which cannot be broken. Let not our minds rest upon any creature, but only upon the creator; not upon goods, things, houses, lands, inventions or vanities, or foolish fashions, lest, our peace being broken, we become cross and brittle and given over to envy. From all such deliver us, O God, and grant us your peace.
GEORGE FOX

MY PRAYER STARTER: God of peace, nothing in this world can compare with the joy and ultimate satisfaction You bring. Let my focus never drift away from You.

God's breath is creative and powerful. As it gave Adam life, it enlivens you. As Jesus' breath gave the disciples sustaining power, it strengthens you. As Holy Spirit's rushing wind forever transformed the first believers, it forever changes you. As God inspired the recorders of His Word, it inspires you to live out that Word.

Today, ask God to breathe upon you. To refuel, renew, and refresh you. As you do, know that you'll receive God's overwhelming love in return, enabling you to do as Jesus would.

> *God formed man of the dust of the ground, and breathed into his nostrils the breath of life; and man became a living soul. . . . Then said Jesus to them again, Peace be unto you: as my Father hath sent me, even so send I you. And when he had said this, he breathed on them, and saith unto them, Receive ye the Holy Ghost. . . . Suddenly there came a sound from heaven as of a rushing mighty wind, and it filled all the house. . . . And they were all filled with the Holy Ghost. . . . All scripture is given by inspiration of God.*
> GENESIS 2:7; JOHN 20:21–22; ACTS 2:2, 4; 2 TIMOTHY 3:16

Breathe on me, Breath of God,
Fill me with life anew,
That I may love what Thou dost love,
And do what Thou wouldst do.
EDWIN HATCH

MY PRAYER STARTER: Lord God, I need Your life-giving Spirit to animate my soul. Without You, I am nothing but a sinful shell of a man.

The "our" in Genesis 1:26—"Let us make man in *our* image, after *our* likeness" (emphasis added)—is the first clear indication of the Trinity: God, Jesus, and the Spirit. And you have been made in Their likeness. Their traits lie within you.

Yet to discover, water, and fertilize that God seed, you need to go deep within. You need your spirit to commune with God's, to be where "deep calleth unto deep" (Psalm 42:7).

Use today's prayers to take that journey. Discover the divine likeness in which you've been made. . .and into which you are destined to grow.

> *And God said, Let us make man in our image, after our*
> *likeness: and let them have dominion over the fish of the sea,*
> *and over the fowl of the air, and over the cattle, and over all*
> *the earth, and over every creeping thing that creepeth upon*
> *the earth. So God created man in his own image, in the image*
> *of God created he him; male and female created he them.*
> GENESIS 1:26–27

Help me, O Lord, to descend into the depths of my being, below my conscious and sub-conscious life until I discover my real self, that which is given me from thee, the divine likeness in which I am made and into which I am to grow, the place where your Spirit communes with mine, the spring from which all my life rises.
GEORGE APPLETON

MY PRAYER STARTER: Triune God, thank You for placing traces of Your attributes inside my soul. Help me to never ignore or hide them; instead, help me to nurture them until they become undeniable to all who see me.

Even on days of impermanence and uncertainty, one thing is forever sure: God. He never changes. And He gives you every good and perfect gift.

With today's prayers, ask God for guidance, good thoughts, and whatever else you need. He'll give you what you ask for.

If any of you lack wisdom, let him ask of God, that giveth to all men liberally. . .and it shall be given him. But let him ask in faith. . . . Every good gift and every perfect gift is from above.
JAMES 1:5–6, 17

Our heavenly Father. . . We desire to go out today under Your eye and to keep close to You all the time. Show us the way, for we cannot find it ourselves, and could never get home without Your guidance. Put good thoughts into our hearts, for we can think beautiful thoughts only when they first drop from Heaven, like stars, and begin to glow in us! Every good thing comes down from above. As every stream is born in the skies, in the clouds—so every good thing in life is born in Heaven, comes out of Your very heart! Send down into our hearts, good and beautiful thoughts and feelings—that from our lives, may go divine blessings to all whom we come into contact with. . . . We ask all this in the name of Jesus Christ our Lord. Amen.

J. R. MILLER

MY PRAYER STARTER: Lord, thank You for being the unchanging constant in this changing world. Please stay by my side and fix my mind on the pure thoughts found in Your Word.

First Chronicles 4 lists Jabez under the descendants of Judah. His mom, the Bible says, named him Jabez—which means "pain" or "sorrow maker" —because she bore him in pain and sorrow (1 Chronicles 4:9). Jabez probably thought this label would follow him for life, so he prayed that God would bless him and keep His hand upon him, enlarging his territory and protecting him from sadness and evil. And God granted his request!

God will bless you as well. . .if you ask Him. He'll even teach you what to pray for! Go to God today in the power of prayer, expecting Him to bless you in ways beyond imagining.

And Jabez called on the God of Israel, saying, Oh that thou wouldest bless me indeed, and enlarge my coast, and that thine hand might be with me, and that thou wouldest keep me from evil, that it may not grieve me! And God granted him that which he requested.

1 CHRONICLES 4:10

O Lord, my God, teach me to pray for the right blessings. Steer the vessel of my life towards yourself, the peaceful harbour for storm-tossed souls. Show me the course I should sail, renew a willing spirit within me. May your Spirit curb my wandering senses and help me to observe your laws. Gladden my heart with your glorious presence within. For yours is the glory and the praise of all the saints forever.
SAINT BASIL THE GREAT

MY PRAYER STARTER: God of second chances, thank You for allowing my past not to define me. Continue helping me walk in Your will, and protect me from the evils of this world.

CONTRIBUTOR BIOS

Alcuin, c. 735–804; English scholar, poet, and teacher.

Alfred the Great, 849–899; king of Wessex, England.

Andrewes, Lancelot, 1555–1626; English bishop, scholar, and writer.

Appleton, George, 1902–1993; Anglican bishop and writer.

Arndt, Johann, 1555–1621; German Lutheran author and theologian.

Arnold, Thomas, 1795–1842; English educator and historian.

Astley, Jacob, 1579–1652; First Baron Astley of Reading, England, and infantry commander.

Baillie, John, 1886–1960; Scottish minister and author.

Barclay, William, 1907–1978; Scottish author and minister.

Baring-Gould, Sabine, 1834–1924; Anglican priest, novelist, and hymn writer.

Becon, Thomas, c. 1511–1567; English cleric and reformer.

Beecher, Henry Ward, 1813–1887; American preacher, reformer, author, and speaker.

Beethoven, Ludwig van, 1770–1827; German composer.

Blake, William, 1757–1827; English artist and poet.

Böhme, Jakob, 1575–1624; German shoemaker, writer, mystic, and theologian.

Bonhoeffer, Dietrich, 1906–1945; German Lutheran pastor, theologian, and writer.

Bounds, E. M. [Edward McKendree], 1835–1913; American attorney, author, and clergyman.

Bright, William, 1824–1901; English historian and Anglican priest.

Brother Lawrence, c. 1614–1691; French lay brother in a Carmelite monastery and author.

Browning, Robert, 1812–1889; English poet and playwright.

Buechner, Frederick, 1926– ; American writer and minister.

Calvin, John, 1509–1564; French theologian and father of Calvinism.

Carpenter, Mary, 1807–1877; English educator, social reformer, and writer.

Carpenter, William Boyd, 1841–1918; English clergyman, bishop, and author.

Cassian, John, c. 360–435; Christian monk and theologian.

Catherine of Siena, 1347–1380; Dominican nun and saint.

Chambers, Oswald, 1874–1917; Scottish evangelist, teacher, and author.

Channing, William Ellery, 1780–1842; Unitarian preacher in the US.

Chrysostom, John, c. 347–407; archbishop of Constantinople and saint.

Cosin, John, 1594–1672; English bishop.

Dawson, George, 1821–1876; English preacher and speaker.

de Chardin, Teilhard, 1881–1955; French philosopher and Jesuit priest.

de Foucauld, Charles, 1858–1916; French Catholic priest.

Donne, John, 1572–1631; English poet, lawyer, and priest.

Dostoevsky, Fyodor, 1821–1881; Russian novelist.

Élisabeth of France, 1764–1794; French princess known for her piety.

Erasmus [a.k.a. Desiderius Erasmus Roterodamus], 1466–1536; Dutch Catholic priest, teacher, and author.

Eusebius of Caesarea [a.k.a. Eusebius Pamphili], 260/265–339/340; Roman historian, writer, and bishop.

Fénelon, François, 1651–1715; Roman Catholic archbishop, poet, and writer.

Foote, Henry W., 1794–1869; American minister and author.

Fox, George, 1624–1691; English founder of the Quakers.

Fuller, Thomas, 1608–1661; English historian, churchman, and author.

Gordon, Charles George, 1833–1885; British army officer and committed Christian.

Gordon, S. D. [Samuel Dickey], 1859–1936; American speaker and author.

Goudge, Elizabeth, 1900–1984; English author.

Grey, Lady Jane [a.k.a. Lady Jane Dudley or the Nine-Day Queen], 1536/1537–1554; English noblewoman and committed Protestant.

Grou, Jean Nicholas, 1731–1803; French Roman Catholic author.

Guyon, Jeanne [a.k.a. Jeanne-Marie Bouvier de la Motte-Guyon, Madam Guyon], 1648–1717; French mystic and writer.

Hallesby, Ole, 1879–1961; Norwegian theologian, author, and educator.

Hammarskjöld, Dag, 1905–1961; Swedish diplomat, author, and second secretary-general of the United Nations.

Hare, Maria [a.k.a. Twtaria Lycester/Mrs. Augustus Hare], 1798–1870; English writer.

Hatch, Edwin, 1835–1889; English theologian and composer.

Herbert, George, 1593–1633; Welsh poet, speaker, and priest.

Hickes, George, 1642–1715; English rector, chaplain, and writer.

Houselander, Caryll, 1901–1954; English writer, artist, and poet.

Hunter, Leslie, 1890–1983; bishop of Sheffield and author.

Jarrett, Bede, 1881–1934; English Dominican friar, Catholic priest, and author.

Jenks, Benjamin, 1646–1724; English curate and author.

Johnson, Samuel, 1709–1784; English author, poet, and moralist.

Jowett, John Henry, 1863–1923; British Protestant preacher and author.

Julian of Norwich, c. 1342–c. 1416; Englishwoman, author, and theologian.

Kelly, Blanche Mary, 1881–1966; American journalist and writer.

Kempis, Thomas à, 1380–1471; Dutch author of *The Imitation of Christ*.

Kierkegaard, Søren, 1813–1855; Danish poet, philosopher, theologian, and author.

King, Martin Luther, Jr., 1929–1968; American preacher, activist, humanitarian, and leader of the African American civil rights movement in the US.

Lewis, C. S. [Clive Staples], 1898–1963; British writer of fiction and nonfiction, teacher, poet, speaker, and theologian.

Livingstone, David, 1813–1873; Scottish doctor, missionary, and explorer of Africa.

Luther, Martin, 1483–1546; German professor, composer, monk, and leader of the Protestant Reformation.

MacDonald, George, 1824–1905; Scottish author, poet, and minister.

Mansfield, Katherine, 1888–1923; New Zealand short story writer.

Marshall, Catherine, 1914–1983; American writer and wife of minister Peter Marshall.

Marshall, Peter, 1902–1949; Scottish American preacher, pastor, and chaplain of the US Senate.

Martineau, James, 1805–1900; Unitarian minister, philosopher, theologian, and writer.

Matheson, George, 1842–1906; Scottish clergyman, writer, and hymn writer.

McComb, Samuel, 1864–1938; Irish-born, Oxford-educated Canadian professor, and American minister, writer, and speaker.

Mechthild of Magdeburg, c. 1207–1282/1294; German mystic and poet.

Merton, Thomas, 1915–1968; American monk and writer.

Meyer, F. B. [Frederick Brotherton], 1847–1929; Baptist preacher and writer.

Miller, J. R. [James Russel], 1840–1912; American author and pastor.

Milner-White, Eric, 1884–1963; English priest, soldier, and Dean of York in the Church of England.

Moody, D. L. [a.k.a. Dwight L. Moody], 1837–1899; American evangelist, publisher, and author.

More, Sir Thomas, 1478–1535; English author, statesman, lawyer, and Roman Catholic saint.

Mother Teresa [born Anjezë Gonxha Bojaxhiu], 1910–1997; Roman Catholic nun, missionary, and saint.

Muggeridge, Malcolm, 1903–1990; British author and agnostic who became Christian.

Murray, Andrew, 1828–1917; South African–born Scotsman, author, and pastor.

Nayler, James, 1616–1660; English Quaker leader, evangelist, minister, and writer.

Newman, John Henry, 1801–1890; English Roman Catholic cardinal.

Niebuhr, Reinhold, 1892–1971; American minister, theologian, ethicist, seminary professor, and writer.

Oldham, John, 1653–1683; English poet and educator.

Oosterhuis, Huub, 1933– ; Dutch theologian and poet.

Orchard, William Edwin, 1877–1955; minister, priest, writer, and pacifist.

Origen, c. 184–253; early Christian theologian.

Oxenden, Ashton, 1808–1892; English clergyman, author, and bishop of Montreal.

Patrick, Simon, 1626–1707; English theologian, bishop, and writer.

Penn, William, 1644–1718; English Quaker, philosopher, and founder of Pennsylvania.

Pope, Alexander, 1688–1744; English poet.

Pusey, Edward B., 1800–1882; English churchman, professor, and author.

Quoist, Michel, 1918–1997; French Catholic priest and writer.

Rahner, Karl, 1904–1984; German Jesuit priest and writer.

Rauschenbusch, Walter, 1861–1918; American theologian and pastor.

Rice, Helen Steiner, 1900–1981; American writer and poet.

Roberts, Evan, 1878–1951; Welsh revivalist, poet, and speaker.

Rossetti, Christina, 1830–1894; English poet.

Sailer, Michael [a.k.a. Johann Michael Sailer], 1751–1832; German professor and bishop.

Saint Anatolius, 449–458; Greek patriarch of Constantinople.

Saint Anselm, 1033–1109; monk, abbot, and philosopher.

Saint Augustine [a.k.a. Augustine of Hippo], 354–430; theologian, philosopher, and writer.

Saint Basil the Great, c. 329–379; Greek bishop, theologian, and writer.

Saint Bede the Venerable, 672/673–735; English monk, scholar, and author.

Saint Benedict of Nursia, c. 480–543 or 547; saint.

Saint Bernard [a.k.a. Bernard of Clairvaux], 1091–1153; French abbot, author, and "doctor of the church."

Saint Clement of Rome, died AD 99; bishop of Rome.

Saint Columba of Iona, 521–597; Irish abbot and missionary.

Saint Columbanus, 543–615; Irish-born founder of monasteries, preacher, and poet.

Saint Francis of Assisi [born Giovanni di Pietro di Bernardone], 1181/1182–1226; Italian Roman Catholic friar, preacher, writer, and poet.

Saint Francis de Sales, 1567–1622; bishop of Geneva, author, and Roman

Catholic saint.

Saint Gregory of Nazianzus, c. 329–390; archbishop of Constantinople, theologian, and philosopher.

Saint Ignatius of Loyola, 1491–1556; Spanish knight, hermit, and priest.

Saint Jerome, 347–420; priest and theologian; translated most of the Bible into Latin.

Saint Patrick, 5th century; Romano-British Christian missionary, bishop, and saint of Ireland.

Saint Peter Claver, 1580–1654; Spanish priest and missionary.

Saint Richard of Chichester [a.k.a. Richard de Wych], 1197–1253; bishop.

Saint Symeon, 949–1022; Byzantine Christian monk and poet.

Saint Teresa of Ávila, 1515–1582; Spanish nun and author.

Saint Thérèse of Lisieux [a.k.a. Marie Françoise-Thérèse Martin], 1873–1897; French nun.

Saint Thomas Aquinas [a.k.a. Tommaso d'Aquino], 1225–1274; Italian friar, Roman Catholic priest, philosopher, and writer.

Sanford, Agnes, c. 1897–1982; American author.

Shakespeare, William, 1564–1616; English poet, actor, and playwright.

Sherman, Frank Dempster, 1860–1916; American poet and professor.

Smith, Hannah Whitall, 1832–1911; American Quaker, speaker, and author.

Snowden, Rita, 1907–1999; New Zealand missionary and author.

Solzhenitsyn, Aleksandr, 1918–2008; Russian novelist, historian, dramatist, and short story writer.

Spurgeon, Charles, 1834–1892; British preacher and writer.

Starck, Johann Friedrich [a.k.a. John Frederick Stark], 1680–1756; German pastor, author, and hymn writer.

Stevenson, Robert Louis, 1850–1894; Scottish novelist, poet, and essayist.

Steward, Mary; American high school principal, women's club member, and writer. Prayer written in 1904.

Stowe, Harriet Beecher, 1811–1896; author and abolitionist.

Taylor, Jeremy, 1613–1667; English author and cleric.

Temple, William, 1881–1944; English bishop, archbishop, teacher, preacher, and writer.

ten Boom, Corrie, 1892–1983; Dutch Christian and author.

Tersteegen, Gerhard, 1697–1769; German reformed religious writer, speaker, poet, and hymn writer.

Torrey, R. A. [Ruben Archer], 1856–1928; American pastor and writer.

Tozer, A. W. [Aiden Wilson], 1897–1963; American preacher, author, and editor.

Underhill, Evelyn, 1875–1941; English writer and pacifist.

van Dyke, Henry, 1852–1933; American clergyman, educator, and author.

Wells, H. G. [Herbert George], 1866–1946; English writer of novels, history, and textbooks.

Wesley, Charles, 1707–1788; English preacher and hymn writer.

Wesley, John, 1703–1791; English preacher and writer.

Westcott, Brooke Foss, 1825–1901; British bishop, scholar, and writer.

Whittier, John Greenleaf, 1807–1892; American Quaker, poet, and abolitionist.

Wilberforce, William, 1759–1833; English politician and abolitionist.

Wilcox, Ella Wheeler, 1850–1919; poet.

William of Saint-Thierry, 1085–1148; monk, theologian, mystic, and abbot.

Williams, Rowland, 1817–1870; British priest, vicar, and professor.

Wilson, Thomas, 1663–1755; English Anglican bishop.

Woolman, John, 1720–1772; North American merchant, essayist, journalist, and Quaker preacher.

SUBJECT INDEX